ACCA

Applied Skills

Financial Management (FM)

Workbook

For exams in September 2022, December 2022, March 2023 and June 2023

BPP
LEARNING
MEDIA

Third edition 2022

ISBN: 9781 5097 4409 1

Previous ISBN: 9781 5097 3810 6

ISBN (for internal use only): 9781 5097 4701 6

e-ISBN: 9781 5097 4659 0

British Library Cataloguing-in-Publication Data

A catalogue record for this book is available from the British Library

Published by

BPP Learning Media Ltd

BPP House, Aldine Place

142–144 Uxbridge Road

London W12 8AA

www.bpp.com/learningmedia

Printed in the United Kingdom

Your learning materials, published by BPP Learning Media Ltd, are printed on paper obtained from traceable sustainable sources.

The contents of this course material are intended as a guide and not professional advice. Although every effort has been made to ensure that the contents of this course material are correct at the time of going to press, BPP Learning Media makes no warranty that the information in this course material is accurate or complete and accept no liability for any loss or damage suffered by any person acting or refraining from acting as a result of the material in this course material.

Contains public sector information licensed under the Open Government Licence v3.0

We are grateful to the Association of Chartered Certified Accountants for permission to reproduce past examination questions and extracts from the syllabus. The suggested solutions in the further question practice bank have been prepared by BPP Learning Media Ltd, except where otherwise stated.

Contents

Helping you to pass

BPP Learning Media – ACCA Approved Content Provider

As an ACCA Approved Content Provider, BPP Learning Media gives you the opportunity to use study materials reviewed by the ACCA examining team. By incorporating the examining team's comments and suggestions regarding the depth and breadth of syllabus coverage, the BPP Learning Media Workbook provides excellent, ACCA-approved support for your studies.

These materials are reviewed by the ACCA examining team. The objective of the review is to ensure that the material properly covers the syllabus and study guide outcomes, used by the examining team in setting the exams, in the appropriate breadth and depth. The review does not ensure that every eventuality, combination or application of examinable topics is addressed by the ACCA Approved Content. Nor does the review comprise a detailed technical check of the content as the Approved Content Provider has its own quality assurance processes in place in this respect.

BPP Learning Media do everything possible to ensure the material is accurate and up to date when sending to print. In the event that any errors are found after the print date, they are uploaded to the following website: www.bpp.com/learningmedia/Errata.

The PER alert

Before you can qualify as an ACCA member, you not only have to pass all your exams but also fulfil a three-year practical experience requirement (PER). To help you to recognise areas of the syllabus that you might be able to apply in the workplace to achieve different performance objectives, we have introduced the 'PER alert' feature (see the next section). You will find this feature throughout the Workbook to remind you that what you are learning to pass your ACCA exams is equally useful to the fulfilment of the PER requirement. Your achievement of the PER should be recorded in your online My Experience record.

Chapter features

Studying can be a daunting prospect, particularly when you have lots of other commitments. This Workbook is full of useful features, explained in the key below, designed to help you to get the most out of your studies and maximise your chances of exam success.

Key to icons

Key term

Central concepts are highlighted and clearly defined in the Key terms feature. Key terms are also listed in bold in the Index, for quick and easy reference.

Formula to learn

This boxed feature will highlight important formula which you need to learn for your exam.

PER alert

This feature identifies when something you are reading will also be useful for your PER requirement (see 'The PER alert' section above for more details).

Real world examples

These will give real examples to help demonstrate the concepts you are reading about.

Illustration

Illustrations walk through how to apply key knowledge and techniques step by step.

Activity

Activities give you essential practice of techniques covered in the chapter.

Essential reading

Links to the Essential reading are given throughout the chapter. The Essential reading is included in the free eBook, accessed via the Exam Success Site (see inside cover for details on how to access this).

At the end of each chapter you will find a Knowledge diagnostic, which is a summary of the main learning points from the chapter to allow you to check you have understood the key concepts. You will also find a Further study guidance which contains suggestions for ways in which you can continue your learning and enhance your understanding. This can include: recommendations for question practice from the Further question practice and solutions, to test your understanding of the topics in the Chapter; suggestions for further reading which can be done, such as technical articles, and ideas for your own research. The Chapter summary provides more detailed revision of the topics covered and is intended to assist you as you prepare for your revision phase.

Introduction to the Essential reading

The electronic version of the Workbook contains additional content, selected to enhance your studies. Consisting of revision materials and further explanations of complex areas including illustrations and activities, as well as practice questions and solutions and background reading, it is designed to aid your understanding of key topics which are covered in the main printed chapters of the Workbook.

A summary of the content of the Essential reading is given below.

Chapter		Summary of Essential reading content
1	Financial management function	• Discussion of other issues in financial management: planning & control • Further explanation of issues concerning profit-based targets such as EPS • Further discussion of stakeholders and ration analysis including numerical illustrations • Further discussion of not-for-profit organisations and value for money
2	Financial management environment	• Further discussion of fiscal policy, monetary policy and exchange rate policy • Extra examples of supply side policy
3	Working capital investment	• Discussion of different approaches used in different types of business • Extra illustrations of working capital ratios and overtrading • Further illustration of the effect of bulk buying discounts, and of inventory buffers • Example of just-in-time (JIT) • Further discussion and illustrations relating to receivables policy
4	Working capital finance	• Further illustration of cash flow forecasting • Extra discussion of investing cash surpluses
5	Investment decision	• Discussion of investment expenditure compared to revenue expenditure, and of investment decisions in not-for-profit organisations • Discussion of the principles of discounting • Extra discussion of the drawbacks of IRR and of the advantages of DCF methods of investment appraisal
6	Allowing for tax, working capital and inflation	• Supplementary illustration of tax cash flows • Deflating a cost of capital • Further illustration of handling more than one rate of inflation
7	Project appraisal and risk	• Further discussion and illustration of conservative forecasting and simulation
8	Specific investment decisions	• Further discussion and numerical illustrations relating to leasing, including the lessor and lessee • Extra illustration of capital rationing

Chapter		Summary of Essential reading content
9	Sources of finance	• Further examples and discussion of sources of short- and long-term finance • Discussion of the advantages, methods and costs of a stock market listing • Discussion of Islamic finance
10	Dividend policy	• Further discussion of dividend policy
11	Cost of capital	• General discussion of risk and return • Further analysis of the dividend growth model and CAPM
12	Capital structure	• Further discussion and illustrations of practical financial ratios and of net operating income and pecking order theory • Extra illustration of a project specific cost of capital • Further discussion of finance for SMEs
13	Business valuations	• Further discussion of information needed for valuations • Extra illustrations of the valuation of debt • Further discussion of market efficiency
14	Foreign currency risk	• Further discussion and illustration of basic and more complex hedging techniques • Further discussion of purchasing power parity theory
15	Interest rate risk	• Further illustration of FRAs and discussion of future • Further discussion of the yield curve

Introduction to Financial Management (FM)

Overall aim of the syllabus

This exam aims to develop the knowledge and skills expected of a financial manager, relating to issues affecting investments, financing, and dividend policy decisions.

The syllabus

The broad syllabus headings are:

A	Financial management function
B	Financial management environment
C	Working capital management
D	Investment appraisal
E	Business finance
F	Business valuations
G	Risk management
H	Employability and technology skills

Main capabilities

On successful completion of this exam, you should be able to:

- Discuss the role and purpose of the financial management function
- Assess and discuss the impact of the economic environment on financial management
- Discuss and apply working capital management techniques
- Carry out effective investment appraisal
- Identify and evaluate alternative sources of business finance
- Explain and calculate the cost of capital and the factors which affect it
- Discuss and apply principles of business and asset valuations
- Explain and apply risk management techniques in business
- Apply employability and technology skills

Links to other exams

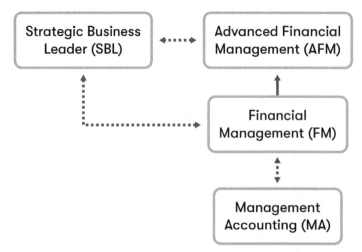

This diagram shows where direct (solid line arrows) and indirect (dashed line arrows) links exist between this exam and others that may precede or follow it.

The Advanced Financial Management (AFM) syllabus assumes auditing knowledge acquired in Financial Management (FM), and develops and applies this further and in greater depth.

Achieving ACCA's Study Guide Outcomes

This BPP Workbook covers all the FM syllabus learning outcomes. The tables below show in which chapter(s) each area of the syllabus is covered.

A	Financial management function	
A1	The nature and purpose of financial management	Chapter 1
A2	Financial objectives and the relationship with corporate strategy	Chapter 1
A3	Stakeholders and impact on corporate objectives	Chapter 1
A4	Financial and other objectives in not-for-profit organisations	Chapter 1

B	Financial management environment	
B1	The economic environment for business	Chapter 2
B2	The nature and role of financial markets and institutions	Chapter 2
B3	The nature and role of money market	Chapter 2

C	Working capital management	
C1	The nature, elements and importance of working capital	Chapter 3
C2	Management of inventories, accounts receivable, accounts payable and cash	Chapter 3
C3	Determining working capital needs and funding strategies	Chapter 4

D	Investment appraisal	
D1	Investment appraisal techniques	Chapter 5
D2	Allowing for inflation and taxation in DCF	Chapter 6
D3	Adjusting for risk and uncertainty	Chapter 7
D4	Specific investment decisions	Chapter 8

E	Business finance	
E1	Sources of and raising business finance	Chapters 9, 10
E2	Estimating the cost of capital	Chapter 11
E3	Sources of finance and their relative costs	Chapter 11
E4	Capital structure theories and practical considerations	Chapter 12
E5	Finance for small and medium-sized enterprises	Chapter 12

F	Business valuations	
F1	Nature and purpose of the valuation of business and financial assets	**Chapter 13**
F2	Models for the valuation of shares	**Chapter 13**
F3	The valuation of debt and other financial assets	**Chapter 13**
F4	Efficient market hypothesis and practical considerations in the valuation of shares	**Chapter 13**

G	Risk management	
G1	The nature and types of risk and approaches to risk management	**Chapters 14, 15**
G2	Causes of exchange rate fluctuations and interest rate fluctuations	**Chapters 14, 15**
G3	Hedging techniques for foreign currency risk	**Chapter 14**
G4	Hedging techniques for interest rate risk	**Chapter 15**

H	Employability and technology skills	
H1	Use computer technology to efficiently access and manipulate relevant information	**Exam skill**
H2	Work on relevant response options, using available functions and technology, as would be required in the workplace	**Exam skill**
H3	Navigate windows and computer screens to create and amend responses to exam requirements, using the appropriate tools	**Exam skill**
H4	Present data and information effectively, using the appropriate tools	**Exam skill**

The complete syllabus and study guide can be found by visiting the exam resource finder on the ACCA website: www.accaglobal.com/gb/en.html.

The exam

Computer-based exams

Applied Skills exams are all computer-based exams (CBE).

Approach to examining the syllabus

The Financial Management syllabus is assessed by a three-hour exam. The pass mark is **50%** and all questions in the exam are **compulsory**.

You will be expected to demonstrate a **broad knowledge** of the syllabus topics, and an ability to **apply** your knowledge and understanding of the subject to answer numerical and discussion-based questions.

The balance of the exam will be approximately 50:50 in terms of the number of marks available for discussion and the number of marks available for numerical calculations.

Format of the exam		Marks
Section A	**Fifteen objective test questions worth two marks each.** Questions will be selected from the entire syllabus. Some of the questions will be numerical and some will be discussion based. The responses to each question are marked automatically as either correct or incorrect by computer.	30
Section B	**Three mini case-study questions worth 10 marks each.** Each mini case-study question consists of five objective test questions worth two marks each. Some of the questions will be numerical and some will be discussion based. The responses to each question are marked automatically as either correct or incorrect by computer. Each mini case-study question will be mainly based on a single syllabus section. Case-study questions can be based on any area of the syllabus.	30
Section C	**Two compulsory 20-mark questions** Each 20-mark question will consist of a variety of numerical sections (to be completed in a spreadsheet) and also discussion sections. Section C questions will mainly focus on the following syllabus areas but a minority of marks can be drawn from any other area of the syllabus: • Working capital management (syllabus area C) • Investment appraisal (syllabus area D) • Business finance (syllabus area E) The responses to these questions are human marked.	40
		100

Essential skills areas to be successful in Financial Management

We think there are three areas you should develop in order to achieve exam success in Financial Management (FM):

(a) Knowledge application

(b) Specific FM skills

(c) Exam success skills

These are shown in the diagram below.

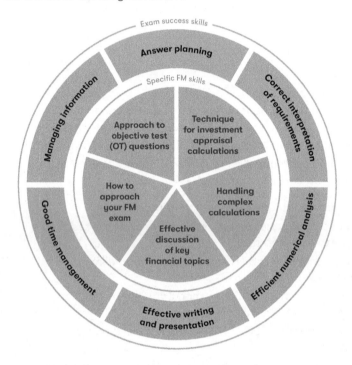

Specific FM skills

These are the skills specific to FM that we think you need to develop in order to pass the exam.

In this Workbook, there are five **Skills Checkpoints** which define each skill and show how it is applied in answering a question. A brief summary of each skill is given below.

Skill 1: Approach to objective test (OT) questions

Section A of the exam will include 15 OT questions worth two marks each. Section B of the exam will include three OT cases, worth 10 marks each. Each OT case contains a group of five OT questions based around a single scenario. 60% of your FM exam is therefore made up of OT questions. It is essential that you have a good approach to answering these questions. OT questions are auto-marked; your workings will therefore not be considered; you have to answer the whole question correctly to earn their two marks.

A step-by-step technique for tackling OT questions is outlined below:

General guidance for approaching OT questions

STEP 1: Answer the questions you know first.

If you're having difficulty answering a question, move on and come back to tackle it once you've answered all the questions you know.

It is often quicker to answer discursive style OT questions first, leaving more time for calculations.

General guidance for approaching OT questions

STEP 2: Answer all questions.

There is no penalty for an incorrect answer in ACCA exams; there is nothing to be gained by leaving an OT question unanswered. If you are stuck on a question, as a last resort, it is worth selecting the option you consider most likely to be correct and moving on. Flag the question, so if you have time after you've answered the rest of the questions, you can revisit it.

Guidance for answering specific OT questions

STEP 3: Read the requirement first!

The requirement will be stated in bold text in the exam. Identify what you are being asked to do, any technical knowledge required and what type of OT question you are dealing with. Look for key words in the requirement such as "which TWO of the following," or " which of the following is NOT".

Guidance for answering specific OT questions

STEP 4: Apply your technical knowledge to the data presented in the question.

Take your time working through calculations, making sure to read through each answer option with care. OT questions are designed so that each answer option is plausible. Work through each response option and eliminate those you know are incorrect.

Skills Checkpoint 1 covers this technique in detail through application to an exam-standard OT case question. It will also look at the different types of OT questions you are likely to see in your FM exam.

Skill 2: Technique for investment appraisal calculations

Section C of the FM exam often includes a question on investment appraisal. You may be asked to calculate the net present value (NPV) of a project and advise whether the investment is financially acceptable. Section C is human marked and therefore it is important that your calculations are laid out clearly.

Key steps in preparing an NPV calculation are outlined below:

STEP 1:
Use a standard NPV proforma. This will help the marker to understand your workings and allocate the marks easily. It will also help you to work through the figures in a methodical and time-efficient way.

STEP 2:
Input easy numbers from the question directly onto your proforma. This will make sure that you pick up as many easy marks as possible before dealing with more detailed calculations.

STEP 3:
Always use formulae to perform basic calculations. Don't write out your working in a single cell; this wastes time and you may make a mistake. Use the spreadsheet formulae instead!

STEP 4:
Show clear workings for any complex calculations.
More complex calculations such as the tax relief on tax allowable depreciation will require a separate working. Keep your workings as clear and simple as possible and ensure they are cross-referenced to your NPV proforma.

Skills Checkpoint 2 covers this technique in detail through application to an exam-standard question.

Skill 3: Handling complex calculations

The business finance section of the syllabus often involves complex calculations such as the weighted average cost of capital (WACC) or ungearing and re-gearing beta factors.

A step-by-step technique for handling complex calculations is outlined below:

> **STEP 1: Understanding the data in the question**
>
> Where a question includes a significant amount of data, read the requirements carefully to make sure that you **understand clearly what the question is asking you to do**. You can use the highlighting function to pull out important data from the question. Use the data provided to think about what formula you will need to use. For example if you are given a beta factor you will use CAPM to calculate the cost of equity; if you are given a dividend growth rate it will be the dividend growth model. If the question states that the debt is redeemable, you will need to use the IRR formula to calculate the cost of debt.

> **STEP 2: Use a standard proforma working.**
>
> For example, if you are asked to calculate the WACC, use your standard proforma or approach for calculating WACC and separately work through the individual parts of the calculation (Ke, Kd, Ve, Vd).

> **STEP 3: Use spreadsheet formulae to perform basic calculations.**
>
> Do not write out your workings; this wastes time and you may make a mistake. Use the spreadsheet formulae instead!

Skills Checkpoint 3 covers this technique in detail through application to an exam-standard question.

Skill 4: Effective discussion of key financial topics

The balance of the FM exam will be approximately 50:50 in terms of the number of marks available for discussion and the number of marks available for numerical calculations. It is very tempting to only practise numerical questions, as they are easy to mark because the answer can only be right or wrong, whereas written questions are more subjective, and a range of different answers will be given credit. Even when attempting written questions, it is tempting to write a brief answer plan and then look at the answer rather than writing a full answer to plan. Unless you practise written questions in full to time, you will never acquire the necessary skills to tackle discussion questions.

A step-by-step technique for effective discussion of key financial topics is outlined below:

STEP 1: Read and analyse the requirement.
The active verb used often dictates the approach that written answers should take. For example, 'discuss' means to examine in detail by using arguments in favour or against.
Work out how many minutes you have to answer each sub requirement.

STEP 2: Read and analyse the scenario.
Identify the type of company you are dealing with and how the financial topics in the requirement relate to that type of company. As you go through the scenario you should be highlighting important information which you think will play a key role in answering the specific requirements.

STEP 3: Plan your answer
Ensure your answer is balanced in terms of identifying the potential benefits **and** limitations of topics that are being discussed or recommended.

Step 4: Write your answer
As you write your answer, **try wherever possible to apply your analysis to the scenario**, instead of simply writing about the financial topic in generic, technical terms.
As you write your answer, explain what you mean – in one (or two) sentence(s) – and then explain **why this matters in the given scenario**. This should result in a series of short paragraphs that address the specific context of the scenario.

Skills Checkpoint 4 covers this technique in detail through application to an exam-standard question.

Skill 5: How to approach your FM exam

You can answer your FM exam in whatever order you prefer. It is important that you adopt a strategy that works best for you. We would suggest that you decide on your preferred approach and practice it by doing a timed mock exam before your real exam.

A suggested approach to tackling your FM exam is outlined below.

Complete Section A first – allocated time 54 minutes

Tackle any easier OT questions first. Often discursive style questions can be answered quickly, saving more time for calculations. Do not leave any questions unanswered. Even if you are unsure make a reasoned guess.

Complete Section B next – allocated time 54 minutes

You will have 18 mins of exam time to allocate to each of the three OT case questions in Section B. Use the same approach to OT questions as discussed for Section A.

There will normally be three discursive and two numerical questions within each case. Again, it is better to tackle the discursive type questions first and make a reasoned guess for any questions you are unsure on.

Finally, complete Section C – allocated time 72 minutes

Start with the question you feel most confident with. The first sub requirement will normally involve some detailed calculations; these tend to be very time pressured. Do not spend so much time on the calculations that you lose out on the easier discursive marks.

Skills Checkpoint 5 covers this technique in more detail.

Exam success skills

Passing the FM exam requires more than applying syllabus knowledge and demonstrating the specific FM skills; it also requires the development of excellent exam technique through question practice.

We consider the following six skills to be vital for exam success. The Skills Checkpoints show how each of these skills can be applied specifically to the FM exam.

Exam success skill 1

Managing information

Questions in the exam will present you with a lot of information. The skill is how you handle this information to make the best use of your time. The key is determining how you will approach the exam and then actively reading the questions.

Advice on developing managing information

You must take an **active approach** to reading each question. Focus on the requirement first, underlining key verbs such as 'evaluate', 'analyse', 'explain', 'discuss', to ensure you answer the question properly. Then read the rest of the question, underlining (using the Word processing functionality) and annotating important and relevant information, and making notes of any relevant technical information you think you will need (using the scratch pad provided).

Exam success skill 2

Correct interpretation of the requirements

The active verb used often dictates the approach that written answers should take (eg 'explain', 'discuss', 'evaluate'). It is important you identify and use the verb to define your approach. The **correct interpretation of the requirements** skill means correctly producing only what is being asked for by a requirement. Anything not required will not earn marks.

Advice on developing correct interpretation of the requirements

This skill can be developed by analysing question requirements and applying this process:

Step 1   **Read the requirement**

Firstly, read the requirement a couple of times slowly and carefully and highlight the active verbs. Use the active verbs to define what you plan to do. Make sure you identify any sub-requirements.

In FM, it is important that you do this not only for section C questions but also for OT questions in sections A and B

Step 2   **Read the rest of the question**

By reading the requirement first, you will have an idea of what you are looking out for as you read through the case overview and exhibits. This is a great time saver and means you don't end up having to read the whole question in full twice. You should do this in an active way – see Exam success skill 1: Managing Information.

Step 3   **Read the requirement again**

Read the requirement again to remind yourself of the exact wording before starting your written answer. This will avoid any misinterpretation of the requirements or any missed requirements entirely. This should become a habit in your approach and, with repeated practice, you will find the focus, relevance and depth of your answer plan will improve.

Exam success skill 3

Answer planning: Priorities, structure and logic

This skill requires the planning of the key aspects of an answer which accurately and completely responds to the requirement.

Advice on developing answer planning: priorities, structure and logic

Everyone will have a preferred style for an answer plan. For example, it may be a mind map, bullet-pointed lists or simply annotating the question paper. Choose the approach that you feel most comfortable with, or, if you are not sure, try out different approaches for different questions until you have found your preferred style.

For a discussion question, annotating the question is likely to be insufficient. It would be better to draw up a separate answer plan in the format of your choosing (eg a mind map or bullet-pointed lists).

Exam success skill 4

Efficient numerical analysis

This skill aims to maximise the marks awarded by making clear to the marker the process of arriving at your answer. This is achieved by laying out an answer such that, even if you make a few errors, you can still get some credit for your calculations. It is vital that you do not lose marks purely because the marker cannot follow what you have done.

Advice on developing efficient numerical analysis

This skill can be developed by applying the following process:

Step 1 **Use a standard proforma working where relevant**

If answers can be laid out in a standard proforma then always plan to do so. This will help the marker to understand your working and allocate the marks more easily. It will also help you to work through the figures in a methodical and time-efficient way.

Step 2 **Show your workings**

Keep your workings as clear and simple as possible and ensure they are cross-referenced to the main part of your answer. Where it helps, provide brief narrative explanations to help the marker understand the steps in the calculation. This means that if a mistake is made you should not lose any subsequent marks for follow-on calculations.

Step 3 **Keep moving!**

It is important to remember that, in an exam situation, it is difficult to get every number 100% correct. The key is therefore ensuring you do not spend too long on any single calculation. If you are struggling with a solution then make a sensible assumption, state it and move on.

Exam success skill 5

Effective writing and presentation

Written answers should be presented so that the marker can clearly see the points you are making, presented in the format specified in the question. The skill is to provide efficient written answers with sufficient breadth of points that answer the question, in the right depth, in the time available.

Advice on developing effective writing and presentation

Step 1   Use headings

Using the headings and sub-headings from your answer plan will give your answer structure, order and logic. This will ensure your answer links back to the requirement and is clearly signposted, making it easier for the marker to understand the different points you are making. Underlining your headings will also help the marker.

Step 2   Write your answer in short, but full, sentences

Use short, concise sentences with the aim that every sentence should say something different and generate marks. Write in full sentences, ensuring your style is professional.

Step 3   Do your calculations first and explanation second

Questions often ask for an explanation with suitable calculations. The best approach is to prepare the calculation first but present it on the bottom half of the page of your answer, or on the next page. Then add the explanation before the calculation. Performing the calculation first should enable you to explain what you have done.

Exam success skill 6

Good time management

This skill means planning your time across all the requirements so that all tasks have been attempted at the end of the 3 hours available and actively checking on time during your exam. This is so that you can flex your approach and prioritise requirements which, in your judgment, will generate the maximum marks in the available time remaining.

Advice on developing Good time management

The exam is 3 hours long, which translates to 1.8 minutes per mark. Each OT question in Section A should be allocated 3.6 mins. Some OT questions involving calculations may take slightly longer than this, however this will be balanced out with other discursive type OT questions that can be answered more quickly. Each OT case in Section B should be allocated 18 minutes to answer the five questions totalling ten marks. Each Section C question is worth 20 marks and therefore should be allocated 36 minutes. It is also important to allocate time between each sub-requirement.

Keep an eye on the clock

Aim to attempt all requirements, but be ready to be ruthless and move on if your answer is not going as planned. The challenge for many is sticking to planned timings. Be aware this is difficult to achieve in the early stages of your studies and be ready to let this skill develop over time.

If you find yourself running short on time and know that a full answer is not possible in the time you have, consider recreating your plan in overview form and then add key terms and details as time allows. Remember, some marks may be available, for example, simply stating a conclusion which you don't have time to justify in full.

Question practice

Question practice is a core part of learning new topic areas. When you practice questions, you should focus on improving the Exam success skills – personal to your needs – by obtaining feedback or through a process of self-assessment.

Financial management function

Learning objectives

On completion of this chapter, you should be able to:

	Syllabus reference
The nature and purpose of financial management	
• Explain the nature and purpose of financial management.	A1(a)
• Explain the relationship between financial management and financial and management accounting.	A1(b)
Financial objectives and the relationship with corporate strategy	
• Discuss the relationship between financial objectives, corporate objectives and corporate strategy.	A2(a)
• Identify and describe a variety of financial objectives, including: shareholder wealth maximisation, profit maximisation, earnings per share growth.	A2(b)
Stakeholders and impact on corporate objectives	
• Identify the range of stakeholders and their objectives.	A3(a)
• Discuss the possible conflict between stakeholder objectives.	A3(b)
• Discuss the role of management in meeting stakeholder objectives, including the application of agency theory.	A3(c)
• Describe and apply ways of measuring achievement of corporate objectives including: ratio analysis (using appropriate ratios such as ROCE, ROE, EPS and DPS) and changes in dividends and share prices as part of total shareholder return.	A3(d)
• Explain ways to encourage the achievement of stakeholder objectives, including: managerial reward schemes (such as share options and performance-related pay), regulatory requirements such as corporate governance codes of best practice and stock exchange listing regulations.	A3(e)
Financial and other objectives in not-for-profit organisations	
• Discuss the impact of not-for-profit (NFP) status on financial and other objectives.	A4(a)
• Discuss the nature and importance of value for money as an objective in NFP organisations.	A4(b)
• Discuss ways of measuring the achievement of objectives in NFP organisations	A4(c)

Exam context

This chapter covers Section A of the syllabus (the financial management function).

This is an important chapter that is commonly examined in Section A of the exam and could also feature in a Section B mini case study scenario question. Part of a Section C exam question could examine some of the themes of this chapter, but these areas will not be the main focus of a Section C question.

This chapter also sets out the main themes of financial management; these will be covered in later chapters.

Chapter overview

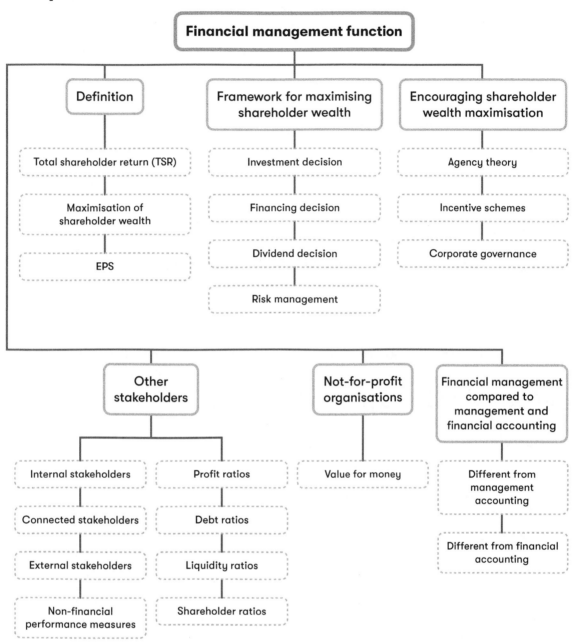

Financial management function

- Definition
  - Total shareholder return (TSR)
  - Maximisation of shareholder wealth
  - EPS

- Framework for maximising shareholder wealth
  - Investment decision
  - Financing decision
  - Dividend decision
  - Risk management

- Encouraging shareholder wealth maximisation
  - Agency theory
  - Incentive schemes
  - Corporate governance

- Other stakeholders
  - Internal stakeholders
  - Connected stakeholders
  - External stakeholders
  - Non-financial performance measures
  - Profit ratios
  - Debt ratios
  - Liquidity ratios
  - Shareholder ratios

- Not-for-profit organisations
  - Value for money

- Financial management compared to management and financial accounting
  - Different from management accounting
  - Different from financial accounting

1 Purpose of financial management

1.1 Definition of financial management

> **Financial management:** The acquisition and deployment of financial resources to achieve key objectives.

We can analyse this definition by breaking it down into its separate parts.

1.1.1 Acquisition of financial resources

This involves obtaining suitable sources of finance and is a **financing decision**.

In selecting sources of finance, **risk will be a consideration** since some sources of finance create risk for a business (eg a variable rate bank loan may expose a company to the risk of interest rate increases).

1.1.2 Deployment of financial resources

This involves using a business's financial resources effectively and can involve deciding whether or not to invest in projects (the **investment decision**), and whether or not to return surplus cash to shareholders (the **dividend decision**).

When making investments, **risk** will again be a consideration.

1.1.3 Key financial objectives – profits

Profit maximisation is often **assumed** to be the main financial objective of a business.

In fact this is **not** the assumption made in financial management and, in reality, shareholders often express disappointment in a company's performance even when profits are rising; this suggests that **profit is not sufficient as a financial objective.**

Activity 1: Financial objectives

B Co has just released its financial results for the year and its profits before tax increased by 38% over the previous year. This was due largely to a doubling of sales in South-East Asia. However, the share price in B Co fell by almost 20% immediately after the profit announcement.

Required

Which of the following is the LEAST likely explanation for the fall in share price?

O Sales in South-East Asia had been expected to increase by more than 100%.

O The depreciation charge was higher due to a change in accounting policy.

O The level of B Co's business risk has increased over the year.

O Delays in the launch of new products are expected in the coming year.

Profit, as a financial objective, has a number of drawbacks:

(a) It is **historic** and is **not future-oriented**

    (i) It therefore **does not measure the future potential of a company**

(b) It does not measure **liquidity or risk**

    (i) Both are important commercial issues

(c) It can be **manipulated**

    (i) eg by the use of accounting policies

However, profit and profit-based ratios such as earnings per share will continue to be monitored by investors as they are evidence of the returns that have actually been achieved by a company.

> **Earnings per share (EPS):** Profits distributable to shareholders/Number of ordinary shares

Distributable profits will be **after interest, tax and preference dividends.**

Other profit-based ratios (such as return on capital employed) are covered later in the chapter.

1.1.4 Key financial objectives – shareholder wealth maximisation

For a for-profit company, **maximisation of shareholder wealth is assumed to be the main financial objective,** although profit-based objectives are still important.

The wealth of the shareholders in a company comes from:

- **Dividends** received
- **Market value** of the shares

The market value of shares will depend on the forecast **future cash flows** of the company, and the perceived **risk** of these cash flows. These forecasts will result from a financial analysis of the impact of a firm's long-term business plans, ie its **corporate strategy.**

The ability of a firm to create wealth for shareholders is measured by total shareholder return (TSR).

Total shareholder return: Dividend + change in share price/Share price at the start of the year

 Illustration 1: TSR

A shareholder purchased 1,000 shares in SJG Co on 1 January 20X1 at a market price of $2.50 per share. On 31 December 20X1 the shares had a market value of $2.82 per share. The dividend paid during 20X1 was $0.28 per share.

Required

Calculate total shareholder return.

Solution

Capital gain during the year is $2.82 - $2.50 = $0.32

The total shareholder return is:

($0.28 + $0.32)/$2.50 = 0.24 or **24%**

This is made up of the capital gain of $0.32/$2.50 = 0.128 or 12.8%

and the dividend return or dividend yield of $0.28/$2.50 = 0.112 or 11.2%

Exam focus point

Students often forget to use the start of year share price as the denominator when calculating the total shareholder return. The start of the period share price needs to be used, as the return being calculated is the return on the share price paid at the start of the period.

Activity 2: Calculation of financial objectives

Magneto plc has objectives to improve **earnings per share (EPS)** and **dividends per share (DPS)** by 10% p.a.

	Last year	Current year
	$m	$m
Profits before interest and tax	22,300	23,726
Interest	3,000	3,000
Tax	5,790	6,218
Profits after interest and tax	13,510	14,508
Preference dividends	200	200
Dividends	7,986	8,585
Retained earnings	5,324	5,723
No. of ordinary shares issued (millions)	100,000	100,000
Ordinary share price at the end of the year	$4.70 per share	$5.16 per share

Required

1   What is the current year earnings per ordinary share?

   O   14.5 cents

   O   14.3 cents

   O   5.7 cents

   O   5.3 cents

2   What is the growth in the dividend per ordinary share?

   O   0%

   O   8.0%

   O   8.6%

   O   7.5%

3   What is the total shareholder return in the current year?

   O   11.6%

   O   10.6%

   O   9.8%

   O   1.8%

Solution

2 A framework for maximising shareholder wealth

Financial management is based on a framework of decisions that are **designed to maximise shareholder wealth**.

2.1 Investment decision

Firstly, and most importantly, the **investment decision** (eg in projects) analyses proposed investments to ensure they are beneficial to the investor and maximise shareholder wealth; this is mainly covered in Chapters 3, 5–8 and 13.

Investments are also crucial in helping a firm to achieve key **corporate objectives** such as market share and quality, and in achieving **financial objectives** such as improving **earnings per share**.

2.2 Financing decision

Financing decisions mainly focus on how much debt a firm should use, and a key aim is to minimise the **cost of capital.**

This area is focused on in Chapters 4 and 9–12.

2.3 Dividend decision

The **dividend decision** considers how much to pay out to shareholders. It is determined by how much a firm has decided to spend on investments (the investment decision) and how much of the finance needed for this it has decided to raise externally (the finance decision) and is a good example of the **interrelationship** between these key decisions.

The dividend decision is covered in Chapter 10.

2.4 Risk management

Risk needs to be considered in determining what type of finance to raise, how to invest it and whether to pay a dividend. Risk matters to shareholders and therefore needs to be carefully managed.

Risk management is mainly covered in Chapters 14–15.

3 Encouraging shareholder wealth maximisation

3.1 Corporate and financial objectives

3.1.1 Corporate strategy and objectives

Corporate strategy is a long-term plan for how an organisation intends to compete, and which markets it intends to compete in.

Corporate objectives are the overall aims of an organisation that should result from the successful implementation of its corporate strategy.

Some corporate objectives, such as shareholder wealth maximisation and profit maximisation, have already been considered. Other corporate objectives reflect the existence of other groups with a powerful interest in how a company is being run (stakeholders). The following tables gives some examples of such objectives.

Examples of other corporate objectives	
Market share	A certain level of market share will often be critical in order to be competitive.
Social responsibility	This might include environmental concerns such as pollution and sustainability, and also treatment of employees and suppliers.
Survival	Especially in an economic recession, the short-term survival of a company is likely to be in the best interest of shareholders.

3.1.2 Relationship to financial objectives

From a financial management perspective, it is argued that corporate objectives should normally only be pursued in support of a **long-run objective to maximise shareholder wealth**.

As such, there are some potential conflicts to be aware of.

Potential conflict between corporate objectives and financial objectives	
Market share	An overly aggressive approach to chasing sales can create pressure on profit if prices are cut in order to do this. Liquidity problems may also arise (see section on overtrading in section 2 of Chapter 3)
Social responsibility	Expenditure on achieving these goals may be in line with achieving shareholder wealth maximisation. However, if excessive spending on achieving this objective compromises the competitiveness of a company, then there may be a conflict that needs to be managed.
Survival	In the longer term, it may be better for a company to close down or sell-out to another company and to cease to exist as an entity; this would release funds back to shareholders to invest in a more productive way. The ability of a company to manage the potential conflict between corporate and financial objectives will depend on the actions of its managers (see section 3.2) and the effectiveness of its corporate governance processes (see section 3.3).

3.2 Agency theory

> **Agency relationship:** A description of the relationship between business owners (eg shareholders) and those acting as agents on their behalf (eg managers), expressing the idea that managers act as agents for the owners, using delegated powers to run the company in the owners' best interests.

In a for-profit company, the ordinary shareholders (equity shareholders) are the owners of the company to whom the board of directors is accountable, the actual powers of shareholders tend to be restricted, except in companies where the shareholders are also the directors. The **day-to-day** running of a company is the responsibility of **management.**

Managers can therefore be said to be acting as the **agents of shareholders.**

However, managers (unless they have a significant equity stake in a business) may not behave in a way that is likely to maximise shareholder wealth. The danger that managers may not act in the best interest of owners (eg shareholders) is referred to as the agency problem.

Examples of the agency problem	
Maximisation of short-term profits at the expense of long-term profits (short-termism)	For example, by cutting back on investments – to ensure short-term profit targets are met and to ensure profit-related bonuses are paid
Minimise dividend payments	To free up funds to use within the business
Neglect risk management	There is often a greater focus on profit
Boost their own pay and perks	Remuneration may be set at excessively generous levels, that damage shareholder wealth

Agency problems can be addressed by monitoring the actions of management (corporate governance) or by the use of incentive schemes.

3.3 Corporate governance

In many countries, including the UK, the **corporate governance** regulations have been developed to **monitor the actions of management**.

> **Corporate governance:** The rules and processes by which the behaviour of a firm is directed.

Here are some common features, which are part of the **listing requirements** for major stock exchanges such as the London Stock Exchange:

Board of directors	Key committees
• Separate MD and chairman (to reduce the power of a single individual) • Significant % of the board consisting of non-executive directors (NEDs – part-time directors who monitor the actions of executives) • NEDs should be independent (three-year contract, no share options)	Remuneration committee • Pay and incentives of executive directors set by NEDs Audit committee • Monitors risk management processes • NEDs only Nomination committee • Choice of new directors by NEDs

3.3.1 Other stock exchange regulations

In addition, other stock exchange requirements increase the scrutiny of directors by shareholders; for example:

- The regular publication of financial accounts (including information on future strategy and risk management policies)
- Regular updates to the stock exchange on trading performance.

Activity 3: Corporate governance

The following statements have been made about corporate governance.

(1) Sound systems of corporate governance involve the establishment of risk management and internal control procedures for the organisation.

(2) Good corporate governance requires the organisation to always act in an ethically acceptable manner even if that is contrary to the law.

(3) A non-executive director should not be paid for his services to the organisation in order to keep him independent.

Required

Which of these statements is/are correct?

- ○ (1) and (2) only
- ○ (1), (2) and (3)
- ○ (1) only
- ○ (3) only

3.4 Incentive schemes

> **Goal congruence:** The alignment between the objectives of agents acting within an organisation and the objectives of the organisation as a whole.

Goal congruence may be better achieved and the 'agency problem' better dealt with by offering organisational **rewards** (more pay and promotion) for the achievement of certain levels of performance.

Examples of such remuneration incentives are:

(a) Performance-related pay (PRP)

Pay or bonuses are usually related to the size of profits, but other performance indicators may be used. PRP may create problems if rewards are based on short-term profits because this may encourage managers to focus on short-term profits at the expense of long-term profits. It may be better to award pay on a broader range of targets (including for example, total shareholder return and key non-financial measures).

Cash or share awards may be given for achieving good performance.

(b) Share options

In a share option scheme, selected employees are given a number of share options, each of which gives the holder the right after a certain date to subscribe for shares in the company at a fixed price. The value of an option will increase if the company is successful and its share price goes up. So, managers now have an interest that aligns with shareholders (ie a higher share price).

However, it is debatable whether share options are really motivational because some managers may feel that there are more powerful forces than their own performance that drive share prices and that these are largely beyond their control (eg market sentiment).

4 Needs of other stakeholders

KEY TERM

Stakeholders: Groups or individuals whose interests are affected by the activities of a firm.

4.1 Types of stakeholder

Stakeholders can be classified as:

(a) **Internal** – staff, managers

(b) **Connected** – finance providers (shareholders, banks), customers, suppliers

(c) **External** – government, trade unions, pressure groups

Shareholders are normally the most important stakeholder group, but the interests of other stakeholders are often important too.

A difficulty in meeting stakeholder needs is that there is often a **conflict between stakeholder objectives**, eg there is a short-term conflict between achieving profit for shareholders and delivering pay rises to staff. Resolving this conflict will require the development of **acceptable compromises**, eg pay rises could be linked to productivity gains.

4.1.1 Examples of stakeholder conflict

Between different shareholder groups

Some shareholders might have a preference for short-term dividends, others for long-term capital gain (requiring more cash to be reinvested, and less to be paid as a dividend).

Shareholders and staff/customers/suppliers

Pursuit of short-term profits may lead to difficult relationships with other stakeholders. For example, relationships with suppliers and customers may be disrupted by demands for changes to the terms of trade. Employees may be made redundant in a drive to reduce costs.

These policies may aid short-term profits, but at the expense of damaging long-term relationships and consequently damaging shareholder value in the long term.

Shareholders and external stakeholders

The impact of a company's activities may impact adversely on its environment, eg noise, pollution.

Managers and shareholders

This has been discussed earlier, in section 3.2 (agency theory).

4.2 Non-financial performance measures

To ensure that the interests of other stakeholder groups are not neglected, non-financial measures can be used in addition to financial measures. Here are some examples:

(a) **Staff** – staff turnover (percentage of staff leaving during a year)

(b) **Customers** – liquidity ratios, complaints, market share

(c) **Suppliers** – payables (creditor) days

4.3 Financial performance measures

Financial ratios are normally split into four categories; each type is likely to be of interest to different stakeholders (note that these ratios need to be learnt):

(a) **Profitability ratios** – important to assess managerial performance

(b) **Debt ratios** – important to banks

(c) **Liquidity ratios** – important to suppliers and customers

(d) **Shareholder investor ratios** – important to shareholders

4.3.1 Profitability ratios

Profitability ratios include:

Return on capital employed (ROCE) = (Profit from operations/Capital employed) %

Profit from operations = before interest and tax

Capital employed = equity plus long-term debt (or total assets less current liabilities)

This is **an important ratio because you cannot assess profits or profit growth properly without relating them to the amount of funds (the capital) employed** in making the profits.

ROE (return on equity) = Profits after interest and tax/Shareholders funds

Another measure of the firm's overall performance is **return on equity**. This compares net profit **after interest and tax** with the equity that shareholders have invested in the firm.

4.3.2 Debt ratios

Debt ratios include:

Gearing = Book value of debt/Book value of equity

(alternatively this could be calculated as debt/(debt + equity) and could use book or market values, so read the question carefully)

Debt ratios are concerned with how much the company owes in relation to its size and whether it is getting into heavier debt or improving its situation. The main debt and gearing ratios are covered in Chapter 12.

The interest cover or coverage ratio is a measure of the affordability of interest payments.

Interest cover = Profit from operations/interest

As a general guide, an interest coverage ratio of **less than three times** is considered low, indicating that profitability is too low given the gearing of the company. However, a better benchmark would be the **industry average interest cover**, and this is often given in a question.

4.3.3 Liquidity ratios

Liquidity ratios include:

Current ratio = Current assets/Current liabilities

Acid Test ratio = Current assets (less inventory)/Current liabilities

A company should have enough current assets that give a promise of 'cash to come' to meet its commitments to pay its current liabilities. Superficially, a current ratio in excess of 1 implies that the organisation has enough cash and near-cash assets to satisfy its immediate liabilities.

Companies are unable to convert all their current assets into cash very quickly. In some businesses where inventory turnover is slow, most inventories are not very liquid assets. For this reason, we calculate an additional liquidity ratio, known as the **quick ratio or acid test ratio**.

4.3.4 Shareholder investor ratios

Shareholder investor ratios include:

Dividend yield = (Dividend per share/Market price per share) × 100

Earnings per share (EPS) = Profits distributable to ordinary shareholders/Number of ordinary shares issued

Price/earnings (P/E) ratio = Market price per share/EPS

The value of the P/E ratio reflects the market's appraisal of the share's future prospects – the more highly regarded a company, the higher will be its share price and its P/E ratio.

Activity 4: Calculation of financial objectives

Summary financial information for Robertson plc is given below, covering the last two years.

	Previous year	Current year
	$'000	$'000
Turnover	43,800	48,000
Cost of sales	16,600	18,200
Salaries and wages	12,600	12,900
Other costs	5,900	7,400
Profit before interest and tax	**8,700**	**9,500**
Interest	1,200	1,000
Tax	2,400	2,800
Profit after interest and tax	**5,100**	**5,700**
Dividends payable	2,000	2,200
Shareholders' funds	**22,600**	**25,700**
Long-term debt	**11,300**	**9,000**
Number of shares in issue ('000)	9,000	9,000
P/E ratio (average for year) Robertson plc	17.0	18.0

Required

Review Robertson's performance by calculating ROCE, interest cover and total shareholder return.

Solution

Essential reading

See Chapter 1 section 2 of the Essential reading for further discussion of stakeholders and ratio analysis.

The Essential reading is available as an Appendix of the digital edition of the Workbook.

---

5 Not-for-profit organisations

5.1 Value for money

> **Value for money:** This can be defined as getting the best possible combination of services from the least resources, which means maximising the benefits for the lowest possible cost.

Many organisations are not for profit. In this case their key objective will be to ensure that the organisation is getting good **value for money.**

5.1.1 Value for money

Value for money involves measuring economy, efficiency and effectiveness.

(a) **Economy** – purchase of inputs of appropriate quality at minimum cost

(b) **Efficiency** – use of these inputs to maximise output

(c) **Effectiveness** – use of these inputs to achieve its goals (quality, speed of response)

The existence of not-for-profit organisations means that we need to recognise that financial management is not always about shareholder wealth maximisation.

Essential reading

See Chapter 1 section 3 of the Essential reading for further discussion of this area.

The Essential reading is available as an Appendix of the digital edition of the Workbook.

Activity 5: Objectives

Which of the following statements is true?

O The agency problem is not important for a public sector organisation because there are no shareholders.

O Maximisation of shareholder wealth is the primary objective of financial management.

O Value for money is not relevant to a for-profit company.

O The agency problem means that shareholder wealth is not being maximised.

6 Financial management compared to management and financial accounting

From your earlier studies you will be aware of the key functions of management and financial accounting. These are recapped and contrasted in the following table.

Financial accounts	Management accounts
Details the performance of an organisation **over a defined period.**	Used to **aid management to control** activities and to help in **decision making.**
Limited companies must, **by law,** prepare financial accounts.	There is **no legal requirement** to prepare management accounts.
Format of published financial accounts is set by **law** and **accounting standards.**	The **format** of management accounts is entirely at management discretion.
Most financial accounting information is of a **monetary** nature.	Management accounts incorporate **non-monetary** measures.

Financial accounts	Management accounts
Financial accounts present an essentially **historic** picture of **past** operations.	Management accounts are both a **historical** record and a **future** planning tool.

Having introduced the scope of financial management, we can identify some differences between **financial management** and management accounting because financial management is:

- **externally focused** (analysis is focused on what is best for shareholders)
- concerned with **longer-term decision-making** issues.

Also, we can say that **financial management differs** from financial accounting because it is:

- **Forward looking**
- **Useful at providing information that is directly used for decision making**
- **Has no set format.**

Activity 6: Financial management

Mount Co is planning to move into a new foreign market. This will involve acquiring a new warehouse, organising new suppliers and a new distribution network.

Required

Which of the following aspects of the investment in Country A would you expect to be the responsibility of financial management?

- O   Recording the acquisition of new non-current assets in Mount Co's financial statements.
- O   Producing regular profit forecasts for the new operation in Country A
- O   Managing the exchange rate risk faced by the new operation
- O   Choosing the new suppliers that will be used

Chapter summary

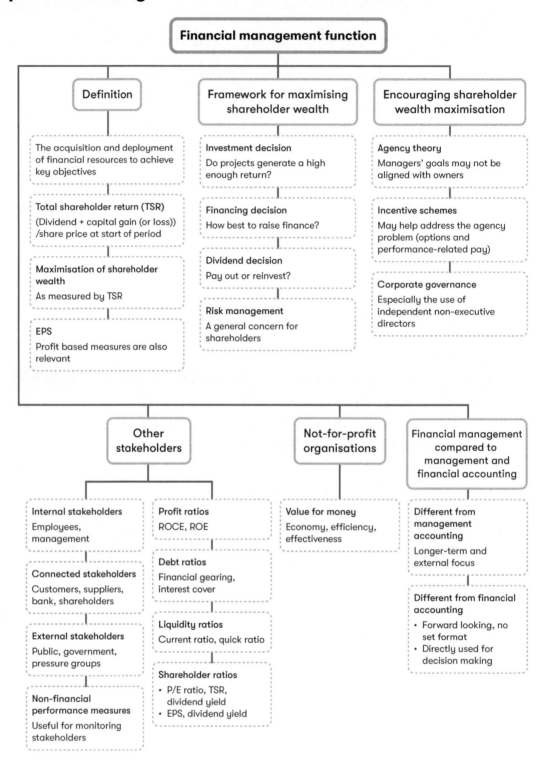

Financial management function

Definition
- The acquisition and deployment of financial resources to achieve key objectives
- Total shareholder return (TSR)
  (Dividend + capital gain (or loss)) /share price at start of period
- Maximisation of shareholder wealth
  As measured by TSR
- EPS
  Profit based measures are also relevant

Framework for maximising shareholder wealth
- Investment decision
  Do projects generate a high enough return?
- Financing decision
  How best to raise finance?
- Dividend decision
  Pay out or reinvest?
- Risk management
  A general concern for shareholders

Encouraging shareholder wealth maximisation
- Agency theory
  Managers' goals may not be aligned with owners
- Incentive schemes
  May help address the agency problem (options and performance-related pay)
- Corporate governance
  Especially the use of independent non-executive directors

Other stakeholders
- Internal stakeholders
  Employees, management
- Connected stakeholders
  Customers, suppliers, bank, shareholders
- External stakeholders
  Public, government, pressure groups
- Non-financial performance measures
  Useful for monitoring stakeholders

- Profit ratios
  ROCE, ROE
- Debt ratios
  Financial gearing, interest cover
- Liquidity ratios
  Current ratio, quick ratio
- Shareholder ratios
  • P/E ratio, TSR, dividend yield
  • EPS, dividend yield

Not-for-profit organisations
- Value for money
  Economy, efficiency, effectiveness

Financial management compared to management and financial accounting
- Different from management accounting
  Longer-term and external focus
- Different from financial accounting
  • Forward looking, no set format
  • Directly used for decision making

Knowledge diagnostic

1. Financial management

Financial management concerns the acquisition and deployment of financial resources to achieve key objectives to maximise shareholder wealth; this can be measured by total shareholder return for a for-profit company.

2. Framework for maximising shareholder wealth

The investment decision is the key mechanism for increasing shareholder wealth, the other key decisions include the financing, dividend and risk management decisions.

3. Agency issues

Corporate governance regulations and incentive schemes are used to combat the agency problem.

4. Ratio analysis

To assess the impact of decisions on shareholders and other stakeholders, it is important to monitor profit, debt, liquidity and shareholder ratios. These ratios need to be learnt.

5. Value for money

Economy – purchase of inputs of appropriate quality at minimum cost

Efficiency – use of these inputs to maximise output

Effectiveness – use of these inputs to achieve its goals (quality, speed of response)

Further study guidance

Question practice

Now try the following from the Further question practice bank (available in the digital edition of the Workbook):

Section A questions

Q1, Q2, Q3

Activity answers

Activity 1: Financial objectives

The correct answer is: Sales in South-East Asia had been expected to increase by more than 100%.

The share price will fall if:

- **expected future returns fall; or**
- **if risk rises.**

This is the case with the other options.

Activity 2: Calculation of financial objectives

1   The correct answer is: 14.3 cents

Earnings after preference dividends divided by the number of shares. $14,308m/100,000 = 14.3 cents

2   The correct answer is: 7.5%

Dividend per share has increased from 8 cents per share to 8.6 cents, a 7.5% increase.

3   The correct answer is: 11.6%

Dividend per share = 8.6 cents

Increase in share price (516 - 470) = 46 cents

As a percentage of the opening share price this is (8.6 + 46)/470 = 11.6%.

Activity 3: Corporate governance

The correct answer is: (1) only

Sound corporate governance does not include breaking the law and a non-executive director can expect to be paid for their services but not in such a way that impairs their independence (eg in shares or share options).

Activity 4: Calculation of financial objectives

The question does not tell us what the share price has been over the period, but it does provide the price/earnings (P/E) ratio. We can derive the share price at the time of the announcement of the results by multiplying the EPS of the company by its P/E ratio which shows the share price as a multiple of its EPS:

	Previous year	Current year
Interest cover	8,700/1,200 = 7.25	9,500/1,000 = 9.5
ROCE	8,700/33,900 = 25.7%	9,500/34,700 = 27.4%
Share price	17 × 5,100/9,000 = 9.63	18 × 5,700/9,000 = 11.40
Total shareholder return		(0.244 dividend + 1.77 increase in share price)/9.63 start of year share price = **21%**

- The debt level does not appear to be a problem, as interest cover is high.
- The P/E ratio, which is influenced by perceived growth potential, has improved.
- Total shareholder return looks impressive, although we would need to know the shareholders' expected return (covered in Chapter 11) to be sure of this.

Activity 5: Objectives

The correct answer is: The agency problem means that shareholder wealth is not being maximised.

If there is an agency problem, it means that the agents of the shareholders (eg managers) are not acting in the best interest of shareholders.

Notes on incorrect answers:

The agency problem also refers to managers not working in the best interest of the organisation; this can also happen in the public sector.

Maximisation of shareholder wealth is the primary objective of financial management – this is true but only for profit-seeking companies, not true for not-for-profit companies.

Value for money is relevant to a for-profit company; even though the term is more commonly associated with not-for profit companies

Activity 6: Financial management

The correct answer is: Managing the exchange rate risk faced by the new operation

Risk management is a key function of financial management, and exchange rate risk is likely to be an issue here.

Notes on incorrect answers:

Recording the acquisition of new non-current assets in the financial statements is the responsibility of the financial accounting function.

Producing regular profit forecasts for the new operation in Country A is a management accounting role.

Financial management may be involved in the terms of trade that will be used with new suppliers, but not the **choice** of suppliers (this will be managed by a purchasing department).

2

Financial management environment

Learning objectives

On completion of this chapter, you should be able to:

	Syllabus reference
The economic environment for business	
• Identify and explain the main macroeconomic policy targets.	B1(a)
• Define and discuss the role of fiscal, monetary, interest rate and exchange rate policies in achieving macroeconomic policy targets.	B1(b)
• Explain how government economic policy interacts with planning and decision-making in business.	B1(c)
• Explain the need for, and the interaction with, planning and decision-making in business of: competition policy, government assistance for business, green policies and corporate governance regulation.	B1(d)
The nature and role of financial markets and institutions	
• Identify the nature & role of money & capital markets, nationally & internationally	B2(a)
• Explain the role of financial intermediaries.	B2(b)
• Explain the functions of a stock market and a corporate bond market.	B2(c)
• Explain the nature and features of different securities in relation to the risk/return trade-off.	B2(d)
• Explain the impact of Fintech in changing the nature and role of financial markets and institutions	B2(e)
The nature and role of money markets	
• Describe the role of the money markets in providing short-term liquidity to the private & public sector, providing short-term trade finance, allowing an organisation to manage its exposure to currency & interest rate risk.	B3(a)
• Explain the role of banks & other institutions in the operation of the money markets.	B3(b)
• Explain & apply the characteristics and role of the principal money market instruments: interest-bearing & discount instruments, & derivatives.	B3(c)

Exam context

This chapter covers Section B of the syllabus (Financial Management Environment).

The topics in this chapter introduce some of the key issues in the financial management environment which impact on a business. It is a very factual chapter and introduces several terms that are examined mainly in section A and B of the exam and mainly as discussion-based OT questions. Part of a section C exam question could examine some of the themes of this chapter but would not test these areas as the main focus of a section C question.

Chapter overview

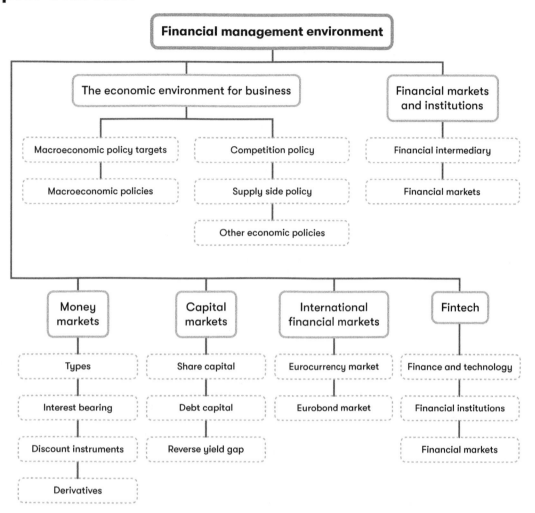

1 The economic environment for business

1.1 Macroeconomic policy targets

KEY TERM

Macroeconomics: Concerned with issues affecting the economy as a whole eg economic growth, inflation, unemployment.

The policies pursued by a government aim to achieve various targets for the economy as a whole.

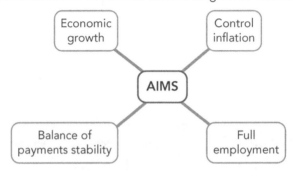

(a) **Economic growth** – 'Growth' implies an increase in national income, which is usually interpreted as a rising standard of living.

(b) **Control price inflation** – This means managing price inflation to a low, stable level. One reason that inflation is viewed as a problem is that if a country has a relatively high rate of inflation, then companies in this country can become less competitive relative to its international trading rivals.

(c) **Full employment** – So that everyone who wants a job has one.

(d) **Balance of payments stability** – It is very difficult for a country to spend more on imports than it earns from exports for a sustained period of time. Where imports exceed exports, this is often called a balance of payments deficit, and governments will often act to correct this situation by manipulating the exchange rate to switch spending away from imports and towards exports (sometimes called an **expenditure switching** policy and covered in the next section).

Expansionary macroeconomic policies can be adopted in order to increase demand (spending) in the economy in order to stimulate **economic growth** and create the need for new **jobs.**

Contractionary macroeconomic policies are required to keep **inflation** within acceptable limits or to reduce domestic spending on imported goods (and so to improve the balance of payments).

1.2 Macroeconomic policies

In order to achieve its objectives, a government will use a number of different policies.

Policy type	Definition
Fiscal policy	Involves using **government spending and taxation** in order to manage demand in order to achieve macroeconomic targets.
Monetary policy	Aims to influence monetary variables such as the **interest rate and the money supply** in order to manage demand to achieve macroeconomic targets.
Exchange rate policy	Governments may try to: • fix the exchange rate (fixed rate policy) • allow it to change in response to market forces (a floating rate policy) • take action to influence its value (a managed exchange rate policy)

These **policy tools** are not mutually exclusive, and a government will adopt a policy mix of monetary policy, fiscal policy and exchange rate policy to achieve its macroeconomic targets.

1.2.1 Impact on business of fiscal policy

A government might intervene in the economy by:

(a) **Spending more** (or less) **money** eg on services such as hospitals and education, or on benefit payments

(b) **Changing the rate of direct taxes** eg taxes on individual or corporate **income**

(c) **Changing the rate of indirect taxes** eg taxes on **spending** (eg VAT)

Each of these may have a **direct impact** on a business (eg changing the rate of tax on corporate income) or an **indirect impact** stemming from changes to the level of **overall (or aggregate) demand** within an economy as a result of fiscal policy (eg increased government spending or lower taxes will boost aggregate demand and is likely to increase sales).

Essential reading

See Chapter 2 Section 1 of the Essential Reading, available in the digital edition of the Workbook, for further discussion of fiscal policy.

The Essential reading is available as an Appendix of the digital edition of the Workbook.

1.2.2 Impact on business of monetary policy

Interest rate changes brought about by government policy affect the **borrowing costs** of businesses.

Increases in interest rates will mean that **fewer investments** show positive returns, deterring companies from borrowing to finance expansion.

Increases in interest rates will also exert a **downward pressure on share prices**, making it more difficult for companies to raise monies from new share issues.

Businesses will also be indirectly affected by **decreases in consumer demand** that result from increases in interest rates.

Essential reading

See Chapter 2 section 2 of the Essential Reading, available in the digital edition of the Workbook, for further discussion of monetary policy.

The Essential reading is available as an Appendix of the digital edition of the Workbook.

BPP LEARNING MEDIA

1.2.3 Impact on business of exchange rate policy

Exchange rate changes brought about by government policy affect the value of sales revenue and costs that are in a foreign currency.

Real life example

Imagine a European car maker is trying to sell cars in the USA. The required revenue per car is 30,000 Euros. If the exchange rate is $1.2 per Euro, then a price of 30,000 x 1.2 = $36,000 is charged.

However, if the value of the Euro falls to $1.0 per Euro then a price of a car falls to $30,000 (30,000 x 1).

The price in $s has fallen significantly, so demand from US customers will increase, and **more cars will be exported to the USA as a result of a fall in the value of the Euro.**

Conversely, a high exchange rate means that any given price in Euros results in a higher price in $s. So, demand in the USA for exports from Europe will be lower.

Fluctuating exchange rates (resulting from exchange rates being determined partly or completely by market forces) create **uncertainties** for businesses involved in international trade, and a **fixed exchange rate policy** may be helpful in reducing this level of uncertainty.

Impact of a lower exchange rate	Impact of a higher exchange rate
Domestic goods are cheaper in foreign markets so **demand for exports increases.**	**Domestic goods are more expensive** in foreign markets so **demand for exports falls.**
Foreign goods are more expensive so **demand for imports falls.**	Foreign goods are cheaper so **demand for imports rises.**
Imported raw materials are more expensive which **increases production costs.**	Imported raw materials are cheaper so **costs of production fall.**

Essential reading

See Chapter 2 section 3 of the Essential Reading, available in the digital edition of the Workbook, for further discussion of exchange rate policy.

The Essential reading is available as an Appendix of the digital edition of the Workbook.

Activity 1: Macroeconomic issues

The following statements have been made in connection with macroeconomic policy.

Which is correct?

(1)   A contractionary fiscal policy involves in part the reduction of government spending.

(2)   Businesses with variable rate debt are likely to see their interest expense increase in the event of an expansionary monetary policy.

O   (1) only

O   (2) only

O   Both (1) and (2)

O   Neither (1) nor (2)

1.3 Competition policy

1.3.1 Market failure

KEY TERM

> **Market failure:** Said to occur when the market mechanism fails to work efficiently and therefore the outcome is sub-optimal.

Types of market failure			
Imperfect competition	**Social costs**	**Imperfect information**	**Fairness**
Where one company's large market share is leading to **inefficiency or excessive profits**, the state may intervene to stimulate competition (see next section for further detail).	These are impacts on a third party (other than the buyer or seller) of an economic transaction (eg pollution), where these effect society as a whole they are called **negative externalities**. These costs may require regulations eg controls on emissions of pollutants, restrictions on car use in urban areas.	This is where false information is being put into the public domain and distorting consumer choice (eg advertisements making false claims).	The government may also resort to regulation to **improve social justice** eg concerns about the fairness of expensive housing.

1.3.2 Imperfect competition

There are two market structures where large firms are often viewed as having excessive market power that may restrict consumer choice, and where competition is often weak.

(a) Oligopoly – this is where **a few large firms** dominate the market.

(b) Monopoly – this is where one large firm dominates the market; in theory this implies 100% market share but **in practice** any firm with a market share of **above 25%** is viewed as having monopoly power.

This power can allow large companies to charge **high prices**, and the lack of incentive of competition may mean companies have **no incentive** to **improve their products** or **offer a wider range of products** or to **improve the efficiency** of its **use of resources**.

However, these market structures are not always viewed as being suboptimal because a large company is often able to benefit from the kinds of **economies of scale** (benefits of conducting operations on a large scale) that can minimise prices (which benefits consumers).

1.3.3 Competition policy

Government regulatory authorities (eg the Competition and Markets Authority in the UK) can be asked to investigate what could be called **'oligopoly situations'** involving explicit or implicit collusion between firms, who together control the market. The Authority must decide whether the monopoly is acting **'against the public interest'**. If so, this may result in several measures, including:

- Price cuts
- Price and profit controls
- The breaking up of the firm (rarely)

A prospective **merger** between two or more companies may be referred to the regulatory authority. In the UK, a referral may be made to the Competition and Markets Authority for investigation if a larger company will gain more than **25% market share** and where a merger

BPP LEARNING MEDIA

appears likely to lead to a substantial lessening of competition in one or more markets in the UK. Many other countries have similar regulatory authorities.

If a potential merger is investigated, the authority again must determine whether the merger would be against the public interest. As with monopolies, it will assess the relative benefits and costs in order to arrive at a decision.

1.4 Supply side policies

Supply side policies aim to improve efficiency, motivation or productive capacity.

Examples include deregulation, re-training, privatisation and cutting income and corporation tax. Competition policy is another example of a supply-side policy.

Essential reading

See Chapter 2 section 4 of the Essential Reading, available in the digital edition of the Workbook, for further discussion of supply-side policies.

The Essential reading is available as an Appendix of the digital edition of the Workbook.

1.5 Other economic policies

(a) **Corporate governance regulation** – this has been introduced in the previous chapter. Tighter regulation imposes costs on a business but increases the confidence of investors and may benefit businesses by making it easier to attract finance.

(b) **Government assistance for business** – grants may be available to attract firms to invest in depressed areas.

(c) **Green policies** – the failure of the free market to recognise positive and negative **externalities** (eg pollution) may lead to government action; this may either threaten a business (eg tax on petrol so 'the polluter pays') or create opportunities (eg subsidies for loft insulation).

2 Financial markets and institutions

When a firm is making its **financing decision** it has two routes to obtaining finance:

- **directly** from investors through **financial markets,** or
- **indirectly** through **financial institutions** that investors have deposited their money in; these financial institutions act as **financial intermediaries**.

2.1 Financial intermediaries

Financial intermediary : An institution bringing together providers of finance and users of finance.

A **financial intermediary** links lenders with borrowers by obtaining deposits from lenders and then re-lending them to borrowers.

2.1.1 Examples of financial intermediaries

- **Retail banks** – offer services to the general public (whether branch-based or online)
- **Investment (or wholesale) banks** – offer finance, services and advice to large corporate clients
- **Mutual societies** – offer banking facilities to its members and those owned by its members, for example building societies
- **Institutional investors** such as pension funds (investing funds built up from pension contributions), insurance companies (investing funds built up from insurance policy payments) and investment trusts and unit trusts (investing shareholders money). **Institutional investors are the biggest investors** in the stock markets.

2.1.2 Benefits of financial intermediaries

Financial intermediaries provide the following functions (remember as **MAP**):

Functions	Description
Maturity transformation	Most importantly, financial intermediaries provide **maturity transformation**, ie borrowing money on shorter timeframes than they lend out. They bridge the gap between the wish of most investors/lenders for **liquidity** and the desire of most borrowers for **loans** over longer periods. Eg a bank can make a ten-year loan (long term) while still allowing its depositors to take money out whenever they want; so short-term deposits become long-term investments.
Aggregation of funds	A financial intermediary can **aggregate** smaller savings deposited by savers and lend on to borrowers in larger amounts.
Pooling losses	**Risk** for individual lenders is reduced by **pooling.** Since financial intermediaries lend to many individuals and organisations, any losses suffered through default by borrowers or capital losses are effectively pooled and **borne** as **costs** by the **intermediary.** Risky investments are therefore effectively changed into low risk investments for individual investors, this is sometimes referred to as risk transformation.

2.2 Financial markets

A financial market brings a **firm** into direct contact with its investors. The trend towards borrowing directly from investors is sometimes called disintermediation.

> **Disintermediation:** Describes a **decline** in the traditional deposit and lending relationship between banks and their customers and an increase in direct relationships between the ultimate suppliers and users of financing.

A contributing factor to the development of disintermediation is the ability of companies to borrow by issuing debt securities (eg, loan notes). This is often referred to as **securitisation**.

This term is also used to describe the process of converting existing previously untradeable (ie, illiquid) **assets** into **marketable securities**; for example the conversion by banks of mortgages into a tradeable security (a mortgage backed security).

Financial markets are split into those that provide short-term finance (for up to one year) and those that provide medium and long-term finance.

The **money market** is the market for short-term finance.

The **capital market** is the term used to describe the market(s) for medium to long-term finance.

In both money and capital markets there is a distinction between:

- primary markets (where companies issue new securities to investors to raise new funding), and
- secondary markets (where investors buy and sell from/to each other).

3 Money markets

3.1 Types of money market instruments

There are three different types of money market instruments: interest-bearing, discount instruments and derivatives.

3.1.1 Interest-bearing instruments

These instruments pay interest and the investor receives face value plus interest at maturity.

3.1.2 Discount instruments

These instruments do not pay interest. They are issued and traded at a discount to the face value and they are redeemed at their par value at maturity.

The discount is equivalent to interest and is the difference between the issue price of the instrument and the redemption price at maturity.

 Illustration 1: Discount instruments

A bill with a face value of $100 is issued at a price of $98.50 and redeemed at maturity at the face value of $100.00 in one years' time (assume 360 days).

Required

1 Calculate the annualised yield on this bill.

2 Calculate the annualised yield if this bill was due to mature in 120 days' time.

Solution

1 The discount of $1.50 represents interest on the investment of $98.50. This is an interest rate of 1.5 ÷ 98.5 × 100 = 1.52% per year (assuming that the bill is redeemed in one years' time).

2 If the bill was redeemable in 120 days' time, and assuming a 360-day year, the annual implied interest rate is calculated as 1.52% × 360/120 = 4.56%.

3.1.3 Derivatives

These instruments derive their value from the value of another asset or variable such as exchange rates and interest rates. Examples of derivatives include futures, options and swaps.

A summary of some of the main interest-bearing and discount instruments is given in the following table (derivatives instruments are discussed in Chapters 14 and 15).

Note that where an instrument is said to be a negotiable instrument, it means that the instrument is **tradeable** and therefore **can be sold before maturity**.

Interest-bearing instruments	Discount instruments
Money market deposits – very short-term loans normally between banks. The rate at which banks lend to each other in the London market is called the **Sterling Overnight Index Average (SONIA)**.	**Treasury bill** – debt instruments issued by the Government with maturities ranging from one month to one year. A **negotiable instrument**.
Certificates of deposit – a certificate of receipt for funds deposited at a financial institution for a specified term and paying interest (called the coupon rate) at a specified rate (in annual terms) on a specified date. For example, if the coupon on three-month US dollar CDs is 2%, this means that the interest payment after three months will be 0.5% (ie one quarter of 2%). A **negotiable instrument**.	**Bank bills** or **acceptance credits** – sold by and guaranteed by a bank on behalf of a company for up to 180 days of credit. They are not tied to a specific transaction. A **negotiable instrument**.
Repurchase agreements (Repo) – an agreement between two parties under which one party agrees to sell a financial instrument to the other on an agreed date for an agreed price and simultaneously buy back the instrument at a later date for a higher price (agreed in advance).	**Commercial paper** – short-term unsecured corporate debt with maturity of up to 270 days. Usually issued by the largest organisations with good credit ratings. A **negotiable instrument**.
	Bill of exchange – an IOU signed by a customer. It can be sold on the money market to raise finance. Bills of exchange are only used for significant transactions (eg above £75,000). A **negotiable instrument**.

3.1.4 Risk and return

Not all money market instruments offer the same return to investors.

Higher risk investments require a higher return to be paid and instruments that are **non-negotiable** require a higher return because they cannot be sold on.

Increasing risk to the investor

1. Treasury bills (issued by governments)

2. Certificates of deposit (shows an entitlement to a deposit)

3. Commercial paper (issued by companies with a high credit rating)

4. Bills of exchange (higher risk unless guaranteed or 'accepted' by a bank).

Activity 2: Money markets

Hoddor Co is a large company and frequently participates in the money markets as both a lender and borrower.

Required

Indicate which of the following instruments are described in the box below.

Repurchase agreement	Money market deposit	Commercial paper

Instruments		
1	Hoddor Co makes a short-term loan to a bank. The interest rate has been agreed in advance along with the maturity date.	
2	Hoddor Co sells an unsecured debt instrument which matures in 180 days, after which it redeems the instrument at face value.	
3	Hoddor Co sells some shares to Cersei Co for $1m on 1 May 20X6 and agrees to buy the shares back from Cersei Co for $1.05m on 1 November 20X6.	

Essential reading

See Chapter 2 section 5 of the Essential reading, available in the digital edition of the Workbook, for further discussion of money market instruments.

The Essential reading is available as an Appendix of the digital edition of the Workbook.

4 Capital markets

Capital markets are markets for raising **long-term finance**, in the form of long-term financial instruments such as equities and corporate bonds or loan notes.

In the UK, the principal capital markets are:

(a) The Stock Exchange **'main market'** (for companies with a full stock market listing)

(b) The more loosely regulated 'second tier' **Alternative Investment Market (AIM)**

4.1 Capital market instruments

Firms obtain long-term or medium-term capital in one of the following ways:

(a) By issuing **share capital**. Most new issues of share capital are in the form of ordinary share capital. Firms that issue ordinary share capital are inviting investors to take an equity stake in the business, or to increase their existing equity stake.

(b) By issuing **debt capital**. Long-term debt capital might be raised in the form of loan notes which are IOUs committing a company to paying interest over a significant time periods, normally 5 years or more.

4.1.1 Risk and return

Not all capital market instruments offer the same return to investors, higher risk investments require a higher return to be paid.

Increasing risk to the investor

1. Bonds/loan notes (secured on an asset or by covenants)

2. Junk bonds (unsecured)

3. Shares traded on the main stock market

4. Shares in the Alternative Investment Market

4.1.2 Reverse yield gap

Because debt involves lower risk than equity investment, we might expect yields (ie the return received as interest or dividend as a percentage of the market price of the asset) on debt to be lower than yields on shares. More usually, however, the opposite applies and the dividend yield on shares is lower than the interest yield on low-risk debt; this situation is known as a reverse yield gap.

A reverse yield gap can occur because shareholders may be willing to accept lower returns on their investment in the short term, in anticipation that they will make capital gains in the future. It can also arise if firms that are desperate to raise finance offer a yield on their debt in excess of the yield on shares.

We return to the link between risk and return again in Chapter 11.

5 International financial markets

5.1 Eurocurrency market

The **eurocurrency markets** involve the borrowing of funds from or depositing funds with a bank outside the country of the currency in which the funds are denominated for a **short term,** typically three months.

For example, if a UK company borrows US$50,000 from its UK bank, the loan will be a 'eurodollar' loan.

5.2 Eurobonds

The Eurobond **market** involves the borrowing of funds from or depositing funds with a bank outside the country of the currency in which the funds are denominated for a long-term, typically between ten and twenty years.

> **Eurobond:** A bond denominated in a currency which often differs from that of the country of issue.

Eurobonds are, in effect, long-term loans raised by international companies or other institutions and sold to investors in several countries at the same time. Eurobonds are negotiable, ie they can be sold by one holder to another.

A **borrower** who is contemplating a eurobond issue must consider the **exchange risk** of a long-term foreign currency loan. If the money is to be used to purchase assets that will earn revenue in a currency **different to that of the bond issue,** the borrower will run the risk of losses from unfavourable exchange rate movements.

If the money is to be used to purchase assets which will earn revenue in the **same currency**, the borrower can match these revenues with payments on the bond, and so remove or reduce the exchange risk.

6 FinTech

Fintech (financial technology) can be thought of as the software and other modern technologies used by businesses to provide automated and improved financial services.

Developments in FinTech have had, and continue to have, an important impact on financial institutions and markets.

6.1 Finance and technology

Changes in technology have helped to develop new financial institutions and new financial markets which are transforming financial services.

Developments in digital technology (the internet), and the willingness and ability of people to use this technology (eg, via smartphones and apps) to manage their financial transactions have created an internet-based revolution in many businesses. Technology is already enabling people to work from home, to attend virtual meetings, bank online, stream entertainment and to access other services such as food delivery.

Another development is blockchain technology which allows a secure, low-cost database of transactions that automatically update to record new transactions. This has permitted the development of new cryptocurrencies such as Bitcoin.

There are many examples of FinTech, but here we focus on how FinTech has impacted on financial institutions and financial markets.

6.2 Financial institutions

Challenger banks seek to offer a wide range of online financial services normally without the expense of maintaining a 'bricks and mortar' banking network. In 2015 Monzo was among the first so-called 'challenger' banks to launch in the UK; many more have followed since then.

More recently, challenger banks have targeted business customers, seeking to use their **low cost base** to offer competitive products and also offering more flexible services. For example:

- multi-currency accounts which allow business customers collect, store, convert and pay in a wide range of foreign currencies.
- using an app to allow currency hedging eg using forward contracts to fix the exchange rate (forward contracts are covered in Chapter 14).
- allowing greater visibility of the stage of payment of customer invoices (supply chain finance is covered in Chapter 12).

6.3 Financial markets

Another impact of Fintech has been to increase the availability of long-term finance by creating **new financial markets** such as the electronic platforms used for crowdfunding, peer to peer lending and security token offerings.

All of these forms of finance are allowing companies to access a broad pool of (global) investment funds without using a financial intermediary and are all examples of 'disintermediation' (covered in section 2 of this chapter).

6.3.1 Crowdfunding

Crowdfunding allows a company to access finance via an online crowdfunding platform, such as Kickstarter, to pitch for finance from a large number of potential investors. This area is covered in more detail in Chapter 12.

6.3.2 Peer to peer lending

Peer-to-peer (or P2P) lending connects established businesses looking to borrow with investors who want to lend, usually via an online platform.

This can result in cheaper loan finance compared to a bank loan because the lender is not having to support the cost of maintaining the infrastructure of a financial intermediary (eg the branch network).

P2P lending can also be quicker to arrange than a bank loan because the process can be initiated and processed outside normal bank opening hours.

P2P lending is not normally available to start-up companies because investors require an established trading history. Platforms usually require borrowers to have a trading track record, to submit financial accounts, and will perform credit checks as part of the credit assessment.

The use of P2P lending has grown rapidly in recent years.

6.3.3 Security token offering

Blockchain technology has facilitated the use of security token offerings to raise long-term finance.

With a security token offering, an investor receives a token eg a share in exchange for payment made in a cryptocurrency such as Bitcoin.

Historically there have been fewer regulations surrounding security token offerings compared to share issues (which are covered in Chapter 9). This has made them more attractive to companies as a way of raising long-term equity finance.

Chapter summary

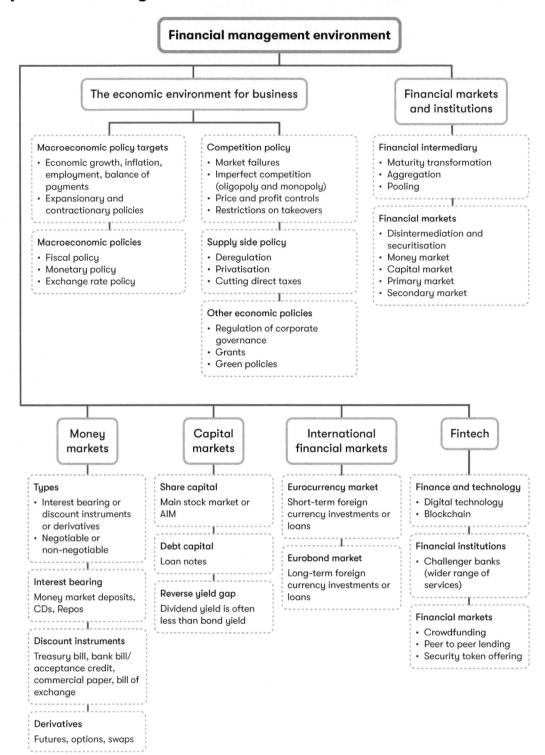

Financial management environment

The economic environment for business

Macroeconomic policy targets
- Economic growth, inflation, employment, balance of payments
- Expansionary and contractionary policies

Macroeconomic policies
- Fiscal policy
- Monetary policy
- Exchange rate policy

Competition policy
- Market failures
- Imperfect competition (oligopoly and monopoly)
- Price and profit controls
- Restrictions on takeovers

Supply side policy
- Deregulation
- Privatisation
- Cutting direct taxes

Other economic policies
- Regulation of corporate governance
- Grants
- Green policies

Financial markets and institutions

Financial intermediary
- Maturity transformation
- Aggregation
- Pooling

Financial markets
- Disintermediation and securitisation
- Money market
- Capital market
- Primary market
- Secondary market

Money markets

Types
- Interest bearing or discount instruments or derivatives
- Negotiable or non-negotiable

Interest bearing
Money market deposits, CDs, Repos

Discount instruments
Treasury bill, bank bill/ acceptance credit, commercial paper, bill of exchange

Derivatives
Futures, options, swaps

Capital markets

Share capital
Main stock market or AIM

Debt capital
Loan notes

Reverse yield gap
Dividend yield is often less than bond yield

International financial markets

Eurocurrency market
Short-term foreign currency investments or loans

Eurobond market
Long-term foreign currency investments or loans

Fintech

Finance and technology
- Digital technology
- Blockchain

Financial institutions
- Challenger banks (wider range of services)

Financial markets
- Crowdfunding
- Peer to peer lending
- Security token offering

BPP LEARNING MEDIA

Knowledge diagnostic

1. Macroeconomic policies

To achieve these macroeconomic policy targets, governments use fiscal policy, monetary policy, and exchange rate policy. Such policies may be expansionary or contractionary.

2. Supply side policies

These aim to improve efficiency and motivation. Key polices include competition policy, deregulation and privatisation.

3. Financial intermediaries

Banks and institutional investors act as a third-party channelling funds from investors to borrowers.

4. Money market

Short-term instruments - either discount instruments, interest-bearing or derivatives.

5. Capital market

Long-term debt and equity can be raised on the capital markets.

6. Fintech

Changes in technology have helped to develop new financial institutions (eg challenger banks) and financial markets (eg crowdfunding) which are transforming financial services.

Further study guidance

Question practice

Now try the following from the Further question practice bank (available in the digital edition of the Workbook):

Section A questions

Q4, Q5, Q6, Q7, Q8, Q9

Activity answers

Activity 1: Macroeconomic issues

The correct answer is: (1) only

A contractionary fiscal policy includes the raising of taxes and/or cutting government expenditure.

Interest rates go down if the Government pursues an expansionary monetary policy.

Activity 2: Money markets

Instruments		
1	Hoddor Co makes a short-term loan to a bank. The interest rate has been agreed in advance along with the maturity date.	Money market deposit
2	Hoddor Co sells an unsecured debt instrument which matures in 180 days, after which it redeems the instrument at face value.	Commercial paper
3	Hoddor Co sells some shares to Cersei Co for $1m on 1 May 20X6 and agrees to buy the shares back from Cersei Co for $1.05m on 1 November 20X6.	Repurchase agreement

3

Working capital investment

Learning objectives

On completion of this chapter, you should be able to:

	Syllabus reference
The nature, elements and importance of working capital	
• Describe the nature of working capital and identify its elements.	C1(a)
• Identify the objectives of working capital management in terms of liquidity and profitability, and discuss the conflict between them.	C1(b)
• Discuss the central role of working capital management in financial management.	C1(c)
Management of inventories, accounts receivable, accounts payable and cash (cash is covered in the next chapter)	
• Explain the cash operating cycle and the role of accounts payable & receivable.	C2(a)
• Explain and apply relevant accounting ratios, including: current ratio and quick ratio, inventory turnover ratio, average collection period and average payable period, sales revenue/net working capital ratio.	C2(b)
• Discuss, apply and evaluate the use of relevant techniques in managing inventory, including the EOQ model and just-in-time techniques.	C2(c)
• Discuss, apply and evaluate the use of relevant techniques in managing accounts receivable, including: assessing creditworthiness, managing accounts receivable, collecting amounts owing, offering early settlement discounts, using factoring and invoice discounting, and managing foreign accounts receivable.	C2(d)
• Discuss and apply the use of relevant techniques in managing accounts payable, including: using trade credit effectively, evaluating the benefits of early settlement and bulk purchase discounts, managing foreign accounts payable.	C2(e)
Determining working capital needs and funding strategies	
• Calculate the level of working capital investment in current assets and discuss the key factors determining this level, including: the length of the working capital cycle and terms of trade, an organisation's policy on the level of investment in current assets and the industry in which the organisation operates.	C3(a)

Exam context

This chapter covers issues relating to the investment in working capital which is part of Section C of the syllabus (Working capital management). This is an important chapter that is examinable in all sections of the exam, including Section A (2-mark questions), B (10-mark question) and Section C (20-mark question). Questions won't just involve **calculations**; exam questions (especially in Section C) may ask you to **discuss** the management of working capital (as a part of a question) or to explain the meaning of a numerical analysis that you have performed.

Chapter overview

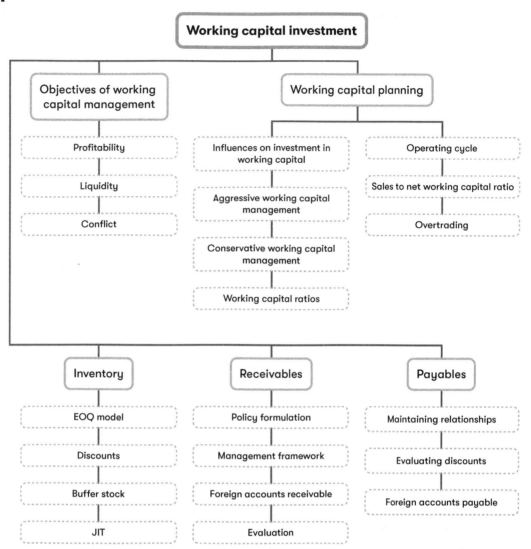

1 Working capital

KEY TERM

Net working capital: The net working capital of a business is its current assets less its current liabilities.

Current assets – examples	Current liabilities – examples
Cash	Overdraft
Inventory	Short-term loans
Amounts receivable from customers	Amounts payable to suppliers

1.1 Objectives of working capital management

Working capital management has two main objectives:

(a) To increase the **profits** of a business

(b) To ensure sufficient **liquidity** to meet short-term obligations as they fall due.

1.1.1 Profitability

If a business operates with **excessively low levels of working capital** then this may lead to trading problems, and **lower profits**.

Examples of problems of operating with excessively low working capital	
Low inventory	This may mean that delivery lead times to customers are excessively high, or that a business does not have enough inventory to meet peaks in demand. This is likely to lead to **lost sales**.
Low receivables	If this means that a business's credit terms are overly strict and that long credit periods are **not** being made available to its customer, this may lead to **lost sales**.

One of the central concerns of working capital management is how much money to **invest** in short-term assets **to address the problems of operating with excessively low levels of working capital**; this can be thought of as a **working capital investment decision and** is the main focus of **this chapter**.

1.1.2 Liquidity

Every business needs adequate **liquid resources** to maintain day to day cash flow such as wages and payments to suppliers.

If money is tied up in short-term assets such as inventory and receivables, this may cause liquidity problems. Liquidity can be maintained by ensuring that the amounts of cash tied up in inventory and receivables is **not excessive**.

This is **the main focus of the next chapter** which looks at cash flow forecasting and how **working capital finance** should be approached.

KEY TERM

Working capital finance: The approach taken to financing the level, and fluctuations in the level, of net working capital.

1.1.3 Conflict between objectives of liquidity and profitability

The objectives of liquidity and profitability **may conflict**.

For example, if a decision is made to **invest** in higher inventory (eg to reduce delivery lead times) or receivables (to allow longer credit terms) in order **to boost sales and profits,** then this will tie up funds in higher net working capital and this will **reduce liquidity**.

However, there will **not always be a conflict** between the objectives of liquidity and profitability.

For example, if the levels of inventory and receivables are high because working capital is not being managed well, then improved management of the warehouse (to keep inventory lower and reduce obsolescence) and credit control (to keep receivables lower and reduce bad debts) may allow **both higher liquidity and higher profitability.**

1.1.4 Role of working capital in financial management

Working capital management involves an **investment decision** and a **financing decision**. We have already seen in Chapter 1 that **these two decisions** are fundamental to financial management in general.

Essential reading

See Chapter 3 section 1 of the Essential reading for more background information on this area.

The Essential reading is available as an Appendix of the digital edition of the Workbook.

2 Working capital planning

2.1 Influences on the level of investment in working capital

Different businesses will have different approaches to **working capital investment,** ie to the **level** of net working capital held, due to:

- **general factors** (eg the industry); and
- **company-specific factors** (eg different working capital strategies).

2.1.1 General factors affecting working capital levels

(a) **The nature of the industry**

The level of working capital required will be influenced by the nature of the industry.

Eg a supermarket will receive much of their sales in cash (or credit or debit card), so it will be able to operate with minimal receivables. However, this would not be possible for a food wholesaler (supplying supermarkets) which is likely to be selling mainly on **credit**.

(b) **Policies of competitors**

A company will be unwilling to lose business to a rival offering its customers more favourable credit terms.

(c) **Seasonal factors**

There may be a need to allow inventory to be higher as a season of peak sales approaches.

2.1.2 Company specific factors

The level of net working capital will also depend on **a company's sales and its working capital strategy.**

If sales are higher, then net working capital will normally rise too (as receivables and inventory will rise). However, different companies will plan to allow net working capital to rise at **different rates** depending on their **working capital investment strategy.**

Aggressive strategy – minimises net working capital	Conservative strategy – maximises net working capital
Aims to keep inventories and receivables as low as possible. Payables are maximised (suppliers paid as late as possible).	Allows high levels of inventories and receivables and plans to pay suppliers on time (which keeps payables low).
This **prioritises liquidity** but may create trading problems.	This aims to reduce the risk of trading problems (eg stock-outs) but **may compromise liquidity**.

2.2 Planning overall working capital needs

2.2.1 Working capital ratios

A company's working capital policies can be quantified by analysing:

- inventory days (the amount of days of sales or production held as inventory)
- payables days (the length of time taken to pay suppliers)
- receivables days (the length of time taken by customers to pay)

These ratios can be used to quantify the level of working capital required to support future sales.

Formula to learn

(a) Inventory days (or inventory turnover period): (Finished goods/Cost of sales) × 365

(b) Inventory turnover: Cost of sales/Average inventory

(c) Receivables days: (Receivables/(credit) sales) × 365

(d) Payables days: (Payables/(credit) purchases) × 365

Exam focus point

Normally, in the exam, inventory can be assumed to be of finished goods. If this is not the case, ie inventory is raw material or WIP, then the calculation will need to be adjusted to reflect the costs incurred in bringing the inventory to its present location and condition as follows:

WIP: (WIP/Cost of Production) × 365 = days of WIP

Raw material: (Raw material/Raw material purchases) × 365 = days of raw material inventory

Exam focus point

Number of days. An exam question may specify that 360 days, not 365, should be assumed. It is even possible that you are given working capital balances for a six-month period in which case 180 days may be appropriate to use in calculating working capital days. So, read the question carefully!

Terminology. In the exam the following terminology will be used:

- Inventory holding period (instead of inventory days)
- Accounts receivable collection period (instead of receivables days)
- Accounts payable payment period (instead of payables days)

Activity 1: Forecasting

Management Co's customers pay after 73 days, on average.

Next year, sales are forecast to be $864,000.

Required

What is the amount of receivables Management Co should forecast for next year, assuming 365 days in the year?

Solution

Basic liquidity ratios (covered in Chapter 1) can also be examined along with these working capital ratios.

Activity 2: Combination of ratios

A business has a current ratio of 2. Current assets consist of inventory of $10 million and current liabilities of $15 million. The company gives on average 36.5 days' credit to its customers.

Required

Assuming that the business has a zero cash balance and that there are 365 days in a year, what is the annual credit sales revenue?

O $150m

O $2

O $20m

O $200m

Solution

2.2.2 The cash operating cycle

The ratio analysis from the previous section can also be used to analyse the impact of higher sales on liquidity using the cash operating cycle (also known as the working capital cycle).

The cash operating cycle measures the length of time (in days, weeks or months), following the receipt of a customer order for:

(a) **Cash to be received**: measured as **inventory days plus receivables days**

(b) **Cash to be paid out to suppliers**: measured as **payables days**

The cash operating cycle is then calculated as:

Cash to be received (in days) <u>minus</u> Cash to be paid out (in days)

> **Cash operating cycle:** The period of time that elapses between the point at which cash begins to be expended on the production of a product or service and the collection of cash from a customer.

Illustration 1: Cash operating cycle

WNS Co is a manufacturer. It buys from suppliers that allow WNS 2.5 months' credit. The raw materials remain in inventory for one month, and it takes WNS two months to produce the goods. The goods are sold immediately after production is completed and customers take on average 1.5 months to pay.

Required

Calculate WNS's cash operating cycle.

Solution

Cash operating cycle

	Months
The average time that raw materials remain in inventory	1.0
The time taken to produce the goods	2.0
The time taken by customers to pay for the goods	1.5
The time taken to pay suppliers	(2.5)
Cash operating cycle	2.0

Activity 3: Operating cycle

The table below gives information extracted from the annual accounts of Management Co for the past year.

	$
Inventory: Finished goods	86,400
Receivables	172,800
Payables	96,400
Purchases	518,400
Cost of goods sold	756,000
Sales	864,000

Required

Calculate the length of the cash operating cycle (assuming 365 days in the year).

Solution

2.2.3 The cash operating cycle: use and meaning

There is no optimal length of the operating cycle for every company (as discussed, working capital investment levels depend on general and company-specific factors). However, by comparing the cash operating cycle from one period to the next or one company to another, it should be possible to identify unwelcome trends. The cash operating cycle can also be used to identify the possibility of a cash shortfall if sales rise too rapidly (this is sometimes called **overtrading** and is covered later in this chapter).

Essential reading

See Chapter 9 section 1 of the Essential reading for further discussion of basic liquidity ratios.

The Essential reading is available as an Appendix of the digital edition of the Workbook.

2.2.4 Sales to net working capital ratio

A more direct way of identifying the possibility of a cash shortfall if sales rise too rapidly is to use the **sales/net working capital ratio**.

> ### Formula to learn
>
> The ratio of:
>
> Sales revenue/(Receivables + Inventory − Payables)

This shows the level of working capital (excluding cash) required to support sales.

For example, if this ratio was 5, then for every $5 increase in sales an extra $1 of cash is required to finance the required increase in net working capital.

The sales to net working capital ratio is a key ratio in demonstrating a company's overall working capital **investment policy** because it considers the level of net current assets used to support revenue generation.

A company adopts an **aggressive** working capital investment policy relative to another company if it uses a **lower level of net current assets** to support a similar level of revenue generation, or a **conservative** working capital investment policy relative to another company if it uses a **higher level of net current assets** to support a similar level of revenue generation.

Exam focus point

The ACCA examining team has confirmed that if cash is included in the calculation of net working capital (which would follow the normal interpretation of the term 'net' working capital) then students will not be penalised.

Activity 4: Sales/net working capital

Management Co – Extracts from annual accounts

	Year 1
	$
Sales	**864,000**
Inventory: Finished goods	86,400
Receivables	172,800
Payables	(96,400)
Net working capital	**162,800**

Sales/net working capital ratio = 864,000/162,800   **= 5.3071**

Required

What increase in the level of net working capital (ie cash) is needed to support higher sales, if sales are forecast to rise by $200,000 over the next year? (Working to the nearest $100)

Solution

2.3 Risk of overtrading

If a business fails to plan how to supply its forecast level of cash flow needs, it will be in danger of **overtrading**.

> **Overtrading:** A situation where a business has inadequate cash to support its level of sales (also known as **undercapitalisation**).

2.3.1 Symptoms of overtrading

Symptoms of overtrading are as follows:

(a) A **rapid increase** in **sales revenue**, and often a **fall in profit margins** as discounts are used to chase higher sales.

(b) A **rapid increase in receivables and inventory,** eg high receivables as better credit terms are used to chase new sales, higher inventory to support higher sales.

(c) Rapid **increase in trade payables** and a **rising bank overdraft** indicating liquidity problems.

(d) Worsening liquidity ratios causing a **significant increase in the operating cycle.**

2.3.2 Managing the risk of overtrading/undercapitalisation

To deal with this risk a business must either:

(a) Plan the introduction of new long-term capital

(b) Improve working capital management

(c) Reduce business activity

Note that it is also possible for a business to hold excessive levels of cash, this is called overcapitalisation.

Essential reading

See Chapter 3 section 3 of the Essential reading for a numerical illustration of overtrading.

The Essential reading is available as an Appendix of the digital edition of the Workbook.

3 Managing inventory

This chapter now moves on to consider each specific component of working capital and the issues surrounding the level of investment that will be required in each type, starting with inventory.

The **inventory days** ratio (see earlier) gives an overview of a company's overall inventory position, but companies may have thousands of items in inventory, and will want to calculate how much to hold of **each individual item**.

This can be established by the **economic order quantity** (EOQ) model which links the level of inventory to the quantity of an order placed with suppliers and aims to minimise the **total inventory related costs** of a company by choosing the optimal order size.

3.1 EOQ model

> **The economic order quantity (EOQ):** The optimal ordering quantity for an item of inventory which will minimise inventory related costs.

The EOQ model links the order quantity placed with a supplier to **inventory related costs**.

Inventory related costs		
Holding costs	**Ordering costs**	**Purchasing costs**
Eg warehousing, insurance, obsolescence, and opportunity cost of capital.	Eg costs of administering orders, and delivery costs.	Eg the amount paid for purchases from suppliers.
Holding costs **increase if the order size increases**.	Ordering costs **decrease if the order size increases**.	Purchasing costs may **decrease if the order size increases** if bulk discounts are offered (although discounts are ignored by the simple EOQ model).

3.1.1 Quantifying inventory holding costs

If a firm orders an amount (Q) from a supplier, holds zero opening inventory and receives the order immediately then **the level of inventory at the start of the period is Q.**

By **the end of the period** we can assume that the **inventory level** has been run down to **zero.**

This can be illustrated as follows:

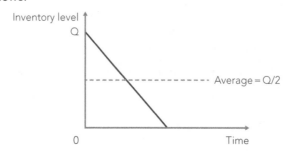

The **average** inventory level is (starting inventory + closing inventory)/2 **which can be expressed as Q/2.**

> **Formula to learn**
>
> Total holding costs can therefore be calculated as:
>
> $$C_h \times \frac{Q}{2}$$
>
> Where Q is the initial order and C_h = Annual cost of holding one unit in inventory

3.1.2 Quantifying inventory ordering costs

If a firm holds zero inventory at the start of the period, the number of orders that it will need to place will be determined by the annual demand in units (D) and the order size (Q).

For example, if 120 units are required (ie demanded) and the order size is 20 units then there will be 120 ÷ 20 = 6. This can be expressed as D/Q.

> **Formula to learn**
>
> If C_o = Cost of placing an order, then total ordering costs can be calculated as:
>
> $$C_o \times \frac{D}{Q}$$

3.1.3 Quantifying purchasing costs

If order size affects the purchase price, purchasing costs will need to be considered.

Purchasing costs are calculated as annual demand × purchase price of one unit.

3.1.4 EOQ formula

To minimise **total inventory related costs** of a company, there is an ideal (economic) order size which can be identified using the EOQ formula (which is given in the exam).

 Formula provided

Economic order quantity (EOQ) =

$$Q = \sqrt{\frac{2C_oD}{C_h}}$$

This formula gives the ideal order quantity **to minimise total inventory related costs.**

Exam focus point

The variables in the EOQ formula need to be based on a consistent time period; normally this is annual. Be alert for questions that present some information, for example D, in non-annual terms. Where this occurs you will need to adjust the variable so that it is in annual terms.

 Illustration 2: Inventory costs

The demand for a commodity is 3,000 units a month, at a steady rate. It costs $20 to place an order, and $0.40 to hold a unit for a year.

Required

Find the order size to minimise inventory costs.

Solution

Annual demand is 3,000 × 12 months = 36,000 units

$$Q = \sqrt{\frac{2C_oD}{C_h}}$$

$$Q = \sqrt{\frac{2 \times 20 \times 36,000}{0.4}} = 1,897 \text{ units}$$

(rounded to the nearest whole unit)

 Activity 5: EOQ

Firm X faces regular demand of 150 units per month. It orders from its supplier at a purchase cost per unit of $25. Each order costs $32, and annual holding cost is $4.50 per unit.

Required

1 Calculate the economic order quantity, and the average inventory level.

2 Calculate total inventory-related cost at this economic order quantity.

Solution

3.2 Drawbacks of EOQ model

The **drawbacks of the EOQ model are** that it:

(a) Assumes **zero lead times**, and **no bulk purchase discounts** – although these can be adjusted for (see next section)

(b) **Ignores the need to increase order sizes** if there is a possibility of supplier shortages or price rises

(c) Ignores the possibility of **fluctuations in demand** (the order quantity is constant)

(d) Ignores the **benefit** of holding inventory to customers (eg shorter lead times)

(e) Ignores the **hidden costs** of holding inventory (see just-in-time, section 3.5).

3.3 Bulk purchase discounts

If bulk purchase discounts are available, the simple EOQ formula cannot be used and we need to adjust our approach as follows:

(a) Calculate EOQ in normal way and inventory related costs at the EOQ

(b) Calculate inventory related costs at the **lower boundary** of each discount **above** the EOQ

(c) Select the order quantity that minimises inventory related costs

Activity 6: Bulk purchase discounts

Using the same information given in the previous activity, calculate whether either of the following bulk purchase discounts should be accepted:

(1) Discount of 2% given on orders of 300 and over

(2) Discount of 4% given on orders of 800 and over

Solution

Essential reading

See Chapter 3 section 4 of the Essential reading for further illustration relating to this area.

The Essential reading is available as an Appendix of the digital edition of the Workbook.

3.4 Buffer inventory

In reality, an organisation would not wait for inventory to fall to zero before placing a new order with its suppliers. One reason for this is the risk of demand being higher than expected while waiting for a new delivery, which creates the risk of stock-outs.

To deal with this an organisation may hold buffer inventory (shown as B in the following diagrams). This has an impact on the average inventory level.

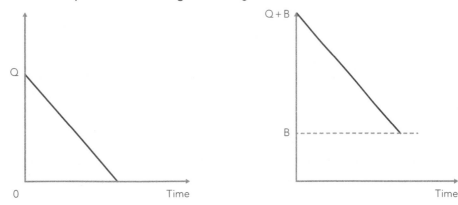

If buffer inventory (**B**) is required, the **average inventory level becomes B + Q/2**

3.5 Just-in-time (JIT)

Just-in-time (JIT) is a philosophy which involves the **elimination of inventory**.

3.5.1 JIT procurement

This is a policy of obtaining goods from suppliers at the latest possible time (ie when they are needed) and so avoiding the need to carry any materials or components as inventory.

3.5.2 JIT production

This describes manufacturing 'to order'. As orders are received, manufacturing is triggered to fulfil those orders. This enables better product customisation, no risk of obsolescence and few holding costs.

It does, however, require a highly flexible and reliable manufacturing process (in terms of what and how much is made).

3.5.3 Benefits of JIT

Proponents of JIT suggest that a key problem with **holding inventory** is that it **allows a firm to compensate for inefficient processes by holding buffer inventory**; this failure to deal with inefficient processes is seen as **hidden costs of holding inventory**.

Examples of hidden costs include: failing to deal with unreliable suppliers, defective production processes and poor labour relations.

In addition, JIT will reduce inventory holding costs.

3.5.4 Drawbacks of JIT

JIT will not be appropriate if **production processes and suppliers are unreliable**, and especially where the consequences of a stock-out are serious. For example, in a hospital, a stock-out could quite literally be fatal and so JIT would be quite unsuitable.

Essential reading

See Chapter 3 Section 5 of the Essential reading for further discussion of re-order levels and a real-life example of JIT.

The Essential Reading is available as an Appendix of the digital edition of the Workbook.

4 Managing receivables

4.1 Policy formulation

A company will have to decide **whether to offer credit** to its customers and **if so on what terms**. These are important decisions and need to be carefully considered by **senior management**.

The decision to **offer credit** can be viewed as an **investment decision**, intended to result in higher profits. For many businesses, offering generous payment terms (or credit period) to customers is essential in order to be competitive.

However, **offering credit comes at a cost**, eg the value of the interest charged on an overdraft to fund the period of credit, and the possibility of bad debts. So, the decision to offer credit will need to be carefully assessed to see **if the benefit from the policy is greater than its cost.**

In some businesses it is possible that the risk of bad debts, or the cost of managing receivables, will mean that it is not commercially viable to offer credit to customers.

4.1.1 Extending the credit period

The decision to **offer extended credit** can also be viewed as an **investment decision,** intended to boost sales and profits.

The **cost** of extended credit is the value of the interest charged on an overdraft to fund the period of extra credit.

The **benefit** is likely to be higher sales and therefore higher profit.

The policy will be assessed by comparing whether the **benefit from higher sales is greater than the finance costs associated with higher receivables.**

Illustration 3: Extending the credit period

Enticement Co currently expects sales of $50,000 a month. Variable costs of sales are $40,000 a month (all payable in the month of sale).

It is estimated that if the credit period allowed to customers was to be increased from 30 days to 60 days, sales volume would increase by 20%.

All customers would be expected to take advantage of the extended credit. The cost of capital is 12.5% a year.

Required

Evaluate whether the extension of the credit period is justifiable in financial terms.

Solution

Evaluation

Workings	$
Current accounts receivable (1 month)	50,000
Accounts receivable after implementing the proposal (2 months) (50,000 × 1.2 × 2)	120,000
Increase in accounts receivable	70,000

Cost

Financing cost (12.5%)	8,750

Benefit

Annual contribution from additional sales ($10,000 × 12 months × contribution/ sales ratio of 20%)	
The 20% contribution to sales ratio is calculated as $10,000 contribution (sales − variable costs) ÷ $50,000 sales revenue.	24,000
Annual net benefit from extending credit period	15,250

Activity 7: Extended credit terms

Greedy Co is considering a proposal to change its credit policy from allowing debtors credit of two months to credit of three months.

Sales are currently $600,000 p.a. and as a result of the proposed change will increase by 15%.

The contribution/sales ratio is 20% and the cost of capital is 10%.

Required

Should the proposed change be made?

Solution

4.1.2 Early settlement discount

Another aspect of credit policy is whether to offer customers a discount for early settlement of amounts due.

Early settlement discounts will result in a **cost** (the discount) but will result in **lower receivables** which can **benefit** a company by **reducing the cost of the interest** charged on an overdraft, since money is being received from customers earlier.

This policy can be assessed by comparing the **cost of the discount to the benefit of lower finance costs associated with lower receivables.**

Illustration 4: Early settlement discount

Lowe and Price Co has annual credit sales of $12,000,000, and three months are allowed for payment. The company decides to offer a 2% discount for payments made within ten days of the invoice being sent, and to reduce the maximum time allowed for payment to two months. It is estimated that 50% of customers will take the discount.

Assume that the volume of sales will be unaffected by the discount, and the company has an overdraft costing 10% per year.

Required

Evaluate the effect of the discount.

Solution

The amount of accounts receivable, if the company policy remains unchanged, would be:

$3/12 \times \$12,000,000 = \$3,000,000$.

If the policy is changed the amount of accounts receivable would be:

$(10/365 \times 50\% \times \$12,000,000) + (2/12 \times 50\% \times \$12,000,000) = \$164,384 + \$1,000,000$

$= \$1,164,384$

Exam focus point

The effect of the settlement discount is not included in the calculation of new receivables. This assumes that sales are recorded before the effect of the settlement discount (which is normally recorded separately). This is the approach that has been adopted in past ACCA Financial Management exam questions.

	$
Current accounts receivable	3,000,000
Accounts receivable after implementing the proposal	1,164,384
Reduction in accounts receivable	1,835,616

Benefit of policy

Since the company has an overdraft costing 10% per year, the value of a reduction in accounts receivable (a source of funds) is 10% of $1,835,616 each year in perpetuity, that is, $183,562 a year.

Cost of policy

Discounts allowed each year (2% × 50% × $12,000,000) = $120,000

Summary

	$
Benefit of policy	183,562
Less cost of policy	120,000
Net benefit of new discount policy each year	63,562

The proposed policy brings a net financial benefit and therefore should be accepted.

Activity 8: Early settlement discounts

Pips Co is considering offering a cash settlement discount to its customers. Currently its annual sales are $10 million and its normal payment terms are 90 days. Customers will be able to take a 2% discount for payments within 10 days. Pips anticipates that 20% of customers will take the discount.

Currently Pips has an overdraft on which it is paying 10% interest.

Required

Assess whether Pips should offer the discount (assume a 365-day year).

Solution

4.2 Framework for managing receivables

After a credit policy has been agreed, a framework is needed to ensure that it is implemented effectively. This will involve **three stages**:

(a) **Planning stage**

(b) **Monitoring stage**

(c) **Collection stage**

4.2.1 Planning stage: credit analysis

Before offering credit to a **particular customer**, it is important to **analyse the risk** of trading with that customer by asking for **bank references** and **trade references**.

A **credit rating agency** will also provide details on a customer's trading history, debt levels and payment performance.

A decision will then need to be taken on the **credit limit** to be offered. A **new customer's credit limit** should be **fixed** at a **low level** and only increased if their payment record subsequently warrants it.

For large value customers, a **file** should be **maintained** of any available financial information about the customer. This file should be reviewed regularly. Information is available from the company's annual report and accounts and **press comments** may give information about what a company is currently doing (as opposed to the historical results in published accounts which only show what the company has done in the past).

4.2.2 Monitoring stage: credit control

Credit customers should be **monitored** to ensure that they are complying with the agreed credit period. It is important that this is not exceeded without senior management approval.

Credit analysis should also be periodically re-applied, especially if dealing with a large customer.

4.2.3 Collection stage

A clear process needs to be in place for chasing late payment. For example, on a regular basis a company could:

(a) Prepare an **aged listing** of receivables

(b) Issue **regular statements** and reminders

(c) Impose **sanctions** after a certain time limit (eg legal action or charging interest)

(d) Consider the use of a **debt factor**.

> **Factoring:** An arrangement to have debts collected by a factor company, which advances a proportion of the money it is due to collect.

A **debt factor** can be used simply to chase late payment or to have a wider role in managing receivables. A debt factor offers a range of potential services:

(a) **Administration** of the client's invoicing, sales accounting and debt collection service.

(b) **Credit insurance** whereby the factor takes over the risk of loss from bad debts and so 'insures' the client against such losses. This is known as a **non-recourse** service. Not all factoring agreements are non-recourse. If this service is not being offered, then this is a with-recourse service.

(c) Making **payments** to the client **in advance** of collecting the debts. A factor will purchase selected invoices and advance a percentage of their value (charging interest on the amount advanced). When the customer pays, the factor will pay over the balance, less charges. This is sometimes referred to as **invoice discounting**.

> **Non-recourse factoring:** The debt factor has no recourse to the client in the event of non-payment, ie bad debts insurance is being provided by the debt factor.

Advantages of debt factor	Disadvantages of debt factor
Saving in internal **administration costs**.	The **fees** charged by a debt factor for its services.
Expertise in **credit analysis** will reduce the potential for bad debts.	Possible **loss of customer goodwill** if the factor is too aggressive in chasing for payment.
A **flexible source of finance**, especially if cash flows are under pressure due to rising sales (ie overtrading).	In the past, was viewed as an indication that the company using the factor is in financial difficulty. As the popularity of factoring has increased, this has become less of an issue.

Activity 9: Debt factor

A company with sales of $240 million p.a. has an average collection period of three months; bad debts are 2%. A factoring company will provide **non-recourse** factoring for a fee of 5% of revenue. As a result of this, administration savings will be made of $8 million p.a. and the credit period will fall to two months. The factor will also advance 75% of the value of invoices in cash for the duration of the credit period. The interest rate on these advances is 13%.

The company has a cost of borrowing of 10%.

Required

Assess whether the factor should be used.

Solution

4.3 Managing foreign accounts receivable

Foreign debts raise the following special problems.

(a) It may be harder to build an accurate credit analysis of a company in a distant country.

(b) It may be harder to chase foreign customers for payments (different time zones and languages).

(c) If a foreign debtor refuses to pay a debt, the exporter must pursue the debt in the debtor's own country and may lack an understanding of the procedures and laws of that country.

Some businesses may decide to **trust** the foreign receivable and not take any special measures to reduce the non-payment risk. This method is known as **open account** and may be suitable for small transactions.

However, there are several measures available to exporters to help overcome the risks of non-payment or late payment on larger transactions.

Methods of reducing risks	
Bill of exchange	An IOU signed by the customer. Until it is paid, shipping documents that transfer ownership to the customer are withheld. As noted in Chapter 2, a Bill of Exchange can also be sold to raise finance.
Letter of credit	The customer's **bank** guarantees it will pay the invoice after delivery of the goods.
Invoice discounting	Sale of selected invoices to a debt factor, at a discount to their face value.
Debt factoring	A local debt factor based in the export market can be especially useful in performing credit analysis and chasing for payment.

BPP LEARNING MEDIA

Essential reading

See Chapter 3 section 6 of the Essential reading for further discussion of this area.

The Essential Reading is available as an Appendix of the digital edition of the Workbook.

5 Managing trade payables

Effective management of **trade accounts payable** involves seeking satisfactory credit terms from supplier and maintaining good relations with suppliers.

Timely payment of invoices, in line with agreed payment terms, will prevent the possibility that late payment of invoices endangers the firm's long-term relationship with the supplier.

5.1 Evaluating discounts

If a supplier offers a discount for the early payment of debts, the evaluation of the decision whether to **accept the discount** is the mirror image of the **evaluation of the decision** whether to **offer a discount to customers**.

Accepting early settlement discounts from a supplier will result in a benefit (the discount) but will result in **lower payables** which will incur a cost to the company by **increasing the cost of the interest** charged on an overdraft, since money is being paid to suppliers earlier.

This can be assessed by comparing the **benefit of the discount to the cost of higher finance costs associated with lower payables.**

Activity 10: Discounts

Pips Co has been offered a discount of 2.5% for an early settlement by a major supplier from which it purchases goods worth $1,000,000 each year. Pip's normal payment terms are 30 days; early settlement requires the payment to be made within 10 days.

Currently Pips has an overdraft on which it is paying 10% interest.

Required

What is the net benefit of accepting the early settlement discount (assuming a 365-day year)?

O $54,795

O $25,000

O $19,520

O $5,480

Solution

5.1.1 Evaluating a supplier discount using percentages

The benefit of an early payment discount can be expressed in **percentage terms**.

Illustration 5: Supplier discounts

A company which has an overdraft costing 10% per year, is evaluating whether to accept a 1% discount for paying its invoices 30 days earlier. Assume a 360-day year.

Required

Evaluate whether to accept the discount.

Solution

No $ amounts are given here, so we must look at this in percentage terms.

If the company **accepted the offer** and did pay 30 days early, it receives a benefit that can be expressed as a **percentage** as follows:

$$\frac{\text{Discount received}}{\text{Amount paid if discount taken}} \times 100$$

Here this is 1%/99% = 0.0101 or 1.01%, where 1% is the discount and 99% is the percentage of the amount due that is paid (after the 1% discount).

This is the benefit of accepting the offer expressed over a 30-day period (since the company is paying 30 days early). This can be converted into an annual equivalent rate using the following formula. (This formula is **not** given in the exam).

$(1+R) = (1+r)^n$

R = annual rate

r = period rate (here 30 days)

n = no. of periods in a year (here 360/30 = 12)

In annual terms this is $1.0101 \wedge 12 = 1.1282$ so R = 12.82%.

Since the benefit of the discount of 12.82% is above the cost of the overdraft (10% per year) the discount should be accepted.

The same formula can be used for accounts receivable.

Activity 11: Discount as a percentage

Hansel Co is to make a payment of $10,000 to a supplier. A 2% discount is available for paying after one month instead of the standard term of three months.

Required

What is the annual percentage cost of the discount?

- ○ 27.4%
- ○ 12.9%
- ○ 26.8%
- ○ 12.6%

Solution

5.2 Managing foreign accounts payable

To avoid the risk of an adverse exchange rate movement by the time a foreign currency invoice is due to be paid, companies sometimes pay the invoice early. This is sometimes called **leading**.

The management of exchange rate risk is covered in Chapter 14.

> **PER alert**
>
> Performance objective 10 requires you to 'prepare and monitor an organisation's cash flow, credit facilities and advise on appropriate actions'. This section covers the management of accounts payable and credit terms.

6 Final exam standard example

This final example shows how this chapter could be tested as a part of a Section C exam question.

Activity 12: Homework example

Velm Co sells stationery and office supplies on a wholesale basis and has annual revenue of $4,000,000. The company employs four people in its sales ledger and credit control department at an annual salary of $12,000 each. All sales are on 40 days' credit with no discount for early payment. Bad debts represent 3% of revenue and Velm Co pays annual interest of 9% on its overdraft.

The most recent accounts of the company offer the following financial information:

VELM CO: STATEMENT OF FINANCIAL POSITION AS AT 31 DECEMBER 20X2

	$'000	$'000
Tangible non-current assets		
Tangible non-current assets		17,500
Current assets		
Inventory of goods for resale	900	
Receivables	550	
Cash	120	
		1,570
Total assets		19,070

	$'000	$'000
Equity and liabilities		
Ordinary shares	3,500	
Reserves	11,640	
		15,140
Non-current liabilities		
12% bonds due 20Y0		2,400
Current liabilities		
Trade payables	330	
Overdraft	1,200	
		1,530
Total equity and liabilities		19,070

Velm Co is considering offering a discount of 1% to customers paying within 14 days, which it believes will reduce bad debts to 2.4% of revenue. The company also expects that offering a discount for early payment will reduce the average credit period taken by its customers to 26 days. The consequent reduction in the time spent chasing customers where payments are overdue will allow one member of the credit control team to take early retirement. Two-thirds of customers are expected to take advantage of the discount.

Required

Using the information provided, determine whether a discount for early payment of 1% will lead to an increase in profitability for Velm Co. Assume a 365-day year.

Solution

Chapter summary

Working capital investment

Objectives of working capital management

Profitability
Increasing the profits of a business

Liquidity
Considering impact on ability to meet short-term liabilities (next chapter)

Conflict
- Possible conflict as investing in working capital to improve profits
- May cause liquidity issues

Working capital planning

Influences on investment in working capital
- General factors (nature of industry, policy of rivals, seasonal factors)
- Company-specific (sales, policies)

Aggressive working capital management
Minimise net working capital increases as sales rise

Conservative working capital management
High levels of net working capital

Working capital ratios
Quantify working capital policies/needs

Operating cycle
Time taken to receive cash less time to pay suppliers

Sales to net working capital ratio
Used to forecast financing impact of sales increases

Overtrading
- Indicated by rapid increases in sales
- And falling margins and worse liquidity
- Rising operating cycle is another indicator
- Also called undercapitalisation

Inventory

EOQ model
- Formula given
- Assumes constant demand
- Assumes zero lead times
- Assumes no discounts

Discounts
Consider impact on inventory related costs

Buffer stock
Increases average inventory

JIT
- Zero inventory approach
- Addresses hidden costs of inventory

Receivables

Policy formulation
- Whether to offer credit
- Credit terms

Management framework
- Credit analysis
- Credit control
- Debt collection
- Use of a debt factor

Foreign accounts receivable
- Bill of exchange
- Letter of credit
- Invoice discounting
- Debt factor

Evaluation
- Credit period
- Early settlement discounts
- Factoring

Payables

Maintaining relationships
Avoid late payment

Evaluating discounts
in $s or %s

Foreign accounts payable
Leading

Knowledge diagnostic

1. Objectives of working capital management

The two main objectives of working capital management are to increase the **profits** of a business and to provide sufficient **liquidity** to meet short-term obligations as they fall due. These two objectives may sometimes **conflict**.

2. Cash operating cycle

The cash operating cycle can be used to determine the amount of working capital investment needed at any sales level, and to identify the possibility of a cash shortfall if sales rise too rapidly.

3. Inventory

The economic order quantity model attempts to identify the optimal level of investment in inventory that is required. The EOQ model ignores the hidden costs of inventory. JIT suggests that inventory should be driven down to as close to zero as possible.

4. Receivables

Requires a four-step approach:

(a) A receivables policy

(b) A planning (credit analysis) system

(c) A monitoring (credit control) system

(d) A debt collection system

5. Payables

Involves controlling the timing of the payment of invoices to exploit attractive early payment discounts, and the credit period offered by suppliers; but ensuring that invoices are not paid so late as to endanger long-term supplier relationships.

BPP LEARNING MEDIA

Further study guidance

Question practice

Now try the following from the Further question practice bank (available in the digital edition of the Workbook):

Section A questions

Q10, Q11, Q12, Q13

Section C questions

Q38 Gustaffson

Q39 H finance

Q40 Victory

Q41 ZX

Further reading

There is a useful Technical Article written by a member of the FM examining team that is available on ACCA's website; it is called 'Management of foreign accounts receivable'. We recommend that you read this article as part of your preparation for the FM exam.

Activity answers

Activity 1: Forecasting

$864,000 × 73/365 = $172,800

Activity 2: Combination of ratios

The correct answer is: $200m

Current assets/Current liabilities = 2

(10 + Receivables)/15 = 2

Receivables = (2 × 15) − 10

= 20

(Receivables/Credit sales) × 365 = 36.5

(20 × 365)/Credit sales = 36.5

Credit sales = (20 × 365)/36.5

= $200m

Activity 3: Operating cycle

46.8 days

1	**Inventory days**			
	Finished goods	86,400/756,000	× 365	= 41.7 days
2	**Receivables days**	172,800/864,000	× 365	= 73.0 days
3	**Payables days**	96,400/518,400	× 365	= (67.9) days
		Cash operating cycle =		46.8

Activity 4: Sales/net working capital

The correct answer is: $37,700

$864,000 + $200,000 = $1,064,000

$1,064,000/5.3071 = **$200,486**

This is an increase of $200,486 − $162,800 = $37,686 or $37,700 to the nearest $100

This represents the increase in cash due to movements in working capital.

Alternative solution:

$200,000 / 5.3071 = $37,685 or $37,700 to the nearest $100

Activity 5: EOQ

1   Annual demand = 12 × 150 = 1,800

    EOQ =

$$Q = \sqrt{\frac{2C_0D}{C_h}} = \sqrt{\frac{2 \times 32 \times 1,800}{4.5}} = 160$$

    Average inventory = Q/2 = 80 units.

2   Total inventory related cost = C_h × Q/2 + C_o × D/Q + purchasing cost

    = $4.50 × 160/2 + $32 × 1,800/160 + $25 × 1,800

    = $45,720

Activity 6: Bulk purchase discounts

If no discount is taken, inventory related costs are $45,720 (previous activity).

Q	Order cost	Holding cost	Purchase cost	Total
	(Co × D/Q)	(Ch × Q/2)	(D × P)	$
300	192	675	44,100	44,967
800	72	1,800	43,200	45,072

∴ **Order 300 units at a time and accept the 2% discount.**

Activity 7: Extended credit terms

The correct answer is: $10,750 benefit

Cost

Finance cost was 600,000 × 2/12 × 10% = $10,000

Finance cost will be 600,000 × 1.15 × 3/12 × 10% = $17,250

Additional cost = $7,250

Benefit

Additional contribution = 600,000 × 15% × 20% = $18,000

Net benefit = $10,750

Activity 8: Early settlement discounts

The correct answer is: $3,836 benefit

Cost

$10m × 0.2 × 0.02 = $40,000

Benefit

Current receivables = 90/365 × $10m = $2,465,753

New receivables = (0.2 × 10/365 × $10m) + (0.8 × 90/365 × $10m) = $54,795 + $1,972,603 = $2,027,398

The effect of the settlement discount is not included in analysing the new receivables. This assumes that sales are recorded before the effect of the settlement discount (this is normally recorded separately). This is the approach that has been adopted in past ACCA Financial Management exam questions.

Reduction in receivables = $438,355

Saving in overdraft interest = **$43,836**

Net benefit = $3,836

Sales may also rise as a result of the policy.

The policy should be introduced.

Activity 9: Debt factor

Cost of debt factor

	$m
Factors charge	
$240m × 5%	12.0
Interest on advances (13% − 10%) × 75% × $240m × 2/12	0.9
	12.9

Alternative solution for interest on advances:

Amount advanced = 0.75 × annual sales = $180m. This is advanced for 2 months at an annual cost of 3% (13% net of 10%) ie $180m × 2/12 × 0.03 = $0.9m.

Benefit of the debt factor

Impact of lower receivables

Current receivables	$240m × 3/12 = $60m	
New receivables	$240m × 2/12 = $40m	
Reduction in receivables	$20m leads to interest saved of $20m × 0.1 = $2m	2.0
Bad debts		
$240m × 2%		4.8
Administration savings		8.0
		14.8

∴ Use the factor as it is estimated to save $1.9m p.a.

Activity 10: Discounts

The correct answer is: $19,520

Cost

Current payables = 30/365 × 1,000,000 = $82,192

New payables = 10/365 × 1,000,000 = $27,397

(as with receivables the discount is ignored in this calculation)

Reduction in payables causes an increase in overdraft interest of $54,795 × 0.1 =**$5,480**

Benefit

0.025 × $1,000,000 = $25,000

Net Saving = **$19,520**

Activity 11: Discount as a percentage

The correct answer is: 12.9%

Paying $9,800 one month early instead of $10,000 is a benefit of $200.

This is a benefit of 200/9,800 = 0.0204 or 2.04% over a two-month period.

Or as a % = 2%/98% = 0.204

There are six two-month periods in a year so this is an annual benefit of 1.0204 ^ 6 = 1.129 ie 12.9%

Incorrect answers:

12.6% is calculated as 200/10,000 = 1.02 and then 1.02 ^ 6 = 1.126 ie 12.6%

26.8% is calculated as 200/10,000 = 1.02 and then 1.02 ^ 12 = 1.268 ie 26.8%

27.4% is calculated as 200/9,800 = 1.0204 and then 1.0204 ^ 12 = 1.274 ie 27.4%

Activity 12: Homework example

Receivables are currently taking on average ($550,000/$4,000,000) × 365 = 50 days to pay. This is in excess of Velm's stated terms. The discount, to be taken up by 2/3 of customers, will cost the company $4,000,000 × 1% × 2/3 = $26,667. It is stated that this will bring the receivables payment period down to 26 days, which is represented by a new receivables level of $4,000,000 × 26/365 = $284,932.

This is a reduction in receivables of $265,068.

At current overdraft costs of 9%, this would be a saving of $265,068 × 0.09 = $23,856.

Bad debts would decrease from 3% to 2.4% of revenue, which saves a total of $4,000,000 × 0.006 = $24,000. There would also be a salary saving from early retirement of $12,000.

So the net effect on Velm's profitability is as follows:

	$
Saving on overdraft costs	23,856
Decreased bad debts	24,000
Salary saving	12,000
Less cost of discount	(26,667)
Net saving	33,189

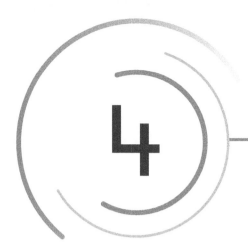

4

Cash management and working capital finance

Learning objectives

On completion of this chapter you should be able to:

	Syllabus reference
Management of inventories, receivables, payables and cash (continued)	C2(f)
• Explain the various reasons for holding cash, and discuss and apply the use of relevant techniques in managing cash, including:	
- preparing cash flow forecasts to determine future cash flows and cash balances	
- assessing the benefits of centralised treasury management and cash control	
- cash management models, such as the Baumol and the Miller-Orr models	
- investing short-term.	
Determining working capital needs and funding strategies	C3(b)
• Describe and discuss the key factors in determining working capital funding strategies, including:	
- the distinction between permanent and fluctuating current assets	
- the relative cost and risk of short-term and long-term finance	
- the matching principle	
- the relative costs and benefits of aggressive, conservative and matching funding policies	
- management attitudes to risk, previous funding decisions & organisation size.	

Exam context

This chapter covers issues relating to liquidity and the finance of working capital, which are part of Section C of the syllabus (Working capital management) and completes this syllabus section. Like the previous chapter, this syllabus area is examinable in all sections of the exam and exam questions won't just involve calculations (eg in section C part of an exam question may ask you to discuss types of working capital funding strategies or to explain the meaning of a numerical cash flow analysis that you have performed).

Chapter overview

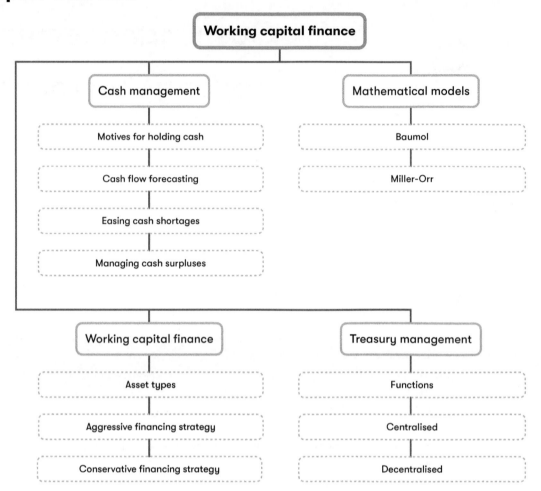

1 Cash management

We saw in the previous chapter that working capital management has two main objectives:

(a) To increase the **profits** of a business

(b) To ensure sufficient **liquidity** to meet short-term obligations as they fall due

This chapter mainly focusses on **liquidity** and covers the importance of **cash flow management** and different strategies that can be followed to provide **working capital finance**

1.1 Motives for holding cash

There are **three main motives** for holding cash.

Transactions motive	Precautionary motive	Speculation motive
A business primarily needs to plan to maintain sufficient cash to meet its forecast transactions eg paying suppliers, employees etc. Cash requirements to cover this motive can be planned using a **cash flow forecast**.	Cash may also be needed to meet unexpected occurrences (eg an unforeseen downturn in sales, or disruption to production). This often means that a business will arrange an **overdraft facility**, or short-term investments which can easily be converted into cash (discussed in section 1.4).	Some businesses hold surplus cash to take advantage of attractive investment opportunities if these arise. For example, the opportunity to take over another company at an attractive price.

However, holding cash (or near equivalents to cash) has a cost: the **loss of profits** which would otherwise have been obtained by using the funds in another way. So, as ever, the financial manager must try to **balance liquidity with profitability**.

1.2 Cash flow forecasting

Cash flow forecast: A detailed forecast of cash inflows and outflows incorporating both revenue and capital items.

Cash flow forecasts will be prepared continuously during the year and will allow a business to **plan how to deal with expected cash flow surpluses or shortages**.

1.2.1 Format of cash flow forecast

A cash flow forecast will tabulate estimated future **cash receipts** and **payments** in such a way as to show the forecast **cash balance** of a business at defined intervals. There is no 'set' format that you are required to use but it is sensible to follow these guidelines:

(a) Have two separate sections, one for cash inflows and one for cash outflows

(b) Don't reproduce the forecast separately for each time period (instead add a new column for each time period being analysed)

(c) Finish each column by netting off the cash flow for the period and adding it to cash brought forward to create a final cash flow carried forward figure. This can be done easily in the exam using the spreadsheet functionality available in the constructive response workspace.

Here is an example of a cash forecast, illustrating a sensible format.

CASH FORECAST FOR THE THREE MONTHS ENDED 31 MARCH 20X1

	January	February	March
Cash receipts			
Sales receipts (W1)	X	X	X
Issue of shares		X	
Cash payments			
Purchase payments (W2)	(X)	(X)	(X)
Dividends/Taxes	(X)		
Purchase of non-current assets			(X)
Wages	(X)	(X)	(X)
Cash surplus/deficit for month	X	(X)	X
Cash balance, beginning	X	X	(X)
Interest on opening cash balance	X	X	(X)
Cash balance, ending	X	(X)	X

Working

	January	February	March
1. Timing of sales receipts			
Revenue from sales 1 month ago (assuming 1-month credit period)	From Dec sales	From Jan sales	From Feb sales
2. Timing of supplier payments			
Supplier invoices from 2 months ago (assuming 2-month credit period)	From Nov purchases	From Dec purchases	From Jan purchases

Exam focus point

In the exam you will need to think carefully about the expected **timing** of receipts and payments of cash during the period and whether a cost is a cash item eg depreciation.

Activity 1: Cash forecast

Ben is a wholesaler of motorcycle helmets. It is 1 January 20X2.

Credit sales in the last quarter of 20X1 were as follows:

	Helmets
October	2,000
November	2,000
December	2,500

His credit sales in the first quarter will be as follows:

	Helmets
January	3,000
February	5,000
March	4,500

Customers are given 60 days' credit and the average selling price is $10, a price rise of $1 is planned in February. His biggest customer, Mickster, is given a 2% discount for paying cash when the sale is made. Mickster is planning to buy 150 helmets in January and 250 Helmets in March. The sales to Mickster are in addition to those credit sales stated above.

Purchases (an average of 30 days' credit) are $4 per helmet. Ben plans to buy in the helmets a month in advance of selling them. Total overheads are $2,000 per month; this includes $400 depreciation and wages of $1,000. All other overheads are paid for after a credit period of 30 days.

Ben plans to inject a further $5,000 of his own money into the business in March to help to buy non-current assets for $29,000. These assets will be depreciated over five years.

Opening cash flow is negative $4,550 which is close to Ben's **overdraft limit of $5,500.**

Required

Prepare a monthly cash flow forecast for the first quarter of 20X2 and comment on your results.

Solution

1.2.2 Working capital movements

If a question provides you with **operating cash flows and working capital movements**, you may be required to adjust the operating cash flows for the **cashflow impact of working capital movements** to calculate monthly cash flows.

Taking the previous activity, if you had been given the operating cash flows in January as being $17,270 and had been told that, during January receivables are forecast to increase by $10,000 (meaning that $10,000 of revenue is deferred to the next period), trade payables are forecast to increase by $7,400 (meaning that $7,400 of cost is deferred to the next period) and inventory is forecast to rise by $7,400 (incurring $7,400 of cost in this period); then the net cash flow in January could be calculated as:

	$
Original operating cash flows	17,270
Less increase in receivables	(10,000)
Plus increase in payables	7,400
Less increase in inventory	(7,400)
Net cash flow for January	7,270

 Essential reading

See Chapter 4 Section 1 of the Essential Reading, available in the digital edition of the Workbook, for further practice on this area.

The Essential reading is available as an Appendix of the digital edition of the Workbook.

1.3 Methods of easing cash shortages

The steps that are usually taken by a company when a need for cash arises, and when it cannot obtain resources from new sources of finance, could include the following:

(a) **Delaying non-essential capital expenditure**

Some new non-current assets might not be needed for the **development and growth of the business,** but it may not be possible to delay some capital expenditures without serious consequences.

For example, if a company's policy is to replace company cars every two years, but the company is facing a cash shortage, it might decide to replace cars every three years.

(b) **Accelerating cash inflows which would otherwise be expected in a later period.**

It might be possible to encourage credit customers to pay more quickly by offering discounts for earlier payment. This was covered in Chapter 3.

(c) **Reversing past investment decisions by selling assets previously acquired**

Some assets are less crucial to a business than others. If cash flow problems are severe, the option of selling investments or property might have to be considered. Sale and leaseback of property could also be considered.

(d) **Negotiating a reduction in cash outflows to postpone or reduce payments**

There are several ways in which this could be done:

- **Longer credit** might be taken from suppliers. Such an extension of credit would have to be negotiated carefully: there would be a risk of having further supplies refused.
- **Loan repayments** could be rescheduled by agreement with a bank.
- **Dividend payments** could be **reduced**. Dividend payments are discretionary cash outflows, however cutting the dividend is likely to be interpreted as sign of weakness by the financial markets so this could be considered as a last resort.

1.4 Managing cash surpluses

If cash surpluses are only forecast for the short-term (eg due to seasonal factors) and will be required to offset cash deficits in the near-future, then it will be important to invest these cash surpluses in a way that **minimises risk** (because the funds will be needed soon).

Desirable investments would generally be **low risk** and **liquid** (ie easy to turn in to cash). These could include:

Definition	
Treasury bills	Short-term government IOUs, can be sold when needed
Term deposits	Fixed period deposits
Certificates of deposit	Issued by banks, entitle the holder to interest plus principal, can be sold when needed
Commercial paper	Short-term IOUs issued by companies, unsecured

If cash surpluses are forecast for the long-term (eg due to seasonal factors) then a different perspective can be taken. **Long-term** cash surpluses may be used to fund:

(a) **Investments** – new projects or acquisitions

(b) **Financing** – repay debt, buy back shares

(c) **Dividends** – returning funds to shareholders

These areas are covered in later chapters.

Essential reading

See Chapter 4 section 2 of the Essential reading, available in the digital edition of the Workbook, for further discussion of this area.

The Essential reading is available as an Appendix of the digital edition of the Workbook.

2 Mathematical models

A number of different cash management models indicate the **optimum amount of cash** that a company should hold.

2.1 Baumol model

The **Baumol model** is based on the idea that deciding on optimum cash balances is like deciding on optimum inventory levels. It assumes that cash is steadily consumed over time and a business holds a stock of marketable securities that can be sold when cash is needed. The Baumol model is an adaptation of the EOQ model to manage cash.

Formula provided

$$\text{Economic order quantity} = \sqrt{\frac{2CoD}{Ch}}$$

The **cost of holding cash (Ch)** is the cost of obtaining the funds net of any interest earned by investing the funds.

The **cost of placing an order (Co)** is the administration cost incurred when selling the securities.

The **demand (D)** is the annual cash required.

Illustration 1: Baumol approach to cash management

Finder Co faces a fixed cost of $400 to obtain new funds. It requires $240,000 of cash each year.

The interest cost on new finance is 12% per year and the interest earned on short-term securities is 9% per year.

Required

How much finance should Finder raise at a time?

Solution

The cost of holding cash is 12% − 9% = 3%

The cost of placing an order is $400

The annual demand is $240,000

Applying the EOQ formula, the optimum level of Q (the 'reorder quantity') is:

$$\sqrt{\frac{2 \times 400 \times 240,000}{0.03}} = \$80,000$$

The optimum amount of new funds to raise is $80,000. This amount is raised three times every year (240,000 ÷ 80,000).

Activity 2: Baumol model

A division requires $1.5m per year; cash use is constant throughout the year. Transaction costs are $150 per transaction and deposit interest is generated at 7.5% and interest on short-term financial securities is 12%.

Required

What is the optimal economic quantity of cash transfer into this division's sub-account and how frequently?

○ $1,500,000 once a year

○ $77,500, 19 times a year

○ $61,200, 25 times a year

○ $100,000, 15 times a year

2.1.1   Drawbacks of the Baumol model

(a)   In reality, it is difficult **to predict amounts required** over future periods with much accuracy.

(b)   It is **unlikely that cash will be used at a constant rate** over any given period (there will points in time when cash out flows will spike as machinery is bought or an interest payment on a loan is made etc).

2.2   Miller-Orr model

Another cash management model is the Miller-Orr model, which recognises that cash inflows and outflows **vary** considerably on a day to day basis. This is clearly more realistic than the Baumol model's assumption of constant usage of cash during a period.

It works as follows:

(a)   A safety level (**lower limit**) of cash is decided upon (often this will be imposed by a bank).

(b)   A statistical calculation is completed to establish the **upper limit** (the maximum cash that will be required) taking into account the variability in a firm's cash flows. The difference between the lower and upper limits is called a **spread**, this is calculated using a formula (which is given):

$$\text{Spread} = 3\left(\frac{3}{4} \times \frac{\text{Transaction cost} \ \times \ \text{Variance of cash flows}}{\text{Interest rate}}\right)^{\frac{1}{3}}$$

The upper limit = lower limit + spread

(c)   The cash balance is managed to ensure that the balance at any point in time is kept between the lower and upper limits.
      If the cash balance reaches an **upper limit** (point A in the following diagram) the firm **buys sufficient securities** to return the cash balance to a normal level (called the 'return point'). When the cash balance reaches a lower limit (point B), the firm sells securities to bring the balance back to the return point.

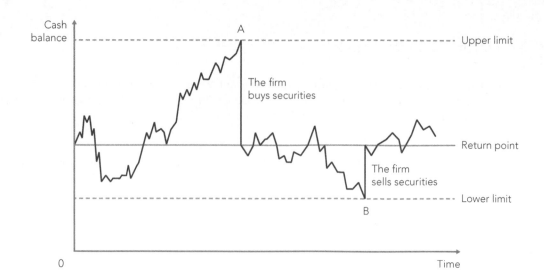

Formula provided

The return point is calculated as: **Lower limit + (1/3 × spread)**

This formula is also given.

Illustration 2: Miller-Orr

The following data applies to a company.

(1)   The minimum cash balance is $8,000.

(2)   The variance of daily cash flows is $4,000,000, equivalent to a standard deviation of $2,000 per day (note: standard deviation is the square root of the variance).

(3)   The transaction cost for buying or selling securities is $50. The interest rate is 0.025% per day.

Required

You are required to formulate a decision rule using the Miller-Orr model.

Solution

(1)   The **spread** between the upper and lower cash balance limits is calculated as follows.

$$\text{Spread} = 3\left(\frac{3}{4} \times \frac{\text{Transaction cost} \ \times \ \text{Variance of cash flows}}{\text{Interest rate}}\right)^{\frac{1}{3}}$$

$$\text{Spread} = 3\left(\frac{3}{4} \times \frac{50 \times 4{,}000{,}000}{0.00025}\right)^{\frac{1}{3}} =$$

$$3 \times (6 \times 10^{11})^{\frac{1}{3}} = 3 \times 8{,}434.33 = \$25{,}303 \text{ say } \$25{,}300$$

(2)   The upper limit and return point are now calculated.

Upper limit = lower limit + $25,300   = $8,000 + $25,300 = $33,300

Return point = lower limit + 1/3 × spread = $8,000 + 1/3 × $25,300

= $16,433, say $16,400

(3) The decision rules are as follows.

- If the cash balance reaches $33,300, buy $16,900 (= 33,300 - 16,400) in marketable securities.
- If the cash balance falls to $8,000, sell $8,400 of marketable securities for cash.

> ### Exam focus point
>
> Variance = standard deviation^2 so if you are given the standard deviation, you will need to square it to calculate the **variance**.
>
> If you are given the annual interest rate, you will need to divide it by 365 to obtain the **daily** interest rate.

2.2.1 Drawbacks of the Miller-Orr model

The **usefulness of the Miller-Orr model** is limited by the assumptions on which it is based:

- The estimates used (for example of variability) are likely to be based on **historic information** which may unreliable as a predictor of future variability (for example if the economic or competitive environment changes).
- The model does not incorporate the impact of **seasonality**: for example, for a retailer, seasonal factors are likely to affect cash inflows.

3 Working capital finance

As a business grows, its non-current asset and current asset base need to grow and this has implications for financing. Here we consider different strategies for financing working capital.

> **Working capital finance:** The approach taken to financing the level, and fluctuations in the level, of net working capital.

In order to understand working capital financing decisions, **assets** will be divided into three different types.

(a) **Non-current (fixed) assets**

Long-term assets from which an organisation expects to derive benefit over a number of periods; for example, buildings or machinery.

(b) **Permanent current assets**

The **minimum current asset base** (eg inventory, receivables) required to sustain normal trading activity.

(c) **Fluctuating current assets**

The variation in current assets during a period, for example due to **seasonal variations**.

3.1 Working capital finance strategies

There are different ways in which **long- and short-term sources of funding** can be used to finance current and non-current assets.

Chapter 9 will examine specific types of short- and long-term finance in more detail, here we discuss some of the **general characteristics of short- and long-term finance.**

3.1.1 Long-term finance and short-term finance compared

Long-term finance is usually **more expensive** than short-term finance because investors require a higher return for locking their money away for longer time periods.

However, **long-term finance** provides **higher security to the borrower** than short-term finance, because there is no guarantee that short-term finance will be available to them when it is needed in the future.

3.1.2 Aggressive and conservative working capital financing strategies

In the previous chapter we identified that **working capital investment** strategies can be **aggressive** (low net working capital) or **conservative** (high net working capital).

Similar terminology exists when we discuss **working capital financing** strategies.

Aggressive financing strategy	Conservative financing strategy
Minimal long-term finance for working capital	High level of long-term finance for working capital
Mainly uses cheaper short-term sources of finance – short-term funds are used to finance **fluctuating current assets and a proportion of permanent current assets.** Leads to problems if short-term finance is not available when required. This strategy is therefore risky	Mainly uses more secure long-term sources of finance – long-term funds are used to finance **permanent current assets and a proportion of fluctuating current assets.** This strategy is safer but can be expensive

The following diagram relates these types of strategy to the investment in non-current assets and current assets of a business.

The curved line represents the finance required at any point in time.

The dotted lines A, B and C are **different possible levels of long-term finance**, depending on the working capital finance strategy being followed.

Assets **above the relevant dotted line are financed by short-term funding** while **assets below the dotted line are financed by long-term funding.**

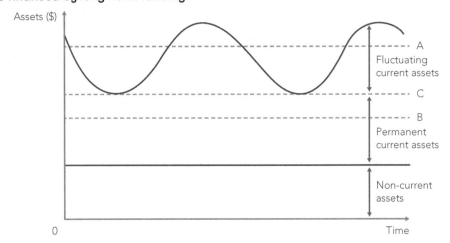

(a) Policy A is a **conservative working capital finance strategy.**

All non-current assets and permanent current assets, as well as a significant part of the fluctuating current assets, are financed by long-term funding.

At times when fluctuating current assets are low and total assets fall below line A, there will be **surplus cash** which the company will be able to invest in marketable securities.

(b) Policy B is an **aggressive working capital finance strategy.**

All fluctuating current assets all financed out of short-term sources, and also some of the permanent current assets. Minimal long-term finance is used.

(c) Policy C is a **matching (or moderate) approach.**

A **balance** between risk and return is achieved by policy C, a policy of **maturity matching** in which long-term funds finance permanent assets while short-term funds finance non-permanent assets. This means that the maturity of the funds matches the maturity of the assets.

3.2 Choice of working capital finance strategy

The working capital finance strategy that is most appropriate to a company depends on

(a) **Management attitude to risk** – short-term finance is higher risk to the borrower because it may not be available in the future when needed. For example, it may not be possible to access trade credit from suppliers when it is required.

(b) **Strength of relationship with the bank providing an overdraft** – if strong this will encourage the use of short-term finance as it makes it more likely that a bank overdraft will be available when required to provide short-term finance.

(c) **Ability to raise long-term finance** – if this is weak (perhaps because the organisation is small and/or has not used long-term finance wisely in the past) this will mean there is a greater need to use short-term finance because long-term finance is hard to access.

4 Treasury management

The responsibility for arranging short- and long-term finance is part of the responsibility of the Treasury department.

4.1 Functions of treasury management

Treasury management normally has four functions

4.1.1 Liquidity management

This is the short-term management of cash that we have referred to at the start of this chapter.

The aim is to ensure that a company has access to the cash that it needs but does not hold unnecessarily high levels of cash and does not incur high costs from needing to organise unforeseen short-term borrowing.

4.1.2 Funding

This involves deciding on suitable forms of finance and organising suitable bank and capital market debt.

Sources of finance will be covered in Chapter 9.

4.1.3 Corporate finance

This is the examination of a company's financial strategies. For example, is the capital structure appropriate, how are investments appraised, and how are potential acquisitions valued?

These areas are all covered in later chapters.

4.1.4 Risk management

This involves understanding and quantifying the risks faced by a company.

In this exam the main focus is on currency risk and interest rate risk (covered in Chapters 14 and 15).

4.2 Centralisation of treasury management

Within a **centralised** treasury department, the treasury department is normally based at Head Office and acts as an **in-house** bank serving the interests of the group.

This has a number of advantages compared to the alternative of allowing each division to organise their own (decentralised) treasury operations:

Advantages of centralisation	
Economies of scale	Borrowing required for a number of subsidiaries can be arranged **in bulk** (meaning lower administration costs and possibly a better loan rate), also combined cash surpluses can be invested **in bulk.**
Improved risk management	**Foreign exchange risk management** is likely to be improved because a central treasury department can **match foreign currency income** earned by one subsidiary with **expenditure** in the same currency by another subsidiary. In this way, the risk of losses on adverse exchange rate movements can be avoided without incurring the time and expense in managing foreign exchange risk.
Reduced borrowing	Cash surpluses in one area can be used to **match** to the cash needs in another, so an organisation avoids having a mix of overdrafts and cash surpluses in different localised bank accounts.
Lower cash balances	The centralised pool of **funds required for precautionary purposes** will be **smaller** than the sum of separate precautionary balances which would need to be held under decentralised treasury arrangements.
Expertise	Experts can be employed with knowledge of the latest developments in treasury management.

However, some companies prefer to decentralise treasury management because:

(a) Sources of finance can be **diversified** and can match **local assets**.

(b) **Greater autonomy** can be given to **subsidiaries** and divisions because of the closer relationships they will have with the decentralised cash management function.

(c) A decentralised treasury function may be **more responsive** to the needs of individual operating units.

Chapter summary

Working capital finance

Cash management

Motives for holding cash

Transaction, precautionary and speculation motives

Cash flow forecasting
- Neat layout
- Care with timings and non-cash items

Easing cash shortages
- Practical steps designed not to damage the business long-term
- Where possible avoid dividend cuts or cuts to important capital expenditure

Managing cash surpluses
- Short-term investments in low risk, highly liquid assets
- Long-term surplus needs to be used to create shareholder value or returned to shareholders

Mathematical models

Baumol
- Uses EOQ model
- Assumes constant use of cash which is unlikely

Miller-Orr
- Recognises cash variability
- Establishes upper and lower cash limits

Working capital finance

Asset types
- Non-current assets
- Permanent current assets
- Fluctuating current assets

Aggressive financing strategy
- Mainly uses short-term finance for current assets and even for some permanent current assets
- Cheaper but risky

Conservative financing strategy
- Mainly uses long-term finance for non-current assets, permanent current assets and also some fluctuating current assets
- Safer, but more expensive

Treasury management

Functions
- Liquidity management
- Funding
- Risk management
- Corporate finance advice

Centralised
- Economies of scale
- Improved risk management
- Reduced borrowing
- Lower cash balances
- Expertise

Decentralised
- Local finance used
- Autonomy for subsidiaries
- More responsive

Knowledge diagnostic

1. Cash flow forecasting

This is the key tool for cash management. Be careful with cash flow timings and non-cash items.

2. Cash surpluses and shortages

Cash shortages can be eased by postponing capital expenditure, selling assets, taking longer to pay accounts payable and pressing accounts receivable for earlier payment.

Temporary cash surpluses can be invested in a variety of low risk and highly liquid financial instruments. Longer-term surpluses should be returned to shareholders if there is a lack of investment opportunities.

3. Mathematical models

Optimal cash holding levels can be calculated from formal models, such as the Baumol model and the Miller-Orr model.

4. Working capital finance strategies

Aggressive strategy relies mainly on short-term finance to finance working capital, a conservative strategy relies more on long-term finance to finance working capital.

5. Treasury management

A large organisation will have a treasury department to manage liquidity, funding, risk management and corporate finance advice. This is often centralised.

Further study guidance

Question practice

Now try the following from the Further question practice bank (available in the digital edition of the Workbook):

Section A questions

Q14

Section C questions

Q42 Velm

Activity answers

Activity 1: Cash forecast
Cash flow forecast

	Jan	Feb	Mar
Inflows	$	$	$
Sales			
– Mickster (Cash)			
(98% × $10 × 150; 98% × $11 × 250)	1,470		2,695
Sales receipts (W1)			
	20,000	25,000	30,000
Capital			5,000
Total inflows	21,470	25,000	37,695
Outflows	$	$	$
Purchases (W2)	12,600	20,000	19,000
Overheads			
(2,000 – 400 – 1,000)	600	600	600
Wages	1,000	1,000	1,000
Non-current assets			29,000
Total outflows	14,200	21,600	49,600
Net cash flow	7,270	3,400	(11,905)
Balance b/f	(4,550)	2,720	6,120
Balance c/f	2,720	6,120	(5,785)

Working

	Jan	Feb	Mar
Sales receipts from 2 months ago			
Nov credit sales	2,000 × $10 = 20,000		
Dec credit sales		2,500 × $10 = 25,000	
Jan credit sales			3,000 × $10 = 30,000

	Jan	Feb	Mar
Supplier invoices from 1 month ago			
Dec purchases for Jan sales (credit & cash)	3,150 × $4 = 12,600		
Jan purchases for Feb sales (credit only)		5,000 × $4 = 20,000	
Feb purchases for March sales (credit & cash)			4,750 × $4 = 19,000

Activity 2: Baumol model

The correct answer is: $100,000, 15 times a year

The calculation is as follows:

$$EOQ = \sqrt{\frac{2 \times 150 \times 1,500,000}{0.045}} = \$100,000$$

ie 15 transfers of $100,000 are needed.

Skills checkpoint 1

Approach to objective test (OT) questions

Chapter overview

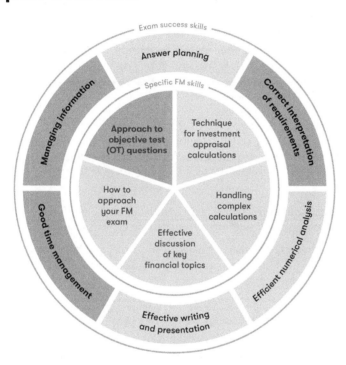

Introduction

Both Sections A and B of the FM exam consist of OT questions.

Section A – Single OT questions

OT questions are single, short questions that are auto-marked and worth two marks each. You must answer the whole question correctly to earn their two marks. There are no partial marks.

The OT questions in Section A aim for a broad coverage of the syllabus, and so all areas of the syllabus need to be carefully studied. You need to work through as many practice objective test questions as possible, reviewing carefully to see how correct answers are derived.

The following types of OT question commonly appear in the FM exam:

Question type	Explanation
Multiple choice (MCQ)	You need to choose one correct answer from four given response options.
Multiple response (MRQ)	These are a kind of multiple choice question, except you need to select more than one answer from a number of given options. The question will specify how many answers need to be selected, but the system won't stop you from selecting more answers than this. It is important to read the requirement carefully.
Fill in the blank (FIB)	This question type requires you to type a numerical answer into a box. The unit of measurement (eg $) will sit outside the box, and if there are specific rounding requirements these will be displayed.
Drag and drop	Drag and drop questions involve you dragging an answer and dropping it into place. Some questions could involve matching more than one answer to a response area and some questions may have more answer choices than response areas, which means not all available answer choices need to be used.
Drop down list	This question type requires you to select one answer from a drop down list. Some of these questions may contain more than one drop down list and an answer has to be selected from each one.

Section B – OT Case questions

Similarly, to Section A, questions can come from any area of the syllabus, reinforcing the need for candidates to study the whole syllabus. Section B will include three OT case questions.

Each OT Case contains a group of five OT questions based around a single scenario. These can be any combination of the single OT question types and they are auto-marked in the same way as the single OT questions.

OT Cases are worth 10 marks (each of the five OTs within it are worth two marks, and as with the OT questions described above, students will receive either two marks or zero marks for those individual questions).

OT cases are written so that there are no dependencies between the individual questions. So, if you did get the first question wrong, this does not affect your ability to get the other four correct. The OT Case scenario remains on screen so you can see it while answering the questions.

Each OT case normally consists of two numerical and three discursive style questions. It is often quicker to tackle the discursive questions first leaving some additional time to tackle calculations.

Skills Checkpoint 1: Approach to OT questions

FM Skill: Approach to OT questions

A step-by-step technique for approaching OT questions is outlined below. Each step will be explained in more detail in the following sections as the OT case question 'Ring Co' is answered in stages.

> **General guidance for approaching OT questions**
>
> **STEP 1: Answer the questions you know first.**
>
> If you're having difficulty answering a question, move on and come back to tackle it once you've answered all the questions you know.
> It is often quicker to answer discursive style OT questions first, leaving more time for calculations.

> **General guidance for approaching OT questions**
>
> **STEP 2: Answer all questions.**
>
> There is no penalty for an incorrect answer in ACCA exams; there is nothing to be gained by leaving an OT question unanswered. If you are stuck on a question, as a last resort, it is worth selecting the option you consider most likely to be correct and moving on. Flag the question, so if you have time after you've answered the rest of the questions, you can revisit it.

> **Guidance for answering specific OT questions**
>
> **STEP 3: Read the requirement first!**
>
> The requirement will be stated in bold text in the exam. Identify what you are being asked to do, any technical knowledge required and what type of OT question you are dealing with. Look for key words in the requirement such as "which TWO of the following," or " which of the following is NOT".

> **Guidance for answering specific OT questions**
>
> **STEP 4: Apply your technical knowledge to the data presented in the question.**
>
> Take your time working through calculations, making sure to read through each answer option with care. OT questions are designed so that each answer option is plausible. Work through each response option and eliminate those you know are incorrect.

Exam success skills

The following question is a Section B OT case question from a past exam worth 10 marks. The technical knowledge required for this question is covered later in the course (in chapter 13), we are looking at it here from a technique viewpoint not a knowledge viewpoint.

For this question, we will also focus on the following **exam success skills**:

- **Managing information.** It is easy for the amount of information contained in an OT case questions in section B to feel a little overwhelming. **Active reading** is a useful technique to use to avoid this. This involves focusing on each of the five requirements first, on the basis that until you have done this the detail in the question will have little meaning and will seem more intimidating as a result.

Focus on the requirements, highlighting key verbs to ensure you understand the requirement properly and correctly identify what type of OT question you are dealing with. Then read the rest of the scenario, underlining and annotating important and relevant information, and making notes of any relevant technical information you think you will need

- **Correct interpretation of requirements.** Identify from the requirement the different types of OT question. This is especially important with multiple response questions to ensure you select the correct number of response options.

- **Good time management.** Complete all OT's in the time available. Each OT is worth 2 marks and should be allocated 3.6 minutes.

Skill activity

The following scenario relates to questions a–e.

Ring Co has in issue ordinary shares with a nominal value of $0.25 per share. These shares are traded on an efficient capital market. It is now 20X6 and the company has just paid a dividend of $0.450 per share. Recent dividends of the company are as follows:

Year	20X6	20X5	20X4	20X3	20X2
Dividend per share	$0.450	$0.428	$0.408	$0.389	$0.370

Ring Co also has in issue loan notes which are redeemable in 7 years' time at their nominal value of $100 per loan note and which pay interest of 6% per year.

The finance director of Ring Co wishes to determine the value of the company.

Ring Co has a cost of equity of 10% per year and a before-tax cost of debt of 4% per year. The company pays corporation tax of 25% per year.

(a) **Using the dividend growth model, what is the market value of each ordinary share?**
- $8.59
- $9.00
- $9.45
- $7.77

Note. This is an MCQ requiring one correct answer to be selected. A calculation of the market value of Ring Co's share using the dividend growth model is required. The required formula is given in the exam.

(b) **What is the market value of each $100 loan note? (give your answer to two decimal places)**

$ [   ]

Note. This is a FIB question, it is important you insert your answer to two decimal places. A calculation of the MV of Ring Co's loan notes is required. This is a popular question in the FM exam. You will need to discount the CF's associated with the loan note to calculate the market value.

(c) **The finance director of Ring Co has been advised to calculate the net asset value (NAV) of the company. Which of the following formulae calculates correctly the NAV of Ring Co?**
- Total assets less current liabilities
- Non-current assets plus net current assets
- Non-current assets plus current assets less total liabilities
- Non-current assets less net current assets less non-current liabilities

Note. This is another MCQ, you need to select one correct definition of the net asset value.

(d) **Which of the following statements about valuation methods is true?**

- The earnings yield method multiplies earnings by the earnings yield.
- The equity market value is number of shares multiplied by share price, plus the market value of debt.
- The dividend valuation model makes the unreasonable assumption that average dividend growth is constant.
- The price/earnings ratio method divides earnings by the price/earnings ratio.

Note. This is an MCQ question requiring you to select one valid statement.

(e) **Which of the following statements about capital market is/are correct?**

Insider information cannot be used to make abnormal gains in a strong form efficient capital market.	
In a weak form efficient capital market, Ring Co's share price reacts to new information the day after it is announced.	
Ring Co's share price reacts quickly and accurately to newly released information in a semi-strong form efficient capital market.	

Pull down list

Correct

Incorrect

STEP 1 **Answer the questions you know first.**

If you're having difficulty answering a question, move on and come back to tackle it once you've answered all the questions you know. It is often quicker to answer discursive style OT questions first, leaving more time for calculations.

Questions c, d and e are discursive style questions. It would make sense to answer these three questions first as it is likely that you will be able to complete them comfortably within the 10.8 minutes allocated to them. Any time saved could then be spent on the more complex calculations required to answer questions a and b.

STEP 2 **Answer all questions.**

There is no penalty for an incorrect answer in ACCA exams, there is nothing to be gained by leaving an OT question unanswered. If you are stuck on a question, as a last resort, it is worth selecting the option you consider most likely to be correct, and moving on. Flag the question, so if you have time after you have answered the rest of the questions, you can revisit it.

Three of the five questions in the OT case are MCQs. With an MCQ you have a 25% chance of getting the question correct so don't leave any unanswered. It is obviously more difficult to get a fill in the blank question (like question b) correct by guessing.

STEP 3 **Read the requirement first!**

The requirement will be stated in bold text in the exam. Identify what you are being asked to do, any technical knowledge required and **what type of OT question** you are dealing with. Look for key words in the requirement such as 'which TWO of the following,' 'which of the following is NOT'.

Question b is a FIB (fill in the blanks) question, you need to follow the instructions carefully and insert your answer to two decimal places. Questions c and d ask you to identify which statements are **correct**. Read through each statement carefully knowing that you are looking to identify the statement that is **correct**.

STEP 4 **Apply your technical knowledge to the data presented in the question.**

Work through calculations taking your time and read through each answer option with care. OT questions are designed so that each answer option is plausible. Work through each response option and eliminate those you know are incorrect.

To answer questions a and b you need to analyse the data given in the question.

Let's look at question a in detail. The question asks you to calculate the market value of Ring Co's shares using the dividend growth model. You will therefore need to find D_0, g and the cost of equity (re) from the data in the question.

Ring Co has in issue ordinary shares with a nominal value of $0.25 per share. These shares are traded on an efficient capital market. It is now 20X6 and the company has just paid a dividend of[1] $0.450 per share. Recent dividends of the company are as follows:[2]

[1] D0 = $0.450

[2] Historical dividend growth rate = 100 x $((0.450/0.370)^{0.25} - 1)$ = 5%

Year	20X6	20X5	20X4	20X3	20X2
Dividend per share	$0.450	$0.428	$0.408	$0.389	$0.370

Ring Co also has in issue loan notes which are redeemable in 7 years' time at their nominal value of $100 per loan note and which pay interest of 6% per year.

The finance director of Ring Co wishes to determine the value of the company.

Ring Co has a cost of equity of 10% per[3] year and a before-tax cost of debt of 4% per year. The company pays corporation tax of 25% per year.

[3] r = 0.10

Taking all 3 variables from the question you can now use the dividend growth model to calculate the value of Ring Co's share.

$P_0 = D_0 (1 + g)/(r_e - g)$

Share price = (0.450 × 1.05)/(0.1 − 0.05) = $9.45

To answer question c you can start by eliminating the response options that do not correctly define the net asset value of a company.

The finance director of Ring Co has been advised to calculate the net asset value (NAV) of the company.

Which of the following formulae calculates correctly the NAV of Ring Co?

- Total assets less current liabilities[4]

- Non-current assets plus net current assets[5]

- Non-current assets plus current assets less total liabilities

- Non-current assets less net[6] current assets less non-current liabilities

[4] This definition wrongly excludes non-current liabilities

[5] This definition wrongly excludes current and non-current liabilities

[6] This definition wrongly deducts net current assets.

The correct definition of net asset value is:

- Non-current assets plus current assets less total liabilities

Exam success skills diagnostic

Every time you complete a question, use the diagnostic below to assess how effectively you demonstrated the exam success skills in answering the question. The table has been completed below for the Ring Co activity to give you an idea of how to complete the diagnostic.

Exam success skills	Your reflections/observations
Managing information	Did you read each of the five requirements first? Did you actively read the scenario highlighting relevant data required such as the dividend just paid, cost of equity and dividend growth pattern?
Correct interpretation of requirements	Did you identify the correct technical knowledge needed to answer each requirement? For example, using the dividend growth model formula to answer question a. Did you identify what type of OT question you were dealing with? For example, knowing that only one correct answer is required for a multiple choice question.
Good time management	Did you manage to answer all five questions within 18 mins? Did you manage your time well by answering questions three, four and five first?
Most important action points to apply to your next question	

Summary

60% of the FM exam consist of OT questions. Key skills to focus on throughout your studies will therefore include:

- Always read the requirements first to identify what you are being asked to do and what type of OT question you are dealing with

- Actively read the scenario highlighting key data needed to answer each requirement.

- Answer OT questions in a sensible order dealing with any easier discursive style questions first.

5

Investment decision

Learning objectives

On completion of this chapter you should be able to:

		Syllabus reference
•	Identify and calculate relevant cash flows for investment projects	D1(a)
•	Calculate payback period and discuss its usefulness as an investment appraisal method	D1(b)
•	Calculate discounted payback and discuss its usefulness as an investment appraisal method	D1(c)
•	Calculate return on capital employed (accounting rate of return) and discuss its usefulness as an investment appraisal method	D1(d)
•	Calculate net present value and discuss its usefulness as an investment appraisal method	D1(e)
•	Calculate internal rate of return and discuss its usefulness as an investment appraisal method	D1(f)
•	Discuss the superiority of discounted cash flow (DCF) methods over non-DCF methods	D1(g)
•	Discuss the relative merits of NPV and IRR	D1(h)

Exam context

This chapter introduces a variety of investment appraisal techniques that are important in Section D of the syllabus (Investment appraisal), it is one of four chapters (along with Chapters 6–8) that covers this important syllabus section. The topics covered here are **commonly examined** in all sections of the exam including section C. Questions won't just involve calculations; you may be asked to discuss the problems with the methods you have used, or their meaning.

Chapter overview

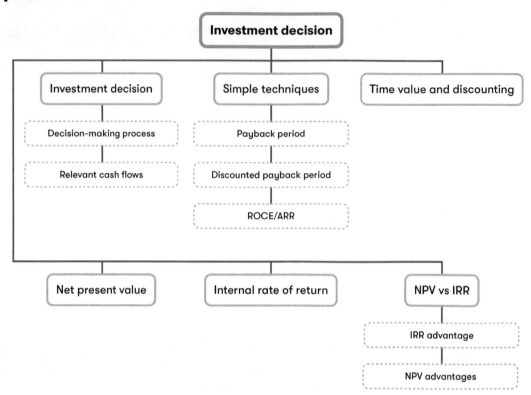

1 Investment decision-making

1.1 Investment decision-making process

PER alert

Performance objective 9 requires you to 'value projects, financial securities and instruments and advise on their costs and benefits to the organisation'. This chapter concentrates on valuing projects using discounted cash flow techniques

Capital investment projects involve the outlay of **large sums of money** in the expectation of **benefits that may take several years to accrue**.

The decision whether to proceed with a capital investment project is normally made by a **capital expenditure committee** overseeing **a process that includes the following phases:**

(a) Idea creation	(b) Screening	(c) Financial analysis	(d) Review
Proposals can be **stimulated** by a regular review of the company's competitive environment and can be encouraged by incentive schemes.	To screen out **unsuitable proposals** by looking at the **impact** of the project **on stakeholders** and whether they support the organisation's **strategy.**	A **detailed appraisal of the project's risk and return,** how it will be financed, any alternatives to it and the implications of not accepting the project.	A post-completion review (or audit) aims to **learn from mistakes** that have arisen in the project appraisal process.

The Financial Management syllabus mainly focusses on **financial analysis** and this area is further considered in this, and the following three chapters.

1.2 Relevant cash flows

Most financial analysis techniques that are used for analysing projects are based on the use of **relevant cash flows.**

Relevant cash flow: A future incremental cash flow caused by a decision (eg to invest in a project).

You will come across many examples in this chapter, and in following chapters, of cash flows that clearly relate to a project. However, a specific and less obvious type of relevant cash flow to look out for is an **opportunity cost.**

Opportunity cost: A cost incurred from diverting existing resources from their best use.

Illustration 1: Opportunity cost

If a team of workers, costing $300,000 per year, is diverted to work on a new project then they will stop work on existing products which earn contribution (ie sales revenue less variable cost) of $500,000, this contribution will therefore be lost (note that this assumes that labour is a variable cost).

Required

Calculate the relevant cost associated with using the team of workers on the new project.

Solution

The relevant cost is the opportunity cost ie the $500,000 of lost contribution plus the cost of the workers. This gives a total relevant cost of $800,000.

1.2.1 Non-relevant costs examples

Questions will expect you to be able to identify costs that are not relevant to decision-making. Some examples are included in the following table.

Examples	Explanation
Non-cash flows	Depreciation and apportioned overheads (ie overheads that are not directly attributable to a project) are **not cash flows**.
Sunk and committed costs	A cost **incurred in the past (ie sunk)**, or **committed to,** will not change whether a project goes ahead or not and is therefore not a relevant cash flow (market research is often an example of this).
Historic cost of materials	If materials that are used by a project need to be replaced, the relevant cost of the materials is the **replacement cost** of the material - not the price originally paid to acquire the material (ie the historic cost).
	If such materials do not need to be replaced, the relevant cost is **zero** (unless there is an opportunity cost from lost revenue if the material could have been sold as scrap).
	The historic cost of materials should only be treated as 'relevant' if no indication of scrap values or replacement costs are given in a question.
Cost of labour	If labour used by a project is:
	(a) **Idle**, then the relevant cost of using that labour is **zero**
	(b) **At full capacity**, then the cost is **wages paid + contribution lost** on the work that they have had to stop doing.
	Only use the labour cost as a relevant cost if no indication of capacity issues are given in a question.
Finance costs	Any finance costs (eg dividend payments, interest payments) should **not** be considered as a cash flow because they are included in the cost of capital used to discount a project (covered in section 3).

Activity 1: Relevant costing

Brenda and Eddie are considering expanding their restaurant business through an investment in a new restaurant, the Parkway Diner. Brenda and Eddie have analysed the profit made in the first year and are concerned that the project could be loss making.

Their Year 1 costs and revenues are forecast as follows:

Year 1	$
Revenue	200,000
Depreciation	25,000
Materials (note 1)	49,000
Labour (note 2)	100,000
Overheads (note 3)	100,000
Profit/(loss)	(74,000)

Notes.

1 The materials include $10,000 of surplus inventory that Brenda and Eddie have in their existing restaurants. This inventory has a scrap value of $1,000.

2 Labour includes 20% of the $50,000 salary of a manager of an existing branch, who will assist the existing manager of the restaurant in its first year of operation.

3 This is an allocation of corporate overheads.

Required

Assess the relevant cash flows of the project in the first year to Brenda and Eddie and advise Brenda and Eddie whether they are right to be concerned.

Solution

Essential reading

See Chapter 5 section 1 of the Essential Reading, available in the digital edition of the Workbook, for further discussion of this area

The Essential reading is available as an Appendix of the digital edition of the Workbook.

2 Simple techniques

2.1 Payback period

> **Payback period:** A measure of how long it takes for the **cash flows affected by the decision to invest** to repay the cost of the original investment.

Payback is often used as part of an initial screening of projects. If a project gets through the payback test it should be **evaluated using a more sophisticated project appraisal technique.**

A project with a long payback period is considered to be **uncertain** because it relies on cash flows that are in the distant future and are therefore highly uncertain.

A company will **reject a project with a payback period that is above the company's target payback period.**

Payback is especially useful if a company has cash flow concerns because it focusses on shorter-term investments.

Payback is based on **relevant cash flows** so any **non-cash flow cost items** (eg depreciation) should be **ignored.**

Activity 2: Payback period

Brenda and Eddie are worried about the length of time it will take for the cash flows from the Parkway Diner to repay their total investment of $500,000 ($350,000 to take over the business and $150,000 to refurbish it).

Cash flow projections from the project are estimated as:

Year	Operating cash flows
	$
1	70,000
2	70,000
3	80,000
4	100,000
5	100,000
6	120,000

After the sixth year, Brenda and Eddie confidently expect that they could sell the business for $350,000.

Required

Calculate the payback period for the project.

Solution

2.1.1 General problems with payback

(a) It **ignores** the **timing** of cash flows **within** the payback period (eg ignores that a project is more uncertain if most of the cash is received at the end of the payback period).

(b) It **ignores the cash flows after the end of the payback period** and therefore the total project return.

(c) It **ignores the time value of money** (a concept incorporated into more sophisticated appraisal methods). This means that it does not take into account that the value of money is lower the further into the future that the money is received.

(d) The choice of any **cut-off** payback period by an organisation is **arbitrary**.

(e) It may lead to **excessive investment** in **short-term projects**.

Because of these drawbacks, a project should **not** be evaluated using payback alone.

2.1.2 Discounted payback period

Payback can be based on **discounted** cash flows (covered in Section 3), in which case it is called discounted payback (or adjusted payback) period. Aside from being based on discounted cash flows, the calculation is the same and most of the drawbacks remain.

2.2 Return on capital employed

Return on capital employed (ROCE) is also called accounting rate of return (ARR) and return on investment (ROI). ROCE is another simple, traditional, approach to evaluating investments.

ROCE compares the profit from an investment project to the amount invested in the project, expressing the result as a percentage.

Using this method, a company will accept a project if it has a ROCE above the company's target.

2.2.1 Calculation (formulae are not given and need to be learnt)

Profit is calculated **after depreciation** which we have seen is **not a relevant cash flow,** this failure to distinguish between relevant and non-relevant cash flows is one of the many drawbacks of this technique.

$$ROCE = \frac{\text{Average annual profit}}{\text{Initial investment}}$$

or

$$ROCE = \frac{\text{Average annual profit}}{\text{Average investment}}$$

Where average investment =

$$\frac{\text{Initial outlay} + \text{scrap value}}{2}$$

Illustration 2: ROCE

An asset costing $120,000 is to be depreciated over 5 years to a nil residual value. Profits **after depreciation** for the 5 years of the project are as follows.

Year	1	2	3	4	5
Profits	12,000	17,000	28,000	37,000	8,000

Required

What is the average accounting rate of return for this project? (Give your answer to the nearest percentage.)

Solution

Average investment = [$120,000 (start) + $0 (end)] ÷ 2 = $60,000

Average profits = [12,000 + 17,000 + 28,000 + 37,000 + 8,000] ÷ 5 (years) = $20,400

ARR = $20,400 ÷ $60,000 = 34% (this can also be referred to as ROI or ROCE).

Activity 3: ARR

Brenda and Eddie are considering expanding their restaurant business through purchase of the Parkway Diner, which will cost $350,000 to take over the business and a further $150,000 to refurbish the premises with new equipment. **Cash flow** projections for this project are as for the previous activity.

The equipment will be depreciated to a zero resale value over the same period and, after the sixth year, Brenda and Eddie confidently expect that they could sell the business for $350,000.

Required

What is the ROCE of this investment (using the average investment method)?

○ 13.0%

○ 15.3%

○ 18.0%

○ 21.2%

Solution

2.2.2 Benefits of using ROCE/ARR

ROCE method is a quick and simple calculation that involves the familiar concept of a percentage return. Unlike payback period **it does consider the whole of a project's life**.

The fact that it gives a **percentage measure** means that ROCE makes it easy to compare two investment options even if they are of different sizes.

2.2.3 General problems with ROCE/ARR

(a) It is based on **accounting profits** and **not relevant cash flows**. ROCE is the only investment appraisal technique not based on relevant cash flows.

(b) It is a **relative measure** (ie a percentage) rather than an absolute measure and therefore takes no account of the size of the investment.

(c) Like the payback method, ROCE **ignores the time value of money**.

> **Exam focus point**
>
> ROCE/ARR is the only project appraisal technique that is based on profit instead of cash flow. So, in this technique (only) you will need to **include depreciation** in your calculations.

3 Time value of money and discounting

A key problem with both payback and ROCE is that they both ignore **the time value of money;** this is an important concept that is used in the more sophisticated investment appraisal techniques that are covered in the remainder of this chapter.

3.1 Time value of money

The idea that receiving $100 in the future is **worth less** than having $100 today is an example of the concept of money having a 'time value'.

Illustration 3: Time value

If a project involved the outlay of $20,000 today and provided a definite return of $21,000 in one year's time.

Required

Would you accept it if you could get a return of 6% on investments of similar risk?

Solution

We can look at this in two ways:

Firstly, if you had $20,000 today and invested it for one year in a project of similar risk at 6% then you would have $20,000 × 1.06 = $21,200 (this approach is called **compounding**).

This is more than is generated by the project, so the **project is not acceptable**.

Alternatively, we can reduce the future cash flow of $21,000 to reflect its worth if it was received today:

$21,000 × 1/1.06 = $19,811

This approach is called discounting.

$19,811 is the **value today,** or the **present value**, of receiving $21,000 in one year's time to reflect the return available to investors.

Again, we can see that the **project is unacceptable** because this present value is below the cost (today) of the project of $20,000.

3.1.1 Discounting and present values

The process of discounting future cash flows back to their **present value** is often called **discounted cash flow (DCF) analysis.** It is important in project appraisal because many projects involve **investing money now** and **receiving returns in many different time periods in the future**.

DCF analysis is an important tool in allowing the value of **future** cash flows to be compared against money invested **today.**

KEY TERM

> **Present value:** The cash equivalent now of money received (or paid) in the future.

3.2 Discount factors

In the previous illustration, a future cash flow received in 1 year was discounted back to a present value by multiplying by 1/1.06.

This is the same as multiplying the cash flows by 0.943 (ie 1/1.06 = 0.943), and this figure is an example of a **discount factor**.

This discount factor reflects the investor's required return (also referred to as a cost of capital) of 6% and the timing of the future cash flow (in one year's time).

In the exam you are provided with a **table of discount factors** to apply depending on the rate of return expected and the timing of the future cash flow.

These are shown as an **Appendix** at the back of this workbook as a **present value table.**

As well as including a wide range of discount factors, this table also shows the formula for calculating any discount factor.

Formula provided

Discount factor = $(1 + r)^{-n}$

Where r = discount/interest rate and n = time period of cash flow

3.3 Conventions used in DCF

- Time 0 is today, it is usual to assume that time 0 is the **first day of a project**, ie the **start** of its first year.
- Time 1 is the last day of the first period (normally a year).
- A cash flow which occurs during the course of a time period is assumed to occur all at once at **the end of the time period** (at the end of the year).
- A cash flow which occurs at the **start** of a time period is taken to occur at **the end of the previous time period** eg a cash outlay of $5,000 at the start of time period 2 is taken to occur at the end of time period 1.

Activity 4: Discounting

Calculate the present value of $100,000 received in seven years' time, if the cost of capital is 12%. (Give your answer to the nearest $100.)

Solution

3.4 Annuities

Annuity: A series of equal cash flows.

If a project involves **equal annual cash flows** (or annuities) then each future cash flow can be discounted separately back to a present value, but it is **quicker to use a single discount factor** (called an annuity factor or a cumulative discount factor).

Illustration 4: Annuities

If a project involved the outlay of $20,000 today and provided a definite return of $8,000 per year for three years would you accept the project?

Assume that you could get a return of 6% on investments of similar risk.

Solution

This can be analysed as a series of individual calculations, obtaining the discount factors from the present value table (from the 6% column for time periods 1, 2 and 3):

Time	0	1	2	3
Cash flow	(20,000)	8,000	8,000	8,000
Discount factors		0.943	0.890	0.840
Present value	(20,000)	7,544	7,120	6,720
Net present value				**+1,384**

Alternatively, this could be analysed more quickly by using a single discount factor provided in the annuity table given in the Appendix to this workbook (here using the 6% column and time period 3). The figure obtained is 2.673: this is called an **annuity** (or cumulative discount) **factor.**

Time	0	1 to 3
Cash flow	(20,000)	8,000
Annuity factor		2.673
Present value	(20,000)	21,384
Net present value		**+1,384**

The annuity factor of 2.673 represents the addition of the individual discount factors used in the first method (0.943 + 0.890 + 0.840).

Formula provided

Formula for an annuity factor:

$$\frac{1-(1 + r)^{-n}}{r}$$

Exam focus point

Annuity tables are provided in the exam, but again only cover integer values of r and up to 15 years ahead. If you need to calculate a discount rate that is not an integer or is not in the range of values covered by the tables, you will need to use the formula provided.

Activity 5: Annuities

A firm has arranged a 10-year lease at an annual rent of $17,264. Each rental payment is to be made at the start of the year.

Required

What is the present value of the lease at 12%? (Give your answer to the nearest $.)

Solution

3.4.1 Perpetuities

> **Perpetuity:** An annuity that occurs for the foreseeable future.

If the series of cash flows does not have an end date (ie it is expected for the foreseeable future) then this is called a **perpetuity**. This can be dealt with by applying a single discount factor, but this requires the use of a formula which you will need to learn:

Formula to learn

The formula for discounting a perpetuity is:

$$\frac{1}{r}$$

Illustration 5: Perpetuities

If a project involved the outlay of $20,000 today and provided a definite return of $3,000 per year **for the foreseeable future.**

Required

Would you accept the project?

(Again, assume that you could get a return of 6% on investments of similar risk.)

Solution

The perpetuity factor here is:

1/0.06

So, the present value of the future cash flows is $3,000 × 1/0.06 =$50,000

And the present value of the inflows exceeds the cost of the project, so the project is acceptable.

3.4.2 Delayed annuities and perpetuities

The approaches demonstrated in the previous sections for annuities and perpetuities **assume that the cash flows begin in time 1** and value these annuities or perpetuities from the perspective of the **preceding time period to when the cash flows begin** (ie time 0, a present value).

Where the first cash flow in an annuity is not received from time 1 this is called a delayed annuity.

Where this is the case, the approach to valuing an annuity or perpetuity must be slightly adjusted.

Illustration 6: Delayed perpetuity

If a project involved the outlay of $20,000 today and provided a definite return of $3,000 per year for the foreseeable future **starting in three years' time.**

Required

Would you accept the project? (Again, assume that you could get a return of 6% on investments of similar risk.)

Solution

As before, the perpetuity factor here is: 1/0.06

So, the value of the future cash flows is $50,000, as before.

However, this value is from the perspective of the **preceding time period to when the cash flows begin** and here the cash flows **begin at time 3** so the value is from the perspective of **time 2** (the preceding time period).

This can be adjusted to a time 0 present value by treating the $50,000 as a one-off cash flow received in time 2 and multiplying it by the discount factor from the present value table for period 2 at 6% of 0.890.

$50,000 × 0.890 = $44,500

This is now a present value and, because this is higher than the cash outflow of $20,000, the project is acceptable.

Activity 6: Delayed annuity

An annuity of $3,000 per annum for eight years starts at the end of the third year and finishes at the end of the tenth year.

Required

What is the present value of the annuity if the discount rate is 6%? (Give your answer to the nearest $.)

Solution

3.4.3 Constant growth

If a series of cash flows does not have an end date (ie it is expected for the foreseeable future) and is growing at a **constant rate,** then this can be converted into present value terms by applying a single discount factor and is known as a growing perpetuity.

This requires the use of the following formula for the annuity factor, this is covered numerically in section 4 of Chapter 13.

Formula to learn

The formula for discounting a constantly growing cash flow is:

$$\frac{1}{r-g}$$

Essential reading

See Chapter 5 Section 2 of the Essential Reading, available in the digital edition of the Workbook, for further discussion of this area mainly for anyone who has not studied this area for a while and would like some further background, the approach used for evaluating constantly growing cashflows is also introduced.

The Essential reading is available as an Appendix of the digital edition of the Workbook.

4 Net present value (NPV)

The NPV method uses the concept of discounting and recognises the time value of money.

This method **compares the present value of all the cash inflows** from a project **with the present value of all the cash outflows** from a project. The difference, the NPV, represents the **change in wealth** of the investor as a result of investing in the project.

Npv Value	
NPV positive	Return from investment's cash inflows in excess of cost of capital (**undertake project**)
NPV negative	Return from investment's cash inflows below cost of capital (**don't undertake project**)
NPV = 0	Return from investment's cash inflows same as cost of capital (**the project will be only just worth undertaking**)

Note. We assume that the cost of capital is the organisation's target rate of return for proposed investment projects.

One of the advantages of NPV is that it gives a clear and objective decision rule which is that a project is acceptable if its **NPV is zero or above**.

Activity 7: NPV

LCH manufactures product X which it sells for $5 per unit. Variable costs of production are currently $3 per unit. Sales of product X are estimated to be 75,000 units per annum.

A new machine is available which would cost $90,000 but which could be used to make product X for a variable cost of only $2.50 per unit. Fixed costs, however, would increase by $7,500 per annum as a direct result of purchasing the machine.

The machine would have an expected life of four years and a disposal value of $10,000.

LCH expects to earn at least 12% per annum from its investments.

Required

Using NPV analysis, should LCH acquire the machine?

Solution

NPV is a very important method of appraising investments, that is commonly examined. NPV will be discussed further in section 6 and developed further in Chapters 6-8.

5 Internal rate of return (IRR)

The IRR method also uses the concept of discounting and recognises the time value of money.

Internal rate of return (IRR): A discounted cash flow technique that calculates **the percentage return given by a project**. If this return is used to discount a project's cash flows, it would deliver an **NPV of zero**.

Internal rate of return (IRR) calculates the **exact rate of return** which a project is expected to achieve; in other words, the rate which, if used as a discount factor, would deliver an **NPV of zero**.

IRR	
IRR is **greater than the required return** (cost of capital)	Return from the investment is above that which is required **(undertake project)**
IRR is **less than the required return** (cost of capital)	Return from investment is below that which is required **(don't undertake project)**
IRR is **equal to the required return** (cost of capital)	Return from investment is the same as cost of capital **(the project will be only just worth undertaking)**

5.1 Calculating IRR

5.1.1 Computer based exam method

In a computer-based exam you can use the =IRR function to calculate the project's IRR.

Real life example

From the previous activity the project cash flows for the NPV calculation could be shown on a **spreadsheet** as follows:

	A	B	C	D	E	F
1	Time	0	1	2	3	4
2	Cash flow	($90,000)	30,000	30,000	30,000	40,000
3	Discount factors	1.0	0.893	0.797	0.712	0.636
4	Present value	($90,000)	26,790	23,910	$21,360	$25,440

To calculate the IRR the correct instruction would be = IRR(B2:F2)

In this example, this would give an IRR of 15.7%.

The **undiscounted** cash flows are used for the IRR calculation. Also, the spreadsheet IRR formula does not work if the cash flows are set up as annuities (eg one cash flow of $30,000 for time 1-3 in the previous illustration).

5.1.2 Interpolation

If a question provides two project NPVs then these can be used to estimate the internal rate of return of a project. This approach is sometimes called interpolation.

Exam focus point

This approach to IRR is more likely to be tested in an OT question.

Formula to learn

$$IRR = a\% + \frac{NPV_a}{NPV_a - NPV_b}(b\% - a\%)$$

Where a is the **lower** discount rate giving NPVa and b is the **higher** discount rate giving NPVb

Real life example

From the previous activity if you had been told that the NPV of the project cashflows was +$7.500 at a cost of capital of 12% and -$540 at 16% then the IRR can be estimated as:

$$IRR = a\% + \frac{NPV_a}{NPV_a - NPV_b}(b\% - a\%)$$

$$IRR = 12 + \frac{7,500}{7,500 + 540}(16 - 12)$$

= 15.7%

If NPVb is a **negative number,** then NPVa-NPVb becomes NPVa+NPVb since subtracting a negative is the same as an addition. Although the interpolation method is slower than the formula method, it does allow some marks to be scored if a minor error is made (follow-through marks) whereas the formula approach will either be 100% correct or will score 0. So, if you are at all unsure about the formula approach then the interpolation method would be better to use in the exam.

Activity 8: Interpolation

A project has a positive NPV of $15,000 when discounted at 6% and a negative NPV of $3,000 when discounted at 12%.

Required

Calculate the internal rate of return.

Solution

Exam focus point

It is easy to confuse internal rate of return (IRR) and accounting rate of return (ARR). One way of remembering the difference is that **accounting** rate of return is based on **accounting** profits (whereas IRR is based on relevant cash flows).

Essential reading

See Chapter 5 Section 3 of the Essential Reading, available in the digital edition of the Workbook, for further discussion of IRR.

The Essential reading is available as an Appendix of the digital edition of the Workbook.

6 NPV compared to IRR

Both NPV and IRR are superior methods for appraising investments compared to the simpler techniques covered in section 2 because:

(a) They are **DCF methods** ie they account for the **time value of money** (unlike **non-DCF methods** like ROCE and payback)

(b) They focus on relevant cash flows (unlike ROCE)

(c) They look at the cash flows over the **whole life of the project** (unlike payback)

Given that there are two methods of using DCF, the NPV method and the IRR method, the relative merits of each method have to be considered.

6.1 Advantage of IRR over NPV

IRR gives the percentage return of a project; this concept **is easy** for non-financial managers **to understand.**

6.2 Advantages of NPV over IRR

6.2.1 Comparing projects of different sizes

Because IRR is a percentage measure it can lead to incorrect choices being made when choosing between mutually exclusive projects.

Real life example: Projects of different sizes

	Project A	Project B
Cost, year 0	$350,000	$35,000
Annual savings, years 1–6	$100,000	$10,000
IRR	18%	18%
NPV at cost of capital of 10%	$85,500	$8,550

If a company had to choose between project A and project B, then it would choose project A which is 10 times bigger (as reflected in the NPV). But if the only information on which the projects were judged were to be their IRR of 18%, project B would be made to seem just as beneficial as project A, which is **not the case.**

6.2.2 Non-conventional cash flows

The projects we have considered so far have had **conventional cash flows (an initial cash outflow followed by a series of inflows).** When flows vary from this they are termed 'non-conventional'.

In general, if the sign of the net cash flow changes in successive periods (inflow to outflow or vice versa), it is possible for the calculations to produce **as many IRRs as there are sign changes.**

This can make IRR **difficult to interpret.**

There are no issues with NPV and non-conventional cash flows.

6.2.3 Re-investment assumption

An assumption underlying the **NPV method** is that any net cash **inflows generated** during the life of the project will be **reinvested** elsewhere **at the cost of capital** (that is, the discount rate).

The **IRR method**, on the other hand, **assumes** these **cash flows** can be **reinvested** elsewhere to earn a **return** equal to the **IRR** of the original project. Assuming that the project is attractive, so that the IRR is above the cost of capital then if this assumption is not valid, the IRR method overestimates the project's actual return.

6.3 Conclusion

There is a general consensus that **NPV is the superior technique** from a technical viewpoint. However, IRR is still extremely useful for explaining the appraisal of an investment to non-financial managers. This is why **both NPV and IRR are both widely used** in practice.

This is not to say that NPV is perfect; like any financial technique, there is the danger that the **non-financial benefits of an investment are ignored** or that the financial estimates are **inaccurate**.

Activity 9: NPV & IRR

DEF Co has a cost of capital of 12%.

Project A has a positive NPV of $5,000 when discounted at 12% and a positive NPV of $3,600 when discounted at 16%.

Project B has a positive NPV of $8,000 when discounted at 12% and a negative NPV of $1,000 when discounted at 16%.

The projects are mutually exclusive.

Required

1   What is the internal rate of return for projects A and B?

    ○   Project A has an IRR of 26.3% and B an IRR of 16.5%.

    ○   Project A has an IRR of 26.3% and B an IRR of 15.6%.

    ○   Project A has an IRR of 14.3% and B an IRR of 16.5%.

    ○   Project A has an IRR of 14.3% and B an IRR of 15.6%.

2   Which of the following statements is correct?

    ○   Both NPV and IRR indicate that Project A is the more financially viable project.

    ○   In order to maximise shareholder wealth Project A is the better project.

    ○   Neither Project A nor Project B should be accepted from a financial perspective.

    ○   Project B will increase shareholder wealth more than Project A at the current cost of capital.

Solution

Essential reading

See Chapter 5 Section 4 of the Essential Reading, available in the digital edition of the Workbook, for further discussion of DCF methods.

The Essential reading is available as an Appendix of the digital edition of the Workbook.

Chapter summary

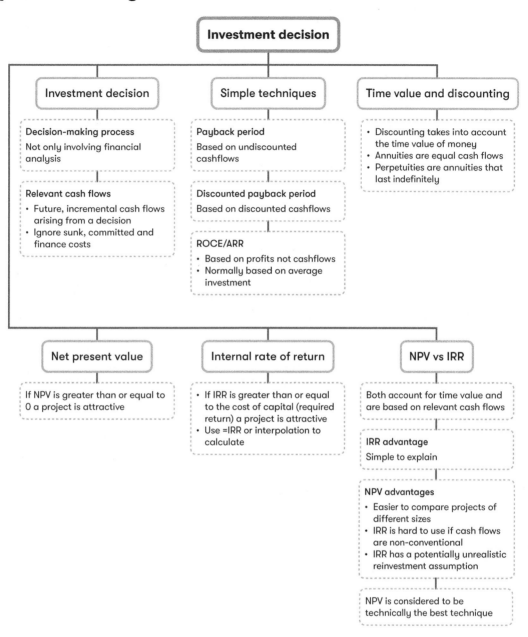

Investment decision

Investment decision

Decision-making process
Not only involving financial analysis

Relevant cash flows
- Future, incremental cash flows arising from a decision
- Ignore sunk, committed and finance costs

Simple techniques

Payback period
Based on undiscounted cashflows

Discounted payback period
Based on discounted cashflows

ROCE/ARR
- Based on profits not cashflows
- Normally based on average investment

Time value and discounting
- Discounting takes into account the time value of money
- Annuities are equal cash flows
- Perpetuities are annuities that last indefinitely

Net present value

If NPV is greater than or equal to 0 a project is attractive

Internal rate of return
- If IRR is greater than or equal to the cost of capital (required return) a project is attractive
- Use =IRR or interpolation to calculate

NPV vs IRR

Both account for time value and are based on relevant cash flows

IRR advantage
Simple to explain

NPV advantages
- Easier to compare projects of different sizes
- IRR is hard to use if cash flows are non-conventional
- IRR has a potentially unrealistic reinvestment assumption

NPV is considered to be technically the best technique

Knowledge diagnostic

1. Relevant costs

Relevant costs include future cash flows and include opportunity costs. Non-relevant costs include sunk costs, committed costs, and finance costs.

2. Simple methods of project appraisal

The payback method of investment appraisal and the ROCE/ARR/ROI methods of investment appraisal are popular appraisal techniques despite their limitations (of which you should be aware).

3. DCF methods

IRR and NPV are both DCF methods and consider the time value of money.

4. Perpetuities and annuities

A perpetuity is a constant annual cash flow (an annuity) that will last forever.

5. Internal rate of return

- The internal rate of return (IRR) of an investment is the cost of capital at which its NPV would be exactly $0.
- The IRR method of investment appraisal is an alternative to the NPV method for investment appraisal. This method's decision rule is to accept investment projects whose IRR exceeds the cost of capital.

Further study guidance

Question practice

Now try the following from the Further question practice bank (available in the digital edition of the Workbook):

Section A questions

Q15, Q16, Q17, Q18

Section B questions

Q33 sub-questions a–e

Section C questions

Q43 Knuckle Down

Q44 Mezen

Activity answers

Activity 1: Relevant costing
Relevant cash flows

Year 1	$
Revenue	200,000
Depreciation	0
Materials (49,000 – 10,000 not relevant + 1,000 scrap value)	40,000
Labour (100,000 – 10,000 not relevant)	90,000
Overheads (not a cash flow)	0
Cash flow	70,000

This is less concerning than the losses figure of $74,000 that we started with but requires further analysis to see if the project is worth pursuing (eg analysis of later time periods).

Activity 2: Payback period
Payback period

Year	Cumulative cash flow	Workings
	$	
0	(500,000)	
1	(430,000)	Calculated as (500,000) + 70,000
2	(360,000)	Calculated as (430,000) + 70,000
3	(280,000)	Calculated as (360,000) + 80,000
4	(180,000)	Calculated as (280,000) + 100,000
5	(80,000)	Calculated as (180,000) + 100,000
6	40,000	Calculated as (80,000) + 120,000

Payback occurs between year 5 and year 6.

After year 5 a further $80,000 is needed for the investment to pay back.

During the 6th year $120,000 of cash is generated (ignoring the residual disposal value that occurs at the end of this year).

So, if cash flows arise evenly used during the year then approximately 80/120 of the 6th year is needed for the project to pay back.

The payback period can be estimated as

∴ Payback = 5 years + (80/120) or 5 years 8 months

This may be considered to be a long payback period (although we are not told the payback period that Brenda and Eddie will find acceptable) and means that if there is no buyer for the business in six years' time, then they will only just have recouped their costs.

This project is beginning to look risky, but it may not be rejected because this analysis **has not considered all of the cash flows of the project.**

Activity 3: ARR

The correct answer is: 15.3%

Profit calculation:

	$
Total cash flows from operations	540,000
Total depreciation (500,000 – 350,000)	(150,000)
Total profits	390,000
Average profits (÷ 6)	65,000 p.a.

Investment calculation

(500,000 + 350,000)/2 = 425,000

ARR = 65/ 425 = 15.3%

Activity 4: Discounting

$45,200

$100,000/(1 + 0.12)^7 = 45,234$ or $45,200 to the nearest $100

Or using tables:

100,000 × 0.452 (the discount factor from the 12% column and the time 7 row) = $45,200

Activity 5: Annuities

$109,247

When discounting we are assuming that cash flows arise the end of the year, so the payments at the start of years 1-10 can be viewed as a payment at time 0 and then nine payments at the end of each fo the years 1-9. So, when we use the annuity table we are looking at time periods 1-9.

r = 12%

n = 9 (1st payment now, 10th payment at the end of time 9)

Annuity factor = 5.328 for time periods 1-9 at 12%.

PV = 17,264 (the first payment is not discounted because it is paid in advance) + (5.328 × 17,264) = 109,247

Activity 6: Delayed annuity

$16,581

Annuity factor for 8 years at 6%= 6.210

Present Value = 3,000 × 6.210 = $18,630

This is a value from the perspective of the preceding time period to the annuity (ie a present value at time 2).

Discounting at time 2 discount factor of 0.890 gives a present value at time 0 of 18,630 × 0.890 = $16,581.

There is an alternative approach which you can use if preferred which is to subtract the annuity factor for times 1-2 (when the cash flow is not received) from the annuity factor for times 1-10 (time 10 is the final year of the cash flow).

Annuity factor for time 3–10 = (annuity factor for time 1–10) – (annuity factor for time 1–2)

= 7.360 – 1.833 = 5.527

Present value = 3,000 × 5.527 = $16,581

BPP
LEARNING
MEDIA

Activity 7: NPV

The correct answer is: $7,470

Savings are 75,000 × ($3 – $2.50) = $37,500 per annum.

Additional costs are $7,500 per annum.

Net cash savings are therefore $30,000 per annum. (Remember, depreciation is not a cash flow and must be ignored as a 'cost'.)

The first step in calculating an NPV is to establish the relevant costs year by year. All future cash flows arising as a direct consequence of the decision should be taken into account. It is assumed that the machine will be sold for $10,000 at the end of year 4.

It is quicker to use an annuity approach for the net cash savings in time period 1-4.

Time	0	1 to 4	4
Cash flow $s	(90,000)	30,000	10,000
Discount factors	1.0	3.037	0.636
Present value $s	(90,000)	91,110	6,360

Net present value = (90,000) + 91,110 + 6,360 = $7,470

Alternatively, this could be shown as:

Time	0	1	2	3	4
Cash flow $s	(90,000)	30,000	30,000	30,000	40,000
Discount factors	1.0	0.893	0.797	0.712	0.636
Present value $s	(90,000)	26,790	23,910	21,360	25,440

Net present value = (90,000) + 91,110 + 6,360 = $7,500 (difference due to rounding).

The NPV is positive and so the project is expected to earn more than 12% per annum and is therefore acceptable.

Activity 8: Interpolation

11%

IRR = 6 + (15/(15 + 3) × 6) = 11%

Activity 9: NPV & IRR

1   The correct answer is: Project A has an IRR of 26.3% and B an IRR of 15.6%.

   IRR (A) = 12 + 5,000/(5,000 – 3,600) × (16 – 12) = 26.3%

   IRR (B) = 12 + 8,000/(8,000 + 1,000) × (16 – 12) = 15.6%

2   The correct answer is: Project B will increase shareholder wealth more than Project A at the current cost of capital.

   The NPV at the current cost of capital will be the movement in shareholder wealth as a result of the project being accepted. Project B (not A) will generate more shareholder wealth.

   NPV suggests that Project B is better, but the IRR is better for Project A.

6

Allowing for tax, working capital and inflation

Learning objectives

On completion of this chapter, you should be able to:

	Syllabus reference
• Apply and discuss the real-terms and nominal-terms approaches to investment appraisal	D2(a)
• Calculate the taxation effects of relevant cash flows, including the tax benefits of tax-allowable depreciation and the tax liabilities of taxable profit	D2(b)
• Calculate and apply before- and after-tax discount rates	D2(c)

Exam context

This chapter covers how to allow for tax and inflation in discounted cash flow calculations (introduced in the previous chapter) and is part of Section D of the syllabus (Investment Appraisal).

This is an important chapter that is examinable in all sections of the exam and is commonly examined as a core feature of one of the section C exam questions.

Chapter overview

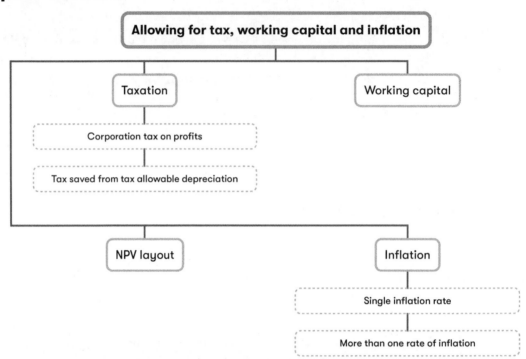

1 Taxation

So far, in looking at project appraisal, we have ignored taxation. However, payments of tax, or reductions in tax payments, are relevant cash flows and ought to be considered in DCF analysis.

The existence of tax on corporate profits gives rise to **two cash flows** that need to be taken into account in project appraisal.

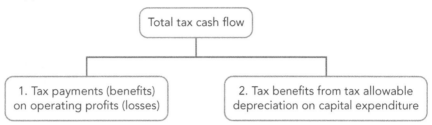

1.1 Corporation tax on profits

The tax rate to be applied will be given in an exam question.

Tax on profits will either be payable in the **same year as the taxable profits are earned or in the following year;** the appropriate timing to apply will be specified in an exam question.

> ### Exam focus point
>
> Check any question involving tax carefully to see what assumptions about the timing of tax payments should be made.

1.2 Tax allowable depreciation

Where tax-allowable depreciation (also called capital allowance or writing down allowance) can be claimed, this will reduce taxable profits, and the consequent reduction in a tax payment should be treated as a **cash saving.**

Tax-allowable depreciation (TAD) is not the same as the accounting depreciation charge for the purpose of reporting profit in the financial statements.

TAD may be applied as **straight-line** depreciation (the same amount each year) **or on a reducing balance basis** based on the written down value (WDV) of the asset **at the start of year.**

Assuming a zero disposal value, in the **final year** of an asset's life TAD **will reduce the WDV of the asset to zero.** This final TAD claim is called a **balancing allowance** and means that the full capital cost of the asset is claimed over the asset's useful life.

> ### Exam focus point
>
> The appropriate basis for tax allowable depreciation, including the rate to claim and the timing of tax cash flows will be specified in an exam question.

Real life example: Tax allowable depreciation

If tax allowable depreciation is available on the cost of **plant and machinery** at a rate of 25% on the written down value (WDV) (ie on a **reducing balance** basis) and a company purchases machinery costing $80,000, with a 4 year useful life and zero residual value the subsequent TAD would be:

Time	1	2	3	4
WDV b/f	$80,000	$60,000	$45,000	$33,750
TAD	**$20,000** (25% of $80,000)	**$15,000** (25% of $60,000)	**$11,250** (25% of $45,000)	**$33,750** (balancing allowance)
WDV c/f	$60,000	$45,000	$33,750	$0

1.2.1 Impact of disposal value

When the asset is eventually sold, the balancing allowance is based on the written down value at the start of the year **less the disposal value obtained from the sale of the asset.**

Real life example: Impact of disposal value

Continuing the previous example, if the asset is sold at the end of year 4 for $25,000 the tax allowable depreciation in time 4 would change (the other time periods are unaffected) to:

Time	4
WDV b/f	$33,750
Disposal value	($25,000)
TAD (balancing allowance)	$8,750
WDV c/f	$0

If the scrap value is **greater than the WDV at the start of the year**, there would be no TAD and the excess would be taxed (this is called a balancing charge).

1.2.2 Tax saved on tax allowable depreciation

In itself, tax allowable depreciation is not a cash flow. However, the **tax saved** due to TAD is a cash flow and this need to be recognised.

The **cash saving on tax-allowable depreciation** is calculated by **multiplying the amount of the tax-allowable depreciation by the tax rate.**

If tax cash flows occur in the year following the year in which the item giving rise to the tax occurs, the cash flow for the tax saving from tax-allowable depreciation will occur in the year following the year in which the allowance is claimed.

Real life example: Tax allowable depreciation (continued)

Using the information from the previous illustration, if the rate of tax on profits is 20%, the **tax saved** from TAD is as follows:

Time	1	2	3	4
TAD	$20,000	$15,000	$11,250	$8,750
Tax saved	**$4,000** (20% of $20,000)	**$3,000** (20% of $15,000)	**$2,250** (20% of $11,250)	**$1,750** (20% of $8,750)

Tax savings **may occur a year after the TAD is claimed** depending on whether tax on profits is payable in the **same year as the taxable profits are earned or in the following year.** The appropriate timing to apply will be specified in an exam question.

1.2.3 Approach to apply to TAD in the exam

In the exam, you should identify the cash flows relating to TAD by:

(a) Calculate the amount of TAD claimed in each year.

(b) Make sure that you remember the balancing allowance in the year the asset is sold.

(c) Calculate the tax saved, noting the timing of tax payments given in the question.

> ### Exam focus point
>
> A common mistake in exams is to include the tax-allowable depreciation itself in the NPV calculation; it is the **cash effect** (ie the tax saved) of the allowance that should be included.

Activity 1: Tax cash flows

Quitongo Co is considering a major investment programme which will involve the creation of a chain of retail outlets throughout the UK.

The following schedule of expected cash flows has been prepared for analysis:

Time	1	2	3	4
	$'000	$'000	$'000	$'000
Revenue	1,000	1,750	2,500	3,200
Direct costs	970	1,350	1,700	1,800
Office overheads	100	100	100	100

Additional information:

(1) 40% of office overhead is an allocation of head office operating costs.

(2) The post-tax cost of capital is 7%.

Quitongo Co is paying tax at 30% and is expected to do so for the foreseeable future. Tax is payable one year after profits are earned.

The costs of investment include $750,000 on fittings and equipment. Tax allowable depreciation is available on fittings and equipment (only) at 25% on a reducing balance basis.

It is estimated that the resale proceeds for fittings and equipment will be $200,000.

Quitongo Co has an accounting year end of 31 December; expenditure on the investment programme will take place in January.

Required

Calculate the tax cash flows to be included in the NPV for this project (ie the tax paid on operating cash flows and tax saved on tax allowable depreciation).

Solution

1.2.4 Cost of capital

When **taxation is ignored** in DCF calculations, the discount rate will reflect the **pre-tax rate of return** required on capital investments.

When **taxation is included** in the cash flows, a **post-tax required rate of return** should be used.

Cost of capital is covered in Chapter 11.

Essential reading

See Chapter 6 Section 1 of the Essential Reading, available in the digital edition of the Workbook, for a further illustration of this area.

The Essential reading is available as an Appendix of the digital edition of the Workbook.

2 Working capital

Investment projects will require an injection of funds to finance the level of working capital required (eg inventory). The effect on cash flows is due to the change in working capital required during the life of the project.

The relevant cash flow associated with working capital is **the change in working capital.**

- An **increase in working capital** required will cause a **cash outflow**
- A **decrease in working capital** required will cause a **cash inflow**.

2.1 Impact of working capital movements on project appraisal

2.1.1 Start of project

In investment appraisal, an investment in working capital at the beginning of the investment period is treated as an outflow of cash.

2.1.2 Each year of operation

In each year of operation of a project the following adjustment is made:

	$
Post tax cash flow from profits in the period	X
Minus working capital **increase**	(X)
or Plus working capital **reduction**	X
Equals adjusted cash flow for the period	X

2.1.3 End of project

Working capital will be released at the end of a project's life, and so there will be a **cash inflow** arising out of the eventual realisation into cash of the project's inventory and receivables in the final year of the project.

Exam focus point

Exam questions will show the total amount of working capital required in each year of the project. **The DCF working should only show the incremental cash flows from one year's requirement to the next.**

Activity 2: Working capital cash flows

Continuation of activity 1.

Quitongo Co plc expects the following working capital requirements during each of the four years of the investment programme (all figures in $'000).

Year 1	Year 2	Year 3	Year 4
250	300	375	400

Quitongo plc has an accounting year end of 31 December; expenditure on the investment programme will take place in January.

Required

Calculate the relevant cash flows relating to working capital.

Solution

3 Net present value (NPV) layout

A neat layout will gain credibility in the exam and will help you make sense of the many different cash flows that you will have to deal with.

The points in bold in the spreadsheet-style table below are the areas already covered in the previous sections of this chapter; the timings of some of the cash flows may alter (eg taxation) depending on the wording of the question.

	A	B	C	D	E	F	G
1	**Time**	**0**	**1**	**2**	**3**	**4**	**5**
2	Sales		X	X	X	X	
3	Costs		(X)	(X)	(X)	(X)	
4	Operating cash flow		X	X	X	X	
5	**Taxation**			(X)	(X)	(X)	(X)
6	Capital expenditure	(X)					
7	Scrap value					X	
8	**Tax benefit of TAD**			X	X	X	X
9	**Working capital changes**	(X)	(X)	(X)	(X)	X	—

	A	B	C	D	E	F	G
1	Time	0	1	2	3	4	5
10	Net cash flows	(X)	X	X	X	X	X
11	Discount factors @ **post-tax cost of capital**	X	X	X	X	X	X
12	Present value	(X)	X	X	X	X	X
13	Net present value	X	-	-	-	-	-

> ### Exam focus point
>
> You can use the spreadsheet function =NPV in the exam to discount the net cash flows arising from time 1 onwards (spreadsheet cells C10 to G10 in the previous table) and **then subtract the time 0 cash flows to determine the overall project NPV**. This two stage approach is required because the NPV function assumes that the first cash flow arises at time 1 (and so ignores the time 0 net cash flow).
>
> If using this approach, you will need to insert the cost of capital (ie the discount rate) into the formula too.
>
> For example, if the cost of capital is 10% then the NPV of the cash flows from time 1 onwards in the previous table would be calculated as:
>
> = NPV(0.1,C10:G10) and then the cash outflow at time 0 would be deducted to calculate the project NPV.
>
> You may prefer to use this method in the exam as it can be quicker than using the discount tables, but either method (ie the =NPV approach or using discount tables) is acceptable.

Activity 3: NPV layout

Continuation of activities 1 and 2.

Extra information:

Quitongo Co's investment programme will also involve the following investment costs and disposal values.

Time	0	1	2	3	4
	$'000	$'000	$'000	$'000	$'000
Land and buildings	3,250				
Fittings and equipment	750				

The cost of land and buildings includes $120,000 which has already been spent on surveyors' and other advisers' fees.

Quitongo Co expects to sell the chain at the end of Year 4 for $4,500,000 after tax (this includes resale proceeds of $200,000 for fittings and equipment).

The post-tax cost of capital is 7%.

Required

Complete the NPV pro-forma below (which includes the results of activities 1 and 2) to calculate the NPV of this project.

Time	0	1	2	3	4	5
	$'000	$'000	$'000	$'000	$'000	$'000
Turnover		1,000	1,750	2,500	3,200	
Direct costs		(970)	(1,350)	(1,700)	(1,800)	
Overheads (60%)		(60)	(60)	(60)	(60)	
Operating cash flow		(30)	340	740	1,340	
Taxation @ 30%			9	(102)	(222)	(402)
Fittings & equipment	(750)					
Sale of business					4,500	
Land and buildings	(3,130)					
Tax saved from TAD			56	42	32	35
Working capital changes	(250)	(50)	(75)	(25)	400	
Net cash flow						
7% discount factors	1	0.935	0.873	0.816	0.763	0.713
Present value						

NPV = [   ]

4 Inflation

Real: The term 'real' when applied to cash flows or to the cost of capital, means **based on current price levels.**

Nominal: The term 'nominal', when applied to cash flows or to the cost of capital, means **after adjusting for the impact of expected inflation.**

4.1 Impact of inflation on project appraisal

So far, we have not considered the effect of **inflation** on the appraisal of capital investment proposals.

Inflation has two impacts on NPV:

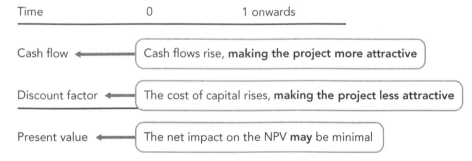

Time	0	1 onwards
Cash flow ←		Cash flows rise, **making the project more attractive**
Discount factor ←		The cost of capital rises, **making the project less attractive**
Present value ←		The net impact on the NPV **may** be minimal

4.2 One rate of inflation

If there is one rate of inflation, inflation has **no net impact on a project's NPV** because the impact of an increase in prices on project cash inflows is exactly offset by the impact of inflation on increasing the cost of capital.

In this case it is normally **quicker to ignore inflation** in the cash flows (ie to use real cash flows, sometimes these are referred to as being at 'current prices') and to use a 'real' cost of capital (ie ignoring the impact of inflation on investors' required return).

Illustration 1: One rate of inflation

Bistro Co is a brewing company trying to decide whether to buy a new bottling machine for $10m to save on rental costs which are currently $6.6m p.a.

Running costs for the new machine would be $1.2m p.a.

The bottling machine has no resale value and has an expected life of three years.

All cash flows are quoted in **current prices** (ie in **real terms**) and are expected to rise in line with the consumer price index (or CPI, a measure of **inflation**) at 5.26% p.a.

Bistro's **real** cost of capital is 14%, and its **nominal** cost of capital is 20%. Ignore tax.

Required

Evaluate whether the new bottling machine should be purchased.

Solution

Because there is **only one rate of inflation**, inflation can be **ignored in the cash flows and the cost of capital.**

Time	0	1–3
	$m	$m
Running costs		(1.20)
Savings		6.60
Purchase costs	(10.00)	
Net	(10.00)	5.40
DF @ 14%	1.0	2.322
PV	(10.00)	12.54
NPV	**+2.54**	

Note that if we had decided to include inflation, we would get the same answer, but it would take **longer to calculate** and therefore is **unnecessary** where there is only one rate of inflation. This approach is shown below.

Time	0	1	2	3
Running costs (× 1.0526 p.a.)		(1.26)	(1.33)	(1.40)
Savings (× 1.0526 p.a.)		6.95	7.31	7.70
Purchase costs	(10.00)			
Net	(10.00)	5.69	5.98	6.30
DF @ 20%		0.833	0.694	0.579
PV	(10.00)	4.74	4.15	3.65
NPV	**+2.54**			

4.3 More than one rate of inflation

If there is more than one rate of inflation, inflation will have an impact on profit margins (as revenue and costs are changing at different rates) and therefore **inflation needs to be included in project appraisal.**

In this case **the cash flows must be inflated, and inflation must also be incorporated into the cost of capital.**

4.3.1 Inflating project cash flows

This will involve adjusting the cash flows by multiplying them by (1 + inflation rate) for each year that inflation is being applied. For example, inflating a cash flow at time 2 will involve multiplying it by $(1 + \text{inflation})^2$.

4.3.2 Inflating the cost of capital

As the inflation rate increases, so will the return required by an investor. For example, you might be happy with a return of 5% in an inflation-free world, but if inflation were running at 15% you would expect a considerably greater yield.

The **nominal (or money) interest rate** incorporates inflation.

The relationship between real and nominal rates of interest is given by the **Fisher formula**.

Formula provided

$(1 + i) = (1 + r)(1 + h)$

Where h = general rate of inflation

          r = real rate of interest

          i = nominal (money) rate of interest

The general inflation rate is often given in an exam question as the retail price index (RPI) or consumer price index (CPI).

4.3.3 Using real cash flows and a real cost of capital if there is more than one rate of inflation

If there is more than one rate of inflation, **it is still possible to calculate an NPV in real terms, but this has to start by an adjustment to nominal cash flows** because where there are multiple rates of inflation then there will be an impact on profit margins due to inflation (as revenue and costs are changing at different rates).

The approach required is to:

(a) Deflate **nominal** (ie inflated) cash flows using the general rate of inflation so that they become real cash flows

      Real cash flow = Nominal cash flow ÷ (1+ inflation rate) ^n

(b) Discount the real cash flows at the **real** cost of capital.

Exam focus point

This approach is more complicated than using nominal cash flows and therefore is rarely used.

Illustration 2: More than one rate of inflation

We will use the details from the previous illustration for Bistro Co with the following amendments:

(1) Running costs rise at the general rate of inflation of 5.26%, but rental costs being saved are expected to increase at 2% p.a.

(2) We are only told that Bistro's **real** cost of capital is 14%.

Required

Evaluate whether the new bottling machine should be purchased.

Solution

Here there is **more than one rate of inflation**, so inflation needs to be incorporated into the cash flows because profit margins are affected by the savings on rental costs inflating at a lower rate than costs are increasing by.

Time	0	1	2	3
Running costs (× 1.0526 p.a.)		(1.26)	(1.33)	(1.40)
Savings (× 1.02 p.a.)		6.73	6.87	7.00
Purchase costs	(10.00)			
Net	(10.00)	5.47	5.54	5.60
DF @ 20% (See working)		0.833	0.694	0.579
PV	(10.00)	4.56	3.84	3.24
NPV	**+1.64**			

Working

1 + Inflated (nominal) cost of capital = (1 + 0.14) × (1.0526) = 1.20 ie 20%

The same answer can also be obtained if the nominal cash flows are **deflated** and a **real cost of capital** is used. This is a slower method and should only be used if requested in a question.

This is demonstrated below:

Time	0	1	2	3
Nominal cash flows (as before)		5.47	5.54	5.60
Deflated ÷ (1.0.526)^n		0.9500	0.9026	0.8575
Real cash flows				
Net	(10.00)	5.20	5.00	4.80
DF @ 14% (real cost of capital)		0.877	0.769	0.675
PV	(10.00)	4.56	3.84	3.24
NPV	**+1.64**			

4.3.4 Working capital and inflation

The working capital requirement each year is a function of sales and costs. It follows that if the sales and purchases figures are to be inflated, then any figure resulting from them (receivables, payables, inventory) should also be inflated.

Only once the total (inflated) working capital required has been calculated should you calculate the incremental cash flows for DCF calculations based on the change in working capital.

Activity 4: Supplementary activity with tax, working capital and inflation

SC Co is evaluating the purchase of a new machine to produce product P, which has a short product life cycle due to rapidly changing technology. The machine is expected to cost $1m.

Production and sales of product P are forecast to be as follows:

Year	1	2	3	4
Production and sales (units/year)	35,000	53,000	75,000	36,000

The selling price of product P (in current price terms) will be $20 per unit, while the variable cost of the product (in current price terms) will be $12 per unit.

Selling price inflation is expected to be 4% per year and variable cost inflation is expected to be 5% per year.

No increase in existing fixed costs is expected since SC Co has spare capacity in both space and labour terms.

Producing and selling product P will call for increased investment in working capital. Analysis of historical levels of working capital within SC Co indicates that at the start of each year, investment in working capital for product P will need to be 7% of sales revenue for that year.

SC Co pays tax of 30% per year in the year in which the taxable profit occurs. Liability to tax is reduced by capital allowances (tax allowable depreciation) on machinery, which SC Co can claim on a straight-line basis over the four-year life of the proposed investment. The new machine is expected to have no scrap value at the end of the four-year period.

SC Co has a real cost of capital of 9.8%, and the general rate of inflation is 2%.

Required

1 Calculate the net present value of the proposed investment in product P. **(13 marks)**

2 Advise on the acceptability of the proposed investment in product P. **(17 marks)**

(Total = 30 marks)

Solution

Essential reading

See Chapter 6 Section 2 of the Essential reading, available in the digital edition of the Workbook, for further discussion of this area.

The Essential reading is available as an Appendix of the digital edition of the Workbook.

Chapter summary

Allowing for tax, working capital and inflation

Taxation

Corporation tax on profits

Apply as an expense using the rate and timing given in an exam question

Tax saved from tax allowable depreciation
- Calculate the amount of TAD to claim in each year
- Final year balancing allowance
- Calculate tax saved noting the timing of tax payments

Working capital
- Relevant cash flow is the change in working capital
- Start year: invest in working capital
- Each year of a project:
  increase in working capital = cash outflow
  decrease in working capital = cash inflow
- Final year: assume working capital is reduced to zero (unless told otherwise in a question)

NPV layout
- Any neat layout is acceptable
- Sensible to group items affecting operating cash flows (affecting tax paid) at the top, and capital items at the bottom

Inflation

Single inflation rate

Easier to use a real cost of capital and not to inflate the cash flows

More than one rate of inflation
- Use a nominal cost of capital
- Inflate each cash flow at the appropriate rate (or deflate the nominal cash flows and use a real cost of capital)

Knowledge diagnostic

1. Taxation

Tax rates and timings will be given in the exam.

Don't forget tax is saved on tax allowable depreciation.

2. Working capital

The relevant cash flow is the change in working capital.

3. Single inflation rate

Use real cash flows and a real cost of capital.

4. More than one rate of inflation

Use nominal cash flows and a nominal cost of capital.

5. NPV layout

Any neat layout will be fine, sensible to start with operating cash flows (which affect tax paid) and then to deal with capital items.

Further study guidance

Question practice

Now try the following from the Further question practice bank (available in the digital edition of the Workbook):

Section A questions

Q19

Section C questions

Q46 Bridgeford

Q47 Dinard

Further reading

There is a useful Technical Article available on ACCA's website, called 'Inflation and investment appraisal', written by a member of the Financial Management examining team. We recommend that you read this article as part of your preparation for the FM exam.

Activity answers

Activity 1: Tax cash flows

Tax cash flow calculations:

(1)   Tax paid on operating cash flows

Only 60% of overheads are a relevant cash flow, the other 40% is not a cash flow because it is an apportionment of an existing overhead.

Time	1	2	3	4	5
	$'000	$'000	$'000	$'000	$'000
Revenue	1,000	1,750	2,500	3,200	
Direct costs	(970)	(1,350)	(1,700)	(1,800)	
Overheads (60%)	(60)	(60)	(60)	(60)	
Operating cash flow	(30)	340	740	1,340	
Taxation @ 30%		9	(102)	(222)	(402)

(2)   Calculation of tax allowable depreciation

Time	1	2	3	4
WDV b/f ($'000)	750	562	421	316
Scrap ($'000)				200
TAD ($'000)	**188**	**141**	**105**	***116**
WDV c/f ($'000)	562	421	316	0

Time	2	3	4	5
Tax saved (TAD × tax rate)	56	42	32	35

* Final year TAD = WDV at time 3 – scrap proceeds = 316 – 200 = 116

Activity 2: Working capital cash flows

Calculation of working capital flows

Time	0	1	2	3	4
Working Capital	250	300	375	400	0*
Change in working capital	250	50	75	25	(400)
Change in cash flow	(250)	(50)	(75)	(25)	400

*Normal assumption

Activity 3: NPV layout

Time	0	1	2	3	4	5
	$'000	$'000	$'000	$'000	$'000	$'000
Turnover		1,000	1,750	2,500	3,200	
Direct costs		(970)	(1,350)	(1,700)	(1,800)	
Overheads (60%)		(60)	(60)	(60)	(60)	
Operating cash flow		(30)	340	740	1,340	
Taxation @ 30%			9	(102)	(222)	(402)
Fittings & equipment	(750)					
Sale of business					4,500	
Land and buildings (3,250 less sunk cost of 120)	(3,130)					
Tax saved from TAD			56	42	32	35
Working capital changes	(250)	(50)	(75)	(25)	400	
Net cash flow	(4,130)	(80)	330	655	6,050	(367)
7% discount factors	1	0.935	0.873	0.816	0.763	0.713
Present value	(4,130)	(75)	288	534	4,616	(262)

NPV = +$971(000)

Alternative solution using the spreadsheet =NPV function:

If the net cash flows from time 1-5 in the table were in spreadsheet cells C10 to G10 then the present value of these cash flows could be calculated as =NPV(0.07,C10:G10) which gives a value of 5,102.

Subtracting the time 0 cash flows of 4,130 then gives the overall NPV as +$972(000).

This is slightly more accurate than using discount tables because discount factors in these tables are rounded to 3 decimal places but either method is accepted in the exam.

Activity 4: Supplementary activity with tax, working capital and inflation

Marking guide		Marks
1	Inflated sales revenue	2
	Inflated variable costs	2
	Taxation	1
	Working capital	3
	Discount factors	2
	Net present value calculation	1
		13
2	Net present value comment	1
	Discussion of limitations	3
		17
Total		30

1 Calculation of NPV

Year	0	1	2	3	4
	$	$	$	$	$
Sales revenue (W1)		728,000	1,146,390	1,687,500	842,400
Variable costs (W2)		(441,000)	(701,190)	(1,041,750)	(524,880)
Contribution		287,000	445,200	645,750	317,520
Taxation @ 30%		(86,100)	(133,560)	(193,725)	(95,256)
Capital expenditure	(1,000,000)				
Working capital (W3)	(50,960)	(29,287)	(37,878)	59,157	58,968
Tax benefit of tax depreciation (W4)		75,000	75,000	75,000	75,000
Net cash flow	(1,050,960)	246,613	348,762	586,182	356,232
Discount factor (W5)	1.000	0.893	0.797	0.712	0.636
Present value	(1,050,960)	220,225	277,963	417,362	226,564
NPV	91,154				

Alternative solution using the spreadsheet =NPV function:

If the net cash flows from time 1-4 in the table were in spreadsheet cells C10 to F10 then the present value of these cash flows could be calculated as =NPV(0.12,C10:F10) which gives a value of 1,141,846.

Subtracting the time 0 cash flows of 1,050,960 then gives the overall NPV as +$90,886.

This is slightly more accurate than using discount tables because discount factors in these tables are rounded to 3 decimal places but either method is accepted in the exam.

Workings

1 **Sales Revenue**

Year	1	2	3	4
Selling price (×1.04)	$20.80	$21.63	$22.50	$23.40
Sales volume in units	35,000	53,000	75,000	36,000
Sales revenue	$728,000	$1,146,390	$1,687,500	$842,400

2 **Variable costs**

Year	1	2	3	4
Variable cost (× 1.05)	$12.60	$13.23	$13.89	$14.58
Sales volume in units	35,000	53,000	75,000	36,000
Variable costs	$441,000	$701,190	$1,041,75	$524,880

3 **Working capital**

Year	0	1	2	3	4
	$	$	$	$	$
Sales revenue		728,000	1,146,390	1,687,500	842,400
Working capital req @7%	50,960	80,247	118,125	58,968	
Incremental working capital cash flow	(50,960)	(29,287)	(37,878)	59,157	58,968

4 **Tax benefit of tax depreciation**

Depreciation = $1,000,000/4 = $250,000 per year

Tax benefit = 30% × $250,000 = $75,000

(W5) *Cost of capital*

1 + Inflated (nominal) cost of capital = (1 + 0.098) × (1.02) = 1.12 ie 12%

A nominal cost of capital needs to be used, as inflation has been included in the cash flows (because there is more than one rate of inflation)

2 The NPV is positive so the proposed investment can be recommended on financial grounds as the project gives a return that is above the cost of capital of 12% used by SC Co for investment appraisal purposes.

Limitations of the evaluations

Forecast sales volumes have been used for both investment appraisal methods and the accuracy of the results is therefore heavily dependent on the accuracy of these forecasts. Product P has a short product life cycle which makes forecast sales volumes particularly unpredictable.

The analysis has used predicted inflation rates for sales price and variable costs which do not change over the four-year period. This is unlikely in reality as price increases will vary according to prevailing economic conditions and unexpected events.

Fixed costs have not been included in the investment appraisal. This is because SC has spare capacity in both space and labour terms so it is assumed that fixed costs will not change as a result of the investment.

This assumption may be questionable in the longer term, especially as production of product P in Year 3 will be double that in Year 1.

7

Project appraisal and risk

Learning objectives

On completion of this chapter, you should be able to:

	Syllabus reference
• Describe and discuss the difference between risk and uncertainty in relation to probabilities and increasing project life	D3(a)
• Apply sensitivity analysis to investment projects and discuss the usefulness of sensitivity analysis in assisting in investment decisions	D3(b)
• Apply probability analysis to investment projects and discuss the usefulness of probability analysis in assisting investment decisions.	D3(c)

• Apply and discuss other techniques of adjusting for risk and uncertainty in investment appraisal, including:
  - simulation
  - adjusted payback
  - risk-adjusted discount rates.
	D3(d)

Exam context

This chapter covers 'adjusting for risk and uncertainty in investment appraisal' which is part of Section D of the syllabus (Investment Appraisal), it introduces the concepts of risk and uncertainty and evaluates their impact on investment appraisal.

This is an important chapter that is often neglected. Remember that this chapter covers a syllabus section that is examinable in all sections of the exam, including Section C.

Chapter overview

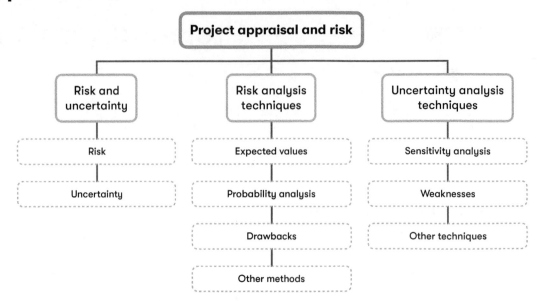

1 Risk and uncertainty

Investment decisions are based on predictions of what will happen in the future and therefore involve an element of unpredictability.

This unpredictability could be described as **risk** or **uncertainty**. However, for this exam there is an important technical **distinction made between these two concepts.**

1.1 Risk

> **Risk:** Arises where there are several possible outcomes and, based on past relevant experience, **probabilities can be assigned to the possible outcomes.**

Risk increases as the **variability of a project's cash flow increases.**

Risk can be **quantified** and **built into** a **net present value** (NPV).

1.2 Uncertainty

> **Uncertainty:** Arises where there are several possible outcomes and **no information** (eg experience) **upon which to create probabilities** so the degree of uncertainty **cannot be quantified.**

The **uncertainty** of project cash flows **increases as the length of a project rises**, since cash flows in the distant future are less certain than cash flows in the short-term.

Uncertainty **cannot be quantified** but it **can be described/analysed.**

> ### Exam focus point
>
> Make sure you can explain the difference between risk and uncertainty, this has been examined in a part of several Section C questions.

2 Risk analysis

There are a number of techniques for **quantifying the risk** of a project's cash flows.

2.1 Probability analysis and expected values

A **probability analysis** of expected cash flows can often be estimated (for example using past experience of similar projects) and used both to calculate an **expected NPV and to measure risk.**

2.1.1 Expected values

An expected value is a weighted average that is calculated using probabilities. It is likely that you have used this technique before.

Activity 1: Expected NPV

Harry Co is choosing between two mutually exclusive projects. The NPV of these projects in $m depends on the rate of growth of the economy over the next five years. Forecast NPV is shown under scenarios of low, medium and high growth:

Probability	Forecast	Project A NPV $m	Project B NPV $m
0.25	Low growth	1.00	−8.00
0.50	Medium growth	2.50	4.00

Probability	Forecast	Project A NPV $m	Project B NPV $m
0.25	High growth	4.00	16.00
1.00	Expected value		

Required

Complete the table (working to two decimal places) to calculate each project's expected NPV and consider which project would be chosen.

Solution

2.1.2 Risk and joint probabilities

A **probability distribution** of 'expected cash flows' can also be used to measure risk, for example by:

(a) calculating the worst possible outcome and its probability

(b) calculating the probability that the project will fail to achieve a positive NPV

This may involve analysing the risk of a single outcome (eg the 25% risk of project B failing to achieve a positive NPV in the previous activity).

Alternatively, risk may be measured by analysing the risk of two risky outcomes occurring at the same time; this is called a **joint probability.**

> **Joint probability:** The probability of two risky outcomes occurring at the same time and is calculated as the probability of one outcome multiplied by the probability of the other.

Illustration 1: Joint probabilities

An investment in a new product is being planned. The product has an expected life of two years. An analysis of similar projects has resulted in the following annual cash flow projections:

	Year 1		Year 2	
Cash flow projection 1 (high)	$56m p.a.	60% chance	$44m p.a.	30% chance
Cash flow projection 2 (low)	$44m p.a.	40% chance	$36m p.a.	70% chance

The outcome in Year 2 is not dependent on the outcome in Year 1.

Set-up costs of $77m are payable immediately. The cost of capital is 10%.

You are the management accountant and you are worried about the risk of the project.

The possible outcomes have been further analysed as follows:

Year 1	Year 2	NPV
$44m (low)	$36m (low)	$-7,268m
$44m (low)	$44m (high)	$-660m
$56m (high)	$36m (low)	$+3,640m
$56m (high)	$44m (high)	$+10,248m

Ignore the impact of taxation.

Required

Identify the mean (expected) NPV of the project. (Give your answer to the nearest $'000.)

Solution

Expected NPV

Possible outcome	Probability Year 1	Probability Year 2	Joint probability
Year 1 low & Year 2 low	0.4	0.7	0.4 × 0.7 = 0.28
Year 1 low & Year 2 high	0.4	0.3	0.4 × 0.3 = 0.12
Year 1 high & Year 2 low	0.6	0.7	0.6 × 0.7 = 0.42
Year 1 high & Year 2 high	0.6	0.3	0.6 × 0.3 = 0.18
			1.0

Expected NPV = (−7,268 × 0.28) + (−660 × 0.12) + (3,640 × 0.42) + (10,248 × 0.18) = **+1,259**

Alternative calculation of expected NPV

Time	0	1	2
Cash flow ($'000)	−77,000	(56,000 × 0.6) + (44,000 × 0.4) = 51,200	(44,000 × 0.3) + (36,000 × 0.7) = 38,400
DF @ 10%	1	0.909	0.826
PV	−77,000	46,541	31,718
NPV	**+1,259**		

Activity 2: Joint probabilities

Using the information from the previous illustration;

Required

1 Identify the probability of the project having a negative NPV. (Give your answer as a percentage to one decimal place.)

2 Identify the NPV of the most likely outcome. (Give your answer to the nearest $'000.)

Solution

2.1.3 Problems with probability analysis

There are a number of problems with using expected values in making investment decisions.

- An investment may be **one-off**, and the 'expected' NPV may never actually occur. Eg if there is a 50% probability that the NPV will be + $10,000 and a 50% probability that it will be $(2,000), the EV of the NPV is + $4,000. On this basis the project will go ahead. However, an NPV of $4,000 is not expected to happen. The NPV will be either positive $10,000 or negative $2,000.

- **Assigning probabilities** to future events and outcomes is usually highly **subjective.**

- Expected values **do not evaluate the range** of possible NPV outcomes. If a company has a neutral attitude to risk it can be assumed that it will select an investment that is forecast to create the highest expected net present value. However, if a company is especially risk-averse or if it is risk-seeking (in the hope of high returns) then a company's decision-making will be influenced by this risk appetite.

2.2 Other techniques for managing risk

Techniques	Description
Simulation	Random numbers are assigned to different values of **variables** to reflect their probability. Risk is assessed as the standard deviation of forecast NPVs (from repeated simulations), and the probability of a negative NPV. However, because random numbers are based on probabilities, there is a danger that they may be highly subjective.
Conservative forecasting	A traditional way of dealing with risk is to reduce estimated project cash inflows to an ultra-safe level (ie the cash could be no worse than…) These cash flows are then discounted as if they are **'risk free'** using a low (risk free) cost of capital. This is sometimes called a certainty-equivalent method. There is a danger with this technique that the likely benefits of investments may be understated, and potentially attractive investments may therefore be rejected.

Finally, later in this Workbook (in Chapter 12) we will see how a **cost of capital** can be adjusted to recognise that investors will want a **higher return on riskier projects**.

This is sometimes referred to as a **risk-adjusted cost of capital**.

Essential reading

See Chapter 7 section 1 of the Essential reading, available in the digital edition of the Workbook, for further discussion of this area.

The Essential reading is available as an Appendix of the digital edition of the Workbook.

---

3 Uncertainty analysis

There are several techniques for **analysing the uncertainty** of a project's cash flows.

3.1 Sensitivity analysis

Sensitivity analysis: A key method of **analysing the uncertainty** surrounding a capital expenditure project and enables an assessment to be made of **how responsive the project's NPV is to changes in a single variable** that affects a project's NPV.

A project's NPV will depend on a number of **uncertain variables** (eg selling price, sales volume, operating costs etc).

The basic approach of sensitivity analysis is to **calculate what the value of a single variable would have to change by, to change a project's NPV to zero.**

Sensitivity analysis therefore **provides an indication of which variables a project's NPV is most sensitive to.**

Management should review critical variables to assess whether or not there is a strong possibility of events occurring which will lead to a negative NPV. Management should also pay particular attention to controlling those variables to which the NPV is particularly sensitive, once the decision has been taken to accept the investment.

A simple approach to calculating sensitivity is as follows

$$\frac{\text{Project NPV}}{\text{Present value of project variable}} \times 100$$

The lower the percentage, the more sensitive the NPV is to that project variable, as the variable would need to change by a smaller amount to make the project non-viable.

Illustration 2: Sensitivity analysis

Kenney Co is considering a project which required an initial investment of $7 million and is expected to result in sales of 100,000 units per year at a selling price of $65 and a variable cost per unit of $20. Kenney Co has a cost of capital of 8%.

The present value (PV) of each these variables has been calculated as follows:

Year	Discount factor 8%	PV of initial investment	PV of variable costs	PV of sales	PV of net cash flow
		$'000	$'000	$'000	$'000
0	1.000	(7,000)			(7,000)
1	0.926		(1,852)	6,019	4,167
2	0.857	–	(1,714)	5,571	3,857

The project has a positive NPV of +$1,024 (000) and therefore would appear to be worthwhile.

The project's IRR has been estimated as 18.5%. Tax can be ignored

Required

Measure the sensitivity of the project to changes in:

(a) The initial investment

(b) Sales volume

(c) Selling price

(d) Variable costs

(e) Cost of capital

Solution

(a) Initial investment

Sensitivity = (1,024/7,000) × 100 = 14.6%

This means that the project will only just provide the required investment return if the cost of the investment is 14.6% higher than estimated, assuming all other variables are unchanged.

(b) Sales volume

This will affect the value of **sales revenue and variable costs (ie contribution).**

Sensitivity = (1,024/(11,590 - 3,566)) × 100 = 12.8%

The project will only just provide the required investment return if sales volume is 12.8% lower than estimated, assuming all other variables are unchanged.

(c) Selling price

This will affect the value of **sales revenue only.**

Sensitivity = (1,024/11,590) × 100 = 8.8%

The project will only just provide the required investment return if the sales price is 8.8% lower than estimated, assuming all other variables are unchanged.

(d) Variable costs

Sensitivity = (1,024/3,566) × 100 = 28.8%

The project will only just provide the required investment return if variable costs per unit are 28.8% higher than estimated, assuming all other variables are unchanged.

(e) Cost of capital

The project's IRR is 18.5% which is 10.5% above the cost of capital of 8%.

The cost of capital can therefore increase by (10.5% / 8%) × 100 = 135% before the NPV becomes negative.

The elements to which the NPV appears to be most sensitive are the selling price followed by the sales volume. Management should pay particular attention to these factors so that they can be carefully monitored.

Note that tax was ignored in this illustration. If tax is given in a question, the sensitivity analysis should be performed on the **post-tax** present value of the cash flows.

Activity 3: Sensitivity analysis

A company is evaluating a three-year project, the NPV has been assessed as follows:

Time	0	1	2	3
	$'000	$'000	$'000	$'000
Sales		4,200	4,900	5,300
Variable costs		(2,850)	(3,100)	(4,150)
Pre-tax cash flow		1,350	1,800	1,150
Tax @ 21%		(284)	(378)	(242)
Investment	(2,000)			
Net cash flow	(2,000)	1,066	1,422	908
DF @ 7%	1	0.935	0.873	0.816
PV	(2,000)	997	1,241	741

NPV = $979,000

Required

Calculate the sensitivity of the NPV to the changes in sales volume, and to changes in the selling price. (Give your answers to one decimal place.)

Solution

3.1.1 Weaknesses of sensitivity analysis

These are as follows.

(a) The method requires that only **one variable changes at a time**. However, management may be more interested in the combination of the effects of changes in two or more key variables.

(b) Looking at factors in isolation is unrealistic since they are often **interdependent** (eg if demand for a product is low then this may also mean that the selling price will not be as high as expected).

(c) It **does not provide a decision rule**. Parameters defining **acceptability** of an investment project, given the uncertainty, must be laid down by managers using their judgement.

3.2 Other techniques for managing uncertainty

Other techniques to be aware of include the following:

Techniques	Description
Scenario building	An analysis of the potential NPV of a project under different scenarios – unlike sensitivity analysis this can be used to show the impact of **more than one variable** changing (eg market share and sales price). However, there is the **danger that the chosen scenarios may be unrealistic** ie unlikely to occur.
Payback period & discounted (or adjusted) payback period	**Covered in Chapter 5**, the quicker the payback the less reliant a project is on the later, more uncertain, cash flows.

Chapter summary

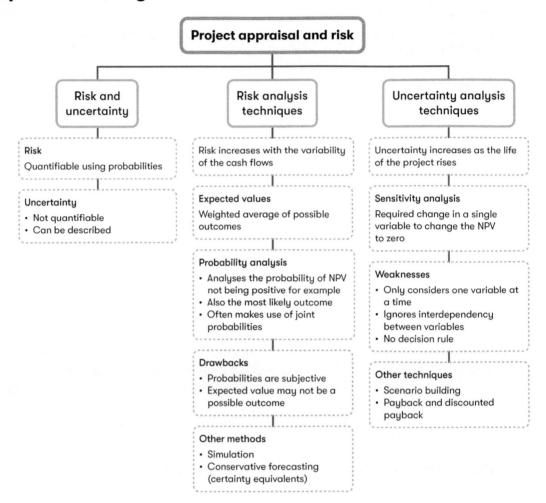

Project appraisal and risk

Risk and uncertainty

Risk
Quantifiable using probabilities

Uncertainty
- Not quantifiable
- Can be described

Risk analysis techniques

Risk increases with the variability of the cash flows

Expected values
Weighted average of possible outcomes

Probability analysis
- Analyses the probability of NPV not being positive for example
- Also the most likely outcome
- Often makes use of joint probabilities

Drawbacks
- Probabilities are subjective
- Expected value may not be a possible outcome

Other methods
- Simulation
- Conservative forecasting (certainty equivalents)

Uncertainty analysis techniques

Uncertainty increases as the life of the project rises

Sensitivity analysis
Required change in a single variable to change the NPV to zero

Weaknesses
- Only considers one variable at a time
- Ignores interdependency between variables
- No decision rule

Other techniques
- Scenario building
- Payback and discounted payback

Knowledge diagnostic

1. Risk analysis

This can be applied to a proposed capital investment where there are several possible outcomes and, based on past relevant experience, probabilities can be assigned to the various outcomes and estimated cash flows that could prevail.

2. Uncertainty analysis

This can be applied to a proposed capital investment where there are several possible outcomes but there is little past relevant experience to enable the probability of the alternative outcomes to be predicted.

3. Sensitivity analysis

This analyses uncertainty by assessing how responsive the project's NPV is to changes in the variables used to calculate that NPV.

4. Expected values

A risk analysis technique that uses probabilities to calculate an expected NPV.

5. Probability analysis

A probability analysis of expected cash flows can often be estimated and used both to calculate to measure risk. This often involves the use of joint probabilities.

Further study guidance

Question practice

Now try the following from the Further question practice bank (available in the digital edition of the Workbook):

Section A questions

Q20, Q21

Section C questions

Q45 Auriga

Q48 Muggins

Activity answers

Activity 1: Expected NPV

Expected values can be calculated as follows

Project A	Project B
(1 × 0.25) + (2.5 × 0.50) + (4 × 0.25) = **2.5**	(−8 × 0.25) + (4 × 0.50) + (16 × 0.25) = **4.0**

Project B has a higher expected value and would therefore be chosen on the basis of this technique.

However, if the company is risk averse, it may be deterred from project B by the 25% change of a negative NPV.

Activity 2: Joint probabilities

1 **40.0%**

Cash flows are low in Years 1 and 2, which has a probability of 0.28 or 28%.

Cash flows are low in Year 1 and high in Year 2, which has a probability of 0.12 or 12%.

Total probability = 0.28 + 0.12 = 0.40 or 40%

2 **3,640**

The most likely outcome in terms of the highest joint probability is that the cash flow in Year 1 is high and Year 2 is low. So, the most likely outcome is +3,640 ($'000).

Activity 3: Sensitivity analysis

Volume

PV of contribution = Project NPV + Outlay = $979,000 + $2,000 = $2,979,000 or the PV of net cash flow for years 1-3 (997 + 1,241 + 741)

Sensitivity = $979,000/$2,979,000 × 100% = **32.9%**

A fall of 32.9% in sales volume is required for the project NPV to fall to zero. This will probably be considered to be unlikely which means that the uncertainty associated with this project looks low with regard to sales volume.

Selling price

PV of sales (including the impact on taxable profit)

	t_1	t_2	t_3
	$'000	$'000	$'000
Sales	4,200	4,900	5,300
Tax @ 21%	(882)	(1,029)	(1,113)
Post tax cash flow	3,318	3,871	4,187
DF @ 7%	0.935	0.873	0.816
PV	3,102	3,379	3,417

Total PV of sales = $9,898,000

Sensitivity = $979,000/$9,898,000 × 100% = **9.9%**

A fall of 9.9% in sales price is required for the project NPV to fall to zero. This will probably be considered to be unlikely which means that the uncertainty associated with this project also looks low with regard to sales price.

BPP
LEARNING
MEDIA

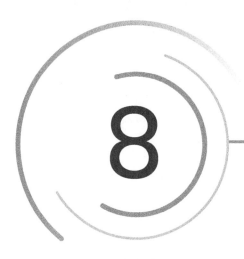

8

Specific investment decisions

Learning objectives

On completion of this chapter you should be able to:

	Syllabus reference
• Evaluate leasing and borrowing to buy using before- and after-tax costs of debt.	D4(a)
• Evaluate asset replacement decisions using equivalent annual cost and equivalent annual benefit.	D4(b)

• Evaluate investment decisions under single-period capital rationing, including:
   - the calculation of profitability indexes for divisible investment projects
   - the calculation of the NPV of combinations of non-divisible investment projects
   - a discussion of the reasons for capital rationing
	D4(c)

Exam context

This chapter covers 'specific investment decisions' which is part of Section D of the syllabus (Investment appraisal). In this chapter, we consider specific applications of discounted cash flow (DCF), including whether to lease or buy an asset, when to replace an asset and how to assess projects when capital is a scarce resource.

This is an important chapter that is often neglected. Remember that this chapter covers a syllabus section that is examinable in all sections of the exam, including Section C.

Chapter overview

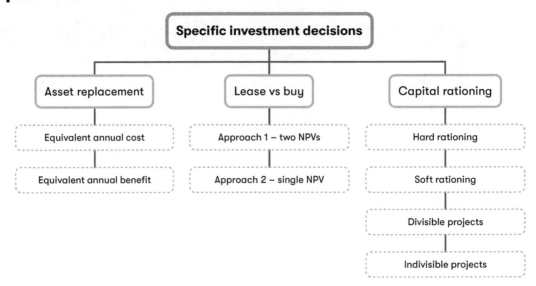

BPP
LEARNING
MEDIA

1 Asset replacement decisions

1.1 Asset replacement cycle

DCF techniques can be useful in **asset replacement decisions** to assess **how frequently** a non-current asset that is **in continual use** in a business (eg delivery vehicles) should be replaced.

If an asset is replaced **less frequently**, then it has a **longer replacement cycle** (the length of time between an asset being purchased and the asset being replaced).

Shorter replacement cycle	Longer replacement cycle
• lower operating costs • a higher residual value when the asset is disposed of • but increased capital expenditure (as the asset is being bought more frequently)	• reduced capital expenditure (since the asset is being bought less frequently) • but as the asset gets older, it may cost more to operate, and residual value will be lower

The ideal replacement cycle will **minimise the costs per year over the replacement cycle**. This is calculated as an **equivalent annual cost** (EAC).

Formula to learn

$$EAC = \frac{NPV \text{ of costs over the replacement cycle}}{\text{Annuity factor for the life of the asset}}$$

Any **revenue** resulting from the **use of the asset** will be disregarded as this revenue will occur in any case, whatever the replacement cycle, and is therefore **not a relevant cash flow**.

Equivalent annual cost: Expresses the present value of the costs of an asset replacement cycle as a cost per year.

Illustration 1: Asset replacement

A company uses machinery which has the following costs and resale values over its three-year life (per machine).

	Year 1	Year 2	Year 3
	$	$	$
Purchase cost: $25,000			
Running costs (cash expenses)	(7,500)	(11,000)	(12,500)
Resale value (end of year)	15,000	10,000	7,500

The organisation's cost of capital is 10%.

Required

Identify how frequently the asset should be replaced.

Solution

Calculations as follows.

Step 1

Year	Discount factors	Replace every year		Replace every 2 years		Replace every 3 years	
		Cash flow	PV at 10%	Cash flow	PV at 10%	Cash flow	PV at 10%
	$	$	$	$	$	$	$
0	–	(25,000)	(25,000)	(25,000)	(25,000)	(25,000)	(25,000)
1	0.909	(7,500)	(6,818)	(7,500)	(6,818)	(7,500)	(6,818)
		15,000	13,635				
2	0.826			(11,000)	(9,086)	(11,000)	(9,086)
				10,000	8,260		
3	0.751					(12,500)	(9,388)
						7,500	5,633
PV of cost over one replacement cycle			(18,183)		(32,644)		(44,659)

Step 2 Calculate the equivalent annual cost (EAC).

We use a discount rate of 10% and an annuity (cumulative discount) factor for each replacement cycle.

(1) **Replacement every year:**

EAC = $(18,183)/0.909 = $(20,003)

(2) **Replacement every two years:**

EAC = $(32,644)/1.736 = $(18,804)

(3) **Replacement every three years:**

EAC = $(44,659)/2.487 = $(17,957)

The optimum replacement policy is the one with the lowest EAC. Here, this is every three years.

Activity 1: EAC

Naurfold regularly buys new delivery vans. Each van costs $30,000, has running costs of $3,000 and a scrap value of $10,000 in its first year. In its second year the van has higher running costs of $4,000, and a lower scrap value of $7,000.

Vehicles are not kept for more than two years for reliability reasons.

Required

Using Naurfold's cost of capital of 15%, identify how often the van should be replaced (ignore tax).

Solution

1.1.1 Assets with different useful lives

The **same technique** is also useful for deciding whether, when considering non-current assets that are **in continual use** within a business, it is better to invest in a cheaper asset with a shorter expected life or a more expensive asset with a longer expected life.

Again, the ideal replacement cycle will **minimise the costs per year over the replacement cycle,** ie the **equivalent annual cost** (EAC).

1.1.2 Drawbacks

This approach only focuses on cost and fails to recognise that as an asset gets older there could be problems with reliability or quality as the asset ages (or that it becomes obsolete as new technology emerges, or new markets emerge).

Exam focus point

A common error is that students include the residual value in more than one year. Be careful to only include the residual value once, in the final year.

1.2 Equivalent annual benefit (EAB)

KEY TERM

Equivalent annual benefit: Expresses the NPV from a project as an annuity, ie a constant cash flow per year.

The equivalent annual benefit = NPV of project/Annuity factor

Real life example

Project A has an NPV of $8.22m and an expected life of six years.

Given a discount rate of 12%, the annuity factor for six years at 12% is 4.111 so project A will have an equivalent annual annuity of 8.22/4.111 = 2.00

An alternative project B with an NPV of $8.90m and an expected life of seven years will have an equivalent annual annuity of 8.90/4.564 = 1.95

(the annuity factor for seven years at 12% is 4.564)

Project A will therefore be **ranked higher** than project B, despite having a lower NPV.

This method is a useful way of comparing projects with **unequal lives.**

1.2.1 Drawbacks

This approach only makes sense if the projects are being **continually renewed** (this assumption of continual replacement was also used in the EAC approach). If this is not the case then the project with the highest NPV (Project B in the previous illustration) would be chosen.

2 Lease vs Buy

After deciding on the viability of an investment using NPV analysis, a separate decision may be needed to determine whether a lease would be a more suitable source of finance than an outright purchase using a loan.

Terminology:

KEY TERM

> **Lessor:** A lessor receives lease payments.
>
> **Lessee:** A lessee makes lease payments.

2.1 Types of leases

2.1.1 Leases that minimise risk to the lessee

Some leases, often short-term leases, are rental agreements between a lessor and a lessee that are structured so that the lessor retains most of the risks of ownership, ie the **lessor** is **responsible** for **servicing and maintaining** the leased equipment.

The risk of ownership is also minimised for the lessee because if there is a change in technology then the lessee can exit from the rental agreement at the end of the lease term and is therefore not tied in to using assets that are technologically out of date.

2.1.2 Leases that are purely a source of finance

Some leases are long-term arrangements that transfer the risks and rewards of ownership of an asset to the lessee. These are agreements between the lessee and the lessor for most or all of the asset's expected useful life.

The **lessee** is responsible for the **upkeep, servicing** and **maintenance** of the asset.

This can be a cheaper source of finance than a bank loan if the lessor buys a large quantity of assets (eg aircraft) and obtains bulk purchase discounts as a result; some of the savings from such discounts can be shared with the lessee in the form of lower rental payments.

2.2 Benefits of leasing

The **benefits of any type of lease to the lessee** include:

Benefits	Discussion
Availability	A firm that cannot get a bank loan to fund the purchase of an asset (**capital rationing** – see next section for further discussion); the same bank that refused the loan will often be happy to offer a lease.
Avoiding loan covenants	Loan covenants may act as a restriction on the ability of a company to borrow in future.

2.3 Numerical analysis

The benefits of leasing compared to using a loan to buy an asset can be assessed using a discounted cash flow approach.

Note that the assessment of the cost of the loan **should not include the interest repayments on the loan.**

For example, the NPV of the repayments on a loan for $10,000 that is repayable in one year at 10% interest is calculated as: $10,000 × 1.1 × 0.909 = $10,000.

The present value of the loan repayment is therefore **the same as the amount borrowed**. So, **the cost of a loan is simply the initial amount of the loan,** here $10,000.

2.3.1 Approach 1: Two separate NPVs

This evaluates the NPV of the cost of the loan and the NPV of the cost of the lease separately, and simply chooses the cheapest option.

Step 1 The **costs of leasing** using the post-tax cost of debt as the discount factor

This could include lease payments, and the tax saved on lease payments.

Step 2 The **costs of the loan** using the post-tax cost of debt as the discount factor

This could include the cost of the loan (ie the initial amount of the loan), netted against the savings from the scrap value of the asset and the tax saved on tax allowable depreciation.

Comparing step 1 to step 2 shows whether a lease or a bank loan is the cheaper cost of finance.

Illustration 2: Simple lease vs buy

Brown Co has decided to invest in a new machine which has a ten-year life and no residual value. The machine can either be:

- Purchased now for $50,000 with a bank loan; or
- It can be leased for ten years with lease rental payments of $8,000 per annum payable at the end of each year.

The cost of capital to be applied is 9% and taxation should be ignored.

Required

Compare the cost of the two financing options.

Solution

Present value of leasing costs

Cash is paid in time periods 1–10

PV = Annuity factor at 9% for 10 years × $8,000

= 6.418 × $8,000 = $51,344

Present value of purchase with a loan

This is simply the amount of the loan, ie $50,000.

If the machine was purchased now, it would cost $50,000 (the cost of a bank loan is simply the amount borrowed).

The purchase with a loan is therefore the least-cost financing option.

Exam focus point

Be careful with the timing of the cash flows with lease payments; sometimes lease payments are made at the start of the year (ie in advance). In the previous illustration this would mean that the cash flows would be received in time periods 0–9, which would affect the discount factor used.

2.3.2 Approach 2: Single NPV

An **alternative method** is to evaluate the NPV of the **cost and benefits of using a lease** in one calculation.

Step 1 The **costs of leasing**

This could include lease payments, and the opportunity costs of not buying the asset including lost tax allowable depreciation and lost scrap revenue.

Step 2 The **benefits of leasing**

By leasing, the lessee avoids the need to buy the asset and therefore saves money by not having to pay for the initial outlay (which, as discussed earlier, reflects the present value of the loan repayments that are saved). The lessee may also save on maintenance costs, if maintenance is provided by the lessor.

Step 3 Discount the net cash flows (ie the costs net of the benefits)

The **post-tax cost of debt** is used.

If the resulting NPV is positive, it means the **lease is cheaper than the post-tax cost of a loan.**

Exam focus point

A common error is to use the weighted average cost of capital (WACC) in a lease vs buy analysis. This is incorrect because the WACC is higher than the cost of debt because it is used to discount project cash flows that have a measure of risk; however, finance cash flows are not risky.

Remember to use the post-tax cost of debt for lease vs buy calculations.

Activity 2: Lease vs buy

A company has decided to undertake an investment project which involves the acquisition of a machine which costs $10,000. The machine has a five-year life with 0 scrap value; 20% straight-line writing down allowances are available.

It could finance the acquisition with a bank loan at 7.143% pre-tax and purchase the asset outright or make five equal lease payments of $2,500 in arrears.

Tax is 30% payable in the same year in which profits are made.

Required

Evaluate the lease from the lessee's viewpoint.

Solution

2.4 Benefits to the lessor

Attract customers	Companies (eg car makers) offer leases to attract customers to acquire their final product.
Returns on finance	The lessor **invests finance** by purchasing assets and making a **return** out of the lease payments from the lessee. The lessor will also get tax-allowable depreciation on the purchase of the equipment.

Essential reading

See Chapter 8 section 1 of the Essential reading, available in the digital edition of the Workbook, for more background information on this area.

The Essential reading is available as an Appendix of the digital edition of the Workbook.

3 Capital rationing

KEY TERM

Capital rationing: Arises when there is insufficient capital to invest in all available projects which have positive NPVs, **ie capital is a limiting factor.**

Exam focus point

In this exam, you only need to be able to analyse situations where this is a problem in a **single year**.

3.1 Reasons

Capital rationing arises for two main reasons:

(a) Hard capital rationing

This is where a firm cannot get finance from the capital markets, because:

- Investors are unwilling or unable to invest more equity finance, or
- Lending institutions consider an organisation to be too **risky** to be granted funds, or
- Capital markets are **depressed** and reluctant to lend to businesses because of fear of an economic downturn.

(b) Soft capital rationing

This is an internal management decision to restrict capital spending and may happen because:

- Management may be **reluctant to issue additional share capital** because of a concern that this may lead to outsiders gaining control of the business or due to the dilutive impact on earnings per share.
- Management may **not want to raise additional debt capital** because they do not wish to be committed to large fixed interest payments and want to keep the firm's gearing under control.
- Creating **competition for a limited pool of funds** encourages divisions to search for the very best possible projects.

Note that when an organisation adopts a policy that restricts funds available for investment, such a policy may be less than optimal as the organisation may reject projects with a positive NPV and forgo opportunities that would have enhanced the market value of the organisation.

3.2 Capital rationing techniques

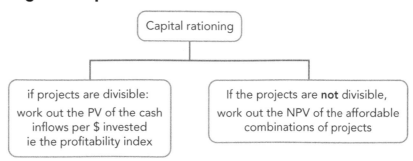

3.2.1 Divisible projects

> **Divisible projects:** A project that can be scaled down and done in part.

When projects are divisible, investment funds are a limiting factor and management should follow the decision rule of maximising the use of this limiting factor by selecting the projects whose cash inflows have the highest return (in present value terms) per $1 of capital invested. This is measured by the **profitability index (PI)**.

> ### Formula to learn
>
> The profitability index = Present value of cash inflows/Initial cash outflow.
>
> **The critical value of the PI is 1.** Any value above this indicates that the project has a positive net present value (ie the present value of the cash inflows is greater than the cash outflows); the higher the PI the higher the return delivered by a project per $1 invested.

Illustration 3: Profitability index

Suppose that Hard Times Co is considering four projects, W, X, Y and Z. Relevant details are as follows:

Project	Investment required	Present value of cash inflows	NPV	Profitability index (PI)	Ranking as per NPV	Ranking as per PI
	$	$	$			
W	(10,000)	11,240	1,240	1.12	3	1
X	(20,000)	20,991	991	1.05	4	4
Y	(30,000)	32,230	2,230	1.07	2	3
Z	(40,000)	43,801	3,801	1.10	1	2

Required

Calculate the NPV from investing in the optimal combination of projects if only $60,000 was available for capital investment.

Solution

If we adopt the profitability index approach, the selection of projects will be as follows:

Project	Priority	Outlay	
		$	
W	1st	10,000	
Z	2nd	40,000	
Y (balance)	3rd	10,000	(1/3 of $30,000)
		60,000	

Because only 1/3 of project Y can be afforded, this means that total NPV will be:

Project	NPV	
	$	
W	1,240	
Z	3,801	
Y (balance)	743	(1/3 of $2,230)
	5,784	

By choosing projects according to the PI, the resulting NPV (if only $60,000 is available) is $5,784.

3.2.2 Non-divisible projects

Non-divisible project: A project that must be undertaken completely or not at all; ie it is not possible to scale down the project and do it in part.

Where a project **cannot** be done in part, the choice facing a company is not how to spend each $1 so the **PI should not be used.**

The appropriate technique here is to:

- Identify which project combinations are **affordable**
- Select the project combination with the **highest NPV**

Exam focus point

The technique that needs to be applied depends on whether projects are divisible or not, so look out for this in assessment questions.

Illustration 4: Non-divisible projects

Short O'Funds has capital of $95,000 available for investment in the forthcoming period. The directors decide to consider projects P, Q and R only. They wish to invest only in whole projects.

Project	Investment required	Present value of inflows at 20%
	$'000	$'000
P	40	56.5
Q	50	67.0
R	30	48.8

Required

Which combination of projects will produce the highest NPV at a cost of capital of 20%?

Solution

The investment combinations we need to consider are the various possible pairs of projects P, Q and R.

The NPV of each affordable combination of projects is calculated as the total Present Value (PV) of inflows from each project minus the required investment for each project.

Projects	Required investment	PV of inflows	NPV from projects
	$'000		$'000
P and Q	90	123.5	33.5
P and R	70	105.3	35.3
Q and R	80	115.8	35.8

The highest NPV will be achieved by undertaking projects Q and R.

Activity 3: Capital rationing

A company has maximum capital to invest of $800,000. Five capital projects have been identified which are of similar risk. The initial analysis shows the following:

Project	Required initial outlay	NPV	Profitability index
No 1	$298,000	$128,000	1.4295
No 2	$240,000	$100,000	1.4166
No 3	$400,000	$160,000	1.4000
No 4	$160,000	$60,000	1.3750
No 5	$798,000	$239,000	1.3000

Projects cannot be postponed, and multiples of the same project are not allowed.

Required

What is the optimal combination of projects to maximise NPV, assuming:

(1) Projects are **divisible**? (Include a working to demonstrate how the profitability index numbers have been calculated for one of the projects.)

(2) Projects are **not divisible**?

Solution

3.3 Drawbacks of methods

The methods used for dealing with capital rationing make a number of assumptions. These can be regarded as limitations. These include:

- Capital rationing is for a **single period** only.
- Projects are **independent, ie** the success of one project is not affected if another project does not proceed.
- It is **not possible to delay** any projects.
- **Multiples** of a single project are **not allowed.**
- It is **not possible to share the investment** in any projects with another organisation (eg by forming a joint venture).

3.3.1 Practical points

The drawbacks of the methods hint at some practical issues that can be used to manage capital rationing, including:

(a) **Delaying one or more projects** to a subsequent period where capital rationing may be less of an issue.

(b) Finding **new sources of finance**, such as leasing or government grants to get around the unwillingness of capital markets to provide finance.

(c) Entering into a **joint venture** with a partner to share the capital outlay on one or more projects.

(d) Issuing **newcapital** (if soft capital rationing exists, this may be possible).

Essential reading

See Chapter 8 Section 2 of the Essential reading, available in the digital edition of the Workbook, for further practice on this area.

The Essential reading is available as an Appendix of the digital edition of the Workbook.

Chapter summary

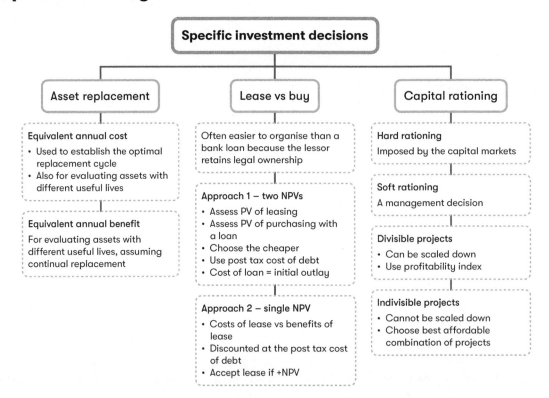

Specific investment decisions

Asset replacement

Equivalent annual cost
- Used to establish the optimal replacement cycle
- Also for evaluating assets with different useful lives

Equivalent annual benefit

For evaluating assets with different useful lives, assuming continual replacement

Lease vs buy

Often easier to organise than a bank loan because the lessor retains legal ownership

Approach 1 – two NPVs
- Assess PV of leasing
- Assess PV of purchasing with a loan
- Choose the cheaper
- Use post tax cost of debt
- Cost of loan = initial outlay

Approach 2 – single NPV
- Costs of lease vs benefits of lease
- Discounted at the post tax cost of debt
- Accept lease if +NPV

Capital rationing

Hard rationing

Imposed by the capital markets

Soft rationing

A management decision

Divisible projects
- Can be scaled down
- Use profitability index

Indivisible projects
- Cannot be scaled down
- Choose best affordable combination of projects

Knowledge diagnostic

1. Equivalent annual cost (or benefit)

Where assets are continually replaced, quantifying their costs (or benefits) over a replacement cycle allows the lifetime costs (or benefits) to be translated into a cost (or benefit) per year. This can be helpful in decision making where asset lives are different.

2. Lease vs buy

This should be evaluated using a post-tax cost of debt.

3. Divisible projects

The profitability index (PI) needs to be calculated to assess the optimal approach to investing where capital is rationed and projects are divisible.

4. Non-divisible projects

The PI approach cannot be used here, instead the best combination of projects needs to be identified using a trial and error approach.

5. Drawbacks of methods for managing capital rationing

The methods used assume that the capital rationing is for a single period only, that there is no interrelationship between the projects and that no project can be delayed.

Further study guidance

Question practice

Now try the following from the Further question practice bank (available in the digital edition of the Workbook):

Section A questions

Q22

Section C questions

Q49 Banden

Q50 ANT

Further reading

There is a useful Technical Article that is available on ACCA's website; it is called 'Equivalent annual costs and benefits'. We recommend that you read this article as part of your preparation for the FM exam.

Activity answers

Activity 1: EAC

Yearly cycles compared:

Every year	Time	0	1
	$	(30,000)	7,000
	DF @ 15%	1.0	0.870
	PV		6,090
	Total PV	23,910	
	Annuity factor for 1 year	0.870	
	EAC	(27,483)	

Every 2 years	Time	0	1	2
	$	(30,000)	(3,000)	3,000
	DF @ 15%	1.0	0.870	0.756
	PV	(30,000)	(2,610)	2,268
	Total PV	30,342		
	2-year annuity factor	1.626		
	EAC	(18,661)		

The two-year replacement cycle is cheaper.

Activity 2: Lease vs buy

Post-tax cost of debt = 7.143% x (1 - 0.3) = 5%

Tax allowable depreciation (TAD) = $10,000/5 = $2,000 per year

Tax saved on tax allowable depreciation = $2,000 × 0.3 = $600

Tax saved on lease payment = $2,500 × 0.3 = $750

Approach 1: two separate NPVs

Cost of a lease

	Time 0	Time 1–5
Lease		−2,500
Tax saved		750
Total		−1,750
DF 5%		4.329
PV		−7,576
NPV	**−7,576**	

Cost of purchase with a loan

	Time 0	Time 1–5
Outlay	(10,000)	
Tax saved on TAD		600
Total	(10,000)	600
DF 5%	1.000	4.329
PV	(10,000)	2,597
NPV	**−7,403**	

∴ the **lease is more expensive by $173**

Approach 2: one single NPV

Benefits and cost of lease

	Time 0	Time 1–5
Cost saved	10,000	
Tax benefit of TAD		−600
Lease		−2,500
Tax saved on lease		750
Total	10,000	−2,350
DF 5%	1.000	4.329
PV	10,000	−10,173
NPV	**−173**	

∴ the **lease is more expensive by $173**

Either approach 1 or approach 2 can be used; there is no need to use both.

Activity 3: Capital rationing

Calculations as follows:

(1)   Profitability index of project no 1 = (128,000 + 298,000)/298,000 = 1.4295

NPV per unit of limiting factor

Rank	Project	NPV per limiting factor	Outlay	Amount of project %	NPV
1st	No 1	1.4295	$298,000	100	$128,000
2nd	No 2	1.4166	$240,000	100	$100,000
3rd	No 3	1.4	$262,000	65.5	$104,800
			$800,000		**$332,800**

(2)   Project 5 gives an NPV of $239,000.

Cumulative NPV from Projects 1, 2 and 4 = $288,000

From projects 2, 3, 4 = $320,000 – **this is the best combination.**

Skills checkpoint 2

Technique for investment appraisal calculations

Chapter overview

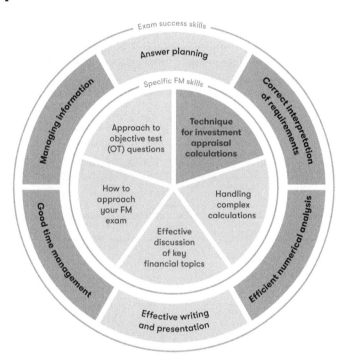

Introduction

Investing in a project with a positive NPV is consistent with the key objective of maximising shareholder wealth. You need to be able to complete an NPV calculation and analyse investments using a range of other techniques such as ROCE, IRR and payback.

Section D of the FM syllabus is 'Investment appraisal' and directly focuses on the skill of **'analysing investment decisions'**. The FM exam will normally contain a question in Section C that will focus on this syllabus area, so this skill is extremely important. OT questions covering investment appraisal can also appear in Sections A and B of the exam.

Analysis of investment decisions requires a sound knowledge of the techniques of investment appraisal. This means that as well as being able to apply techniques numerically you need to be able to discuss the reasons for applying them, compare the techniques and highlight their limitations.

An NPV calculation is normally quite time pressured to complete in the exam, so you need to be able to approach the question in a practical and time-efficient way, making good use of the spreadsheet functions available in the exam.

Skills checkpoint 2: Technique for investment appraisal calculations

FM Skill: Technique for investment appraisal calculations

The key steps in applying this skill are outlined below and will be explained in more detail in the following sections as the past exam question 'BQK' is answered.

> **STEP 1:**
>
> Use a standard NPV proforma. This will help the marker to understand your workings and allocate the marks easily. It will also help you to work through the figures in a methodical and time-efficient way.

> **STEP 2:**
>
> Input easy numbers from the question directly onto your proforma. This will make sure that you pick up as many easy marks as possible before dealing with more detailed calculations.

> **STEP 3:**
>
> Always use formulae to perform basic calculations. Don't write out your working in a single cell; this wastes time and you may make a mistake. Use the spreadsheet formulae instead!

> **STEP 4:**
>
> Show clear workings for any complex calculations.
> More complex calculations such as the tax relief on tax allowable depreciation will require a separate working. Keep your workings as clear and simple as possible and ensure they are cross-referenced to your NPV proforma.

Exam success skills

The following question is an extract from a past exam question; this extract was worth approximately 13 marks.

For this question, we will also focus on the following **exam success skills**:

- Managing information. It is easy for the amount of information contained in a Section C question to feel overwhelming. **Active reading** is a useful technique to use to avoid this. This involves focusing on the requirement first, on the basis that until you have done this the detail in the question will have little meaning.

- This is especially important in investment appraisal questions where there is likely to be a high level of numerical content and questions can be very confusing to read through unless you first have a clear idea of the nature of the required analysis.

- **Correct interpretation of requirements**. At first glance, it looks like the following question just contains one requirement. However, on closer examination you will discover that it contains two.

- **Efficient numerical analysis**. The key to success here is applying a sensible proforma for typical investment appraisal calculations, backed up by clear, referenced, workings wherever needed. Working through the numerical data in a logical manner will ensure that you stay focused.

- **Good time management**. Complete all tasks in the time available.

Skills activity

BQK Co, a house-building company, plans to build 100 houses on a development site over the next four years. The purchase cost of the development site is $4,000,000, payable at the start of the first year of construction. Two types of house will be built, with annual sales of each house expected to be as follows:

Year	1	2	3	4
Number of small houses sold:	15	20	15	5
Number of large houses sold:	7	8	15	15

Houses are built in the year of sale. Each customer finances the purchase of a home by taking out a long-term personal loan from their bank. Financial information relating to each type of house is as follows:

	Small house	Large house
Selling price:	$200,000	$350,000
Variable cost of construction:	$100,000	$200,000

Selling prices and variable cost of construction are in current price terms, before allowing for selling price inflation of 3% per year and variable cost of construction inflation of 4.5% per year.

Fixed infrastructure costs of $1,500,000 per year in current price terms would be incurred. These would not relate to any specific house, but would be for the provision of new roads, gardens, drainage and utilities. Infrastructure cost inflation is expected to be 2% per year.

BQK Co pays profit tax one year in arrears at an annual rate of 30%. The company can claim tax-allowable depreciation on the purchase cost of the development site on a straight-line basis over the four years of construction.

BQK Co has a real after-tax cost of capital of 9% per year and a nominal after-tax cost of capital of 12% per year.

Required

Calculate the net present value of the proposed investment and comment on its financial acceptability. Work to the nearest $1,000. **(13 marks)**

STEP 1 Use a standard NPV proforma. This will help the marker to understand your workings and allocate the marks easily. It will also help you to work through the figures in a methodical and time-efficient way.

This is a 13-mark question and at 1.8 minutes a mark, it should take approximately 23 minutes.

Using a standard NPV proforma will help you to work through the information in the question in a methodical, time efficient way.

Your proforma should look like this:

	A	B	C	D	E	F	G
1		**0**	**1**	**2**	**3**	**4**	**5**
2		**$'000**	**$'000**	**$'000**	**$'000**	**$'000**	**$'000**
3	Revenue						
4	Variable costs						
5	Fixed costs						
6	Taxable CF						
7	Tax @ 30%						
8	Tax relief on TAD						
9	Capital cost						
10	Net CF						
11	DF @ 12%						
12	PV						
13	NPV						
14							
15	***Workings***						
16							
17							
18							

STEP 2   Input easy numbers from the question directly onto your proforma. This will make sure that you pick up as many easy marks as possible before dealing with more detailed calculations.

There are some easy numbers from the question that you can download straight onto your proforma such as the capital cost of the investment, fixed costs and using the nominal cost of capital to discount. This will ensure that you pick up some easy marks before dealing with more complex calculations.

STEP 3   Always use formulae to perform basic calculations. Do not write out your working in a single cell; this wastes time and you may make a mistake. Use the spreadsheet formulae instead!

For inflated fixed costs shown in the following spreadsheet in year 1, the marker will be able to see your working very clearly by clicking on cell D5 for example and viewing the spreadsheet formulae.

This means that there is no value in spending time on detailed explanations of these simple calculations in rows 16 and 17.

D5			fx	=C5*1.02			
	A	B	C	D	E	F	G
1		0	1	2	3	4	5
2		$'000	$'000	$'000	$'000	$'000	$'000
3	Revenue		5,614	7,214	9,015	7,034	
4	Variable costs						
5	Fixed costs		-1530	-1561	-1592	-1624	
6	Taxable CF						
7	Tax @ 30%						
8	Tax relief on TAD						
9	Capital cost	-4000					
10	Net CF						
11	DF @ 12%	1	0.893	0.797	0.712	0.636	0.567
12	PV						
13	NPV						
14							
15	*Workings*						
16	Fixed costs	-1500	-1530	-1561	-1592	-1624	
17			x 1.02	x 1.02	x 1.02	x 1.02	
18							

STEP 4 Show clear workings for any **complex calculations.**

More complex calculations such as the tax relief on tax allowable depreciation will require a separate working. Keep your workings as clear and simple as possible and ensure they are cross-referenced to your NPV proforma.

Clear workings are needed here for sales revenue and variable costs.

Take information from the question, such as selling price and the quantity of each type of house sold, into a clear working. Make use of the spreadsheet formulae to calculate total revenue and link the cell from your working back into the NPV proforma. This makes it easier for your marker to clearly follow through your logic.

For example, we can clearly see from the working that revenue for year 3 is the total of small house and large house sales, inflated at 3% for three cumulative years.

	D28	▼	:	×	✓	fx	=D27*1.03*1.03*1.03		

	A	B	C	D	E
19	**Revenue**				
20	*Year*	*1*	*2*	*3*	*4*
21	Small houses selling price	200	200	200	200
22	Small houses sales quantity	15	20	15	5
23	Small house revenue	3000	4000	3000	1000
24	Large houses selling price	350	350	350	350
25	Large houses sales quantity	7	8	15	15
26	Large house revenue	2450	2800	5250	5250
27	Total sales revenue	5,450	6,800	8,250	6,250
28	Inflated sales revenue	5,614	7,214	9,015	7,034

Exam success skills diagnostic

Every time you complete a question, use the diagnostic below to assess how effectively you demonstrated the exam success skills in answering the question. The table has been completed below for the 'BQK' activity to give you an idea of how to complete the diagnostic.

Exam success skills	Your reflections/observations
Managing information	Did you identify that the cash flows were given in real terms and that you would need to build in inflation each year?
Correct interpretation of requirements	You need to calculate the NPV and comment on whether it is financially acceptable. Did you remember to comment?
Efficient numerical analysis	Did your answer present a neat NPV in a proforma that would have been easy for a marker to follow?
Good time management	Did you manage your time to ensure you tackled all workings and completed the NPV in the time available?
Most important action points to apply to your next question	

Summary

Section C of the FM exam could contain a question that focuses on investment appraisal and asks you to perform an NPV calculation.

This is an important area to revise and to ensure that you understand the variety of techniques available (including their limitations).

It is also important to be aware that in the exam you are dealing with detailed calculations under timed exam conditions and time management is absolutely crucial. You therefore need to ensure that you:

- Use a clear, standard NPV proforma.
- Use spreadsheet formulae to perform basic calculations.
- Score well on the easier parts of the question
- Show clear workings for more complex areas.

Remember that there are no optional questions in the FM exam and that this syllabus section (investment appraisal) will definitely be tested!

9

Sources of finance

Learning objectives

On completion of this chapter, you should be able to:

	Syllabus reference
• Identify and discuss the range of short-term sources of finance available to businesses, including overdraft, short-term loan, trade credit, lease finance	E1(a)
• Identify and discuss the range of long-term sources of finance available to businesses, including: equity finance, debt finance, lease finance, venture capital	E1(b)
• Identify and discuss methods of raising equity finance, including: rights issue, placing, public offer, stock exchange listing	E1(c)

• Identify and discuss methods of raising short- and long-term Islamic finance, including:
  - major differences between Islamic finance and other forms of business finance.
  - the concept of riba and how returns are made by Islamic financial securities.
  - Islamic financial instruments available to businesses including: murabaha, ijara, mudaraba, sukuk, musharaka. (note: calculations are not required)
	E1(d)

Exam context

The financing decision is a key part of financial management and is covered in Section E of the syllabus. This syllabus section is covered in Chapters 9–12 and can be tested in any part of the exam, including Section C where one of the questions normally focuses on this syllabus area.

From this chapter, you may be asked to describe appropriate sources of finance for a company, or to discuss in general terms the characteristics of different types of short-term, long-term and Islamic finance. The mechanics of a rights issue are especially important. This chapter is examinable in all sections of the exam.

Chapter overview

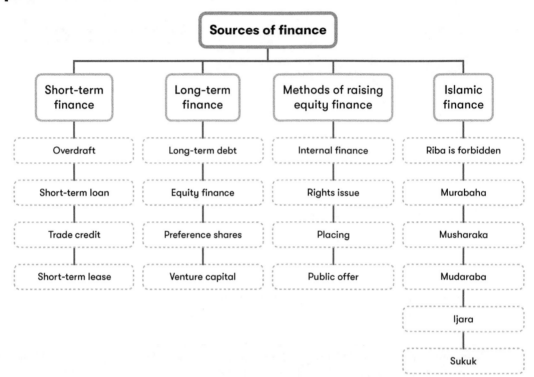

1 Short-term finance

Chapter 4 considered the use of short-term finance as part of a **matching policy** to finance **fluctuating current assets**.

As noted in Chapter 4, **short-term finance is usually cheaper** than long-term finance, so some companies adopt an '**aggressive**' approach and rely mainly on short-term finance as part of an **aggressive working capital finance strategy**. Here we briefly review types of short-term finance.

> **PER alert**
>
> Performance objective 10 requires you to 'source short-term finance to improve an organisation's liquidity'. You can apply the knowledge from this chapter to help to demonstrate this competence.

1.1 Types of short-term finance

Overdraft	The bank grants an overdraft facility (usually for a fee). This facility can be used by the borrower (up to an agreed limit) but does not have to be.
	Overdrafts are the most important source of short-term finance available to businesses. They can be arranged relatively **quickly** and offer a level of **flexibility** with regard to the amount borrowed at any time, while interest is only paid when the account is overdrawn.
	Overdrafts are repayable on demand.
Short-term loan	This is drawn in full at the beginning of the loan period and repaid at a specified time or in defined instalments.
	Once the loan is agreed, the **term of** the loan must be **adhered** to, provided that the customer does not fall behind with their repayments.
	It is not repayable on demand by the bank.
Trade credit	A major source of short-term finance for a business. Current assets such as raw materials may be purchased on credit, and this therefore represents an interest-free short-term loan.
	However, it is important to take into account the **loss of discounts** suppliers may offer for early payment.
	Unacceptable delays in payment will worsen a company's **credit rating** and additional credit may become difficult to obtain.
Short-term lease	Rather than buying an asset outright, using either available cash resources or borrowed funds, a business may **lease** an asset. Leasing is a popular source of finance.
	Leasing was covered in the previous chapter.

Essential reading

See Chapter 9 Section 1 of the Essential reading, available in the digital edition of the Workbook, for more background information on this area.

The Essential reading is available as an Appendix of the digital edition of the Workbook.

2 Long-term finance

Where finance is required over a longer time period, it is possible to rely on short-term finance and to renew it so that it provides finance over a longer time period. However, this exposes the borrower to the risk that this short-term finance may not be available (or may be expensive) at the point that it is being renewed. For this reason, it is more likely that a source of long-term finance will be appropriate where finance is required over a longer time period.

Where a long-term investment is being considered by a firm, there is a strong argument for **matching** the term of the investment to the term of the finance by using long-term finance because:

(a) The **returns being generated by the investment may be required to repay the debt**.

If returns are being gradually generated by a project over, for example, ten years, then it may be difficult to repay a loan that matures in four years (so a ten-year loan may be more appropriate).

(b) A loan whose maturity date was longer than the term of the investment would **expose the company to a potentially unnecessarily long period over which interest repayments must be made**.

Here, we briefly review the types of long-term finance that are available, some of which have already been introduced in Chapter 2. Chapter 12 will then consider the advisability of using different mixtures of these sources of long-term finance, most notably the mix of long-term debt and equity finance, ie the capital structure.

2.1 Long-term debt finance

2.1.1 Bank loans

To obtain a bank loan a firm may need to:

- Present a convincing **business plan** (including information on cash flow forecasts, the management team and investment proposals)
- Provide security by either a **fixed or floating charge** against a firm's assets or provide **personal collateral**, eg director's home.

Because the bank will be committing its funds to a customer for several years, it may insist on building certain written safeguards, **known as loan covenants,** into the loan agreement, to prevent the customer from becoming overextended with their borrowing during the course of the loan.

> **Loan covenant:** A condition that the borrower must comply with. If the borrower does not act in accordance with the covenants, the loan can be considered in **default** and the bank can demand payment.

Examples of loan covenants include:

- **Positive covenants**

Maintaining certain levels of particular financial ratios, eg the debt/equity ratio, interest cover ratio – note that **interest cover** is calculated as:

$$\frac{\text{Profit before interest and tax (or operating profit)}}{\text{Interest paid}}$$

- **Negative covenants**

Limit a borrower's behaviour, eg prevent borrowing from another lender, disposal of key assets, paying dividends above a certain level, acquiring another company.

Activity 1: Debt covenants

A company is funded by 5 million $1 equity shares and a $10 million bank borrowing carrying a fixed rate of interest of 10%.

The bank borrowing carries a covenant specifying the following two conditions:

(1)   Interest cover limit of 2.5

(2)   Debt/cash flow from operations limit of 3

The company currently has no other debt finance and the rate of corporate income tax is 20%.

The company is about to borrow $5 million at an interest rate of 12% in order to fund a new project. The project is expected to increase annual operating profit by 20% from its current level of $4 million and annual cash flow from operations by 15% from its current level of $5 million.

The directors wish to assess the impact of the new financing and investment decisions on the bank covenants before commencing with the project.

Required

What will be the impact on the bank covenants?

O   Covenant (1) breached, Covenant (2) not breached

O   Covenant (1) not breached, Covenant (2) breached

O   Covenant (1) breached, Covenant (2) breached

O   Covenant (1) not breached, Covenant (2) not breached

Solution

2.1.2   Loan notes

Following the banking crisis of 2008–9, **banks have generally been more cautious about lending to companies.** This has led to an increase in the use of loan notes as a source of finance. In Chapter 2 we saw that bypassing bank finance is sometimes referred to as **disintermediation.**

Conventional loan notes are **fixed rate IOUs that are sold on the Stock Market**; they are also referred to as **bonds or debentures.**

Real life example

Here is an example of a loan note that was issued in 2013 by Royal Dutch Shell.

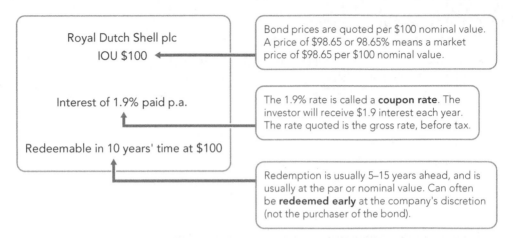

Royal Dutch Shell plc
IOU $100

Bond prices are quoted per $100 nominal value. A price of $98.65 or 98.65% means a market price of $98.65 per $100 nominal value.

Interest of 1.9% paid p.a.

The 1.9% rate is called a **coupon rate**. The investor will receive $1.9 interest each year. The rate quoted is the gross rate, before tax.

Redeemable in 10 years' time at $100

Redemption is usually 5–15 years ahead, and is usually at the par or nominal value. Can often be **redeemed early** at the company's discretion (not the purchaser of the bond).

Features of loan notes	
Coupon rate	The coupon rate is fixed at the time of issue and will be set according to **prevailing market conditions** given the **credit rating** of the company issuing the debt.
Marketable	The ability to sell the debt can mean that investors accept a **lower return compared to the cost of a bank loan**.
Redeemable	Loan notes are **normally** redeemable. Some loan notes are **'irredeemable'** or **'undated'**. These are often called perpetual bonds and are normally issued by banks.
Secured	Loan notes are normally secured – if unsecured, they are likely to carry **debt covenants** (see earlier). Investors are likely to expect a **higher yield** with unsecured bonds to compensate for the extra risk.

KEY TERM

Convertible loan notes: Give the loan note holders the right (but not an obligation) to convert their loan notes at a specified future date **into new equity shares** of the company, at a conversion rate that is also specified when the loan notes are issued.

The possibility of the convertible loan note holders being able to sell these shares at a favourable price means that **the coupon rate of interest is often considerably lower than on similar conventional loan notes.**

If the loan note **holders** choose not to convert their loan notes into shares, the loan notes will be redeemed at maturity, as for a conventional loan note.

The current **market value** of ordinary shares into which a loan note may be converted is known as the **conversion value**. The **conversion value** will be below the value of the loan note at the date of issue but will be expected to increase as the date for conversion approaches, on the assumption that a company's shares ought to increase in market value over time.

Conversion ratio = number of shares a single convertible loan note can be converted to

Conversion value = Conversion ratio × market price per share

KEY TERM

Conversion premium: Conversion premium = Current market value of loan note – current conversion value of shares

A company will aim to issue loan notes with the **greatest possible conversionpremium**, as this will mean that for the amount of capital raised it will, on conversion, have to issue the lowest number of new ordinary shares. The premium that will be accepted by potential investors will depend on the company's growth potential and so on prospects for a sizeable increase in the share price.

Activity 2: Convertible loan notes

Cleethorpe Co has a 3% convertible bond in issue, with a nominal value of $100. Each bond can be converted into 25 ordinary shares at any time over the next 3 years. The bond is currently trading at $120 (ex-interest), and the share price is currently $3.80.

Required

Answer the following questions.

(a) Calculate the conversion value.

(b) Calculate the conversion premium, and comment on its meaning.

(c) Discuss why Cleethorpe may have issued a convertible bond.

Solution

2.1.3 Long-term lease

Long-term leases have been covered in the previous chapter.

2.2 Equity finance

Equity capital refers to finance provided by the owners of the business, and as such normally refers to the capital invested by **ordinary shareholders.**

Ordinary shareowners have the right to vote on directors' appointments, and to receive a share of any dividend that is agreed by the board. The mechanics of raising equity finance are **discussed later in this chapter.**

2.3 Preference shares

Preference shareholders **receive dividends, normally at a fixed rate**; some preference shares will also pay an extra dividend as a fixed percentage of the ordinary dividend (in this case they are called participating preference shares).

Here is an example of a preference share that Barclays Bank has issued.

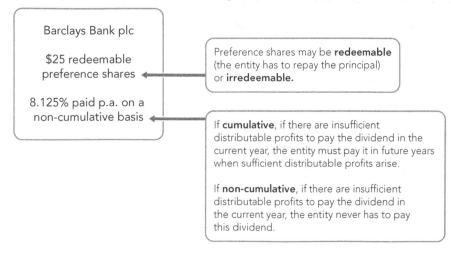

Advantages of preference shares	
Compared to debt	Compared to ordinary shares
More flexible than debt finance (if losses are made, the dividend is not paid).	**No dilution of control** (preference shares carry no voting rights except in exceptional circumstances, eg a proposed liquidation).

Disadvantages of preference shares	
Compared to debt	Compared to ordinary shares
No tax relief is received on dividend payments, whereas debt interest reduces taxable profit and therefore attracts tax relief.	**Creates extra risk** for ordinary shareholders because the preference dividend has to be paid before the ordinary dividend.

2.4 Venture capital

KEY TERM

> **Venture capital:** Risk capital, normally provided by a venture capital firm or individual venture capitalist, in return for an equity stake.

Venture capitalists seek to invest cash in return for shares in private companies with high growth potential. They seek a **high return**, which is often realised through a stock market listing, and accept that this will mean that the investments are often **high risk**.

Venture capital may be invested in young start-up companies but is more commonly invested in small companies that already have a track record of business development and which need additional finance to grow. These companies may have borrowed as much money as their banks are prepared to lend, and do not have enough equity capital (from the existing owners or retained profits) to expand at the rate or scale required.

Failure to hit targets set by the venture capitalist can lead to extra shares being transferred to their ownership at no additional cost. This is called an **equity ratchet**.

Essential reading

See Chapter 9 section 2 of the Essential reading, available in the digital edition of the Workbook, for more background information on this area.

The Essential reading is available as an Appendix of the digital edition of the Workbook.

3 Methods of raising equity finance

Companies often decide to **retain cash** within the business to finance their investment needs (instead of paying this cash to shareholders as a dividend). This cash represents equity finance because it could have been paid out to shareholders and is a significant source of equity finance.

For larger projects it may be necessary to raise **new equity** by **issuing new ordinary shares**.

There are three main ways of issuing new shares:

(1) A rights issue	A legal right for **existing shareholders**
(2) A placing	Shares are issued at a fixed price to **institutional investors**
(3) A public offer	An offer for sale **to the public,** either at a fixed price or by tender

3.1 Rights issues

Rights issue: In a rights issue, ordinary shareholders are invited to apply for shares **in proportion to their existing shareholdings.**

In a rights issue, shareholders have a number of choices; they can:

- Buy the new shares
- Sell their 'right' to buy shares
- Do a mix of the above

A rights issue will normally be at a significant discount (eg 20%) to the existing share price, so the share price after the rights issue will be below the pre-rights share price. However, this does not in itself damage shareholder wealth because shareholders also benefit from buying the shares at a discount (or by selling the rights).

Real life example

In March 2014 Babcock, the UK defence support and engineering services group, agreed to acquire helicopter transport services firm Avincis, funding the deal with a £1.1bn rights issue.

The fully underwritten rights issue offered shareholders **5 new shares at 790p for every 13 held**.

This was a 40% discount to the share price. It is normal for rights issues to be priced at a significant discount to the current share price to create the **impression** that shareholders are getting a bargain.

Rights issues are cheaper than a public share issue, but underwriting costs are still significant (approximately 2% of the amounts raised).

Cum rights price: A 'cum rights' price means that the purchaser of existing shares has the **right to participate** in the rights issue (ie the price prior to the rights issue).

Issue price: The price at which the new shares are being offered for sale.

Theoretical ex-rights price (TERP): The theoretical price **after** the rights issue.

Value of a right: The price at which a right can be sold (calculate as TERP – issue price).

Value of a right per existing share: The value of a right divided by the number of shares that need to be possessed in order to own a right.

Illustration 1: TERP

Fundraiser has 1,000,000 ordinary shares of $1 in issue, which have a market price on 1 September of $2.10 per share. The company decides to make a rights issue and offers its shareholders the right to subscribe for one new share at $1.50 each for every four shares already held. After the announcement of the issue, the share price fell to $1.95, but by the time just prior to the issue being made, it had recovered to $2 per share.

Required

What is the theoretical ex-rights price?

Solution

Value of the portfolio for a shareholder with four shares before the rights issue:

	$
4 shares @ $2.00	8.00
1 share @ $1.50	1.50
5 shares	9.50

So, the value per share after the rights issue (or TERP) is 9.50/5 = $1.90.

The value of rights is the theoretical gain a shareholder would make by exercising their rights.

Here, the **value attaching to a right** is $1.90 – $1.50 (issue price) = $0.40. A shareholder would therefore be expected to gain 40 cents for each new share they buy.

If they do not have enough money to buy the share themselves, they could sell the right to subscribe for a new share to another investor and receive 40 cents from the sale. This other investor would then buy the new share for $1.50, so that their total outlay to acquire the share would be $0.40 + $1.50 = $1.90, the theoretical ex-rights price.

The following formula can be used **but is not essential**

TERP = [(N × cum-rights price) + Issue price]/(N+1)

Where N is the number of shares required to have the right to buy 1 new share

Using the formula: TERP = [(4 x $2) + $1.50]/(4 + 1) = $1.90

The **value of rights attaching to existing shares** is calculated in a similar way.

If the value of rights on a new share is 40 cents, and there is a one for four rights issue, the value of the rights attaching to each existing share is 40/4 = 10 cents.

Activity 3: Fantasia

Fantasia plc is an all equity financed company specialising in animated films. It needs to raise $164m and has decided on a rights issue at a discount of 18% to its current market price.

Currently Fantasia has 500 million shares in issue and a market price of $2.00/share.

Required

Answer the following questions.

(a) Calculate the terms of the rights issue.

(b) Calculate the theoretical ex-rights price (the price after the rights issue).

(c) Calculate the value of a right and the value of a right per existing share

(d) Assess the impact on the wealth of a shareholder who owns 10,000 shares and can only afford to take up half of their rights

Solution

> ### Exam focus point
>
> A question could ask for discussion of the effect of a rights issue, as well as calculations.

3.2 Placing

The cheapest and quickest way of raising equity from new investors is to sell large blocks of shares at a fixed price to a narrow **group of external institutional investors**.

3.3 Offer for sale – fixed price

Here, a prospectus is produced outlining the company's future plans and past performance. The issue is advertised in the national press and is normally underwritten. This is normally used for larger share issues. A **placing** does not incur such significant underwriting and advertising costs.

3.4 Offer for sale – tender

Here, no prior issue price is announced; instead shareholders are invited to bid for shares at a variety of different prices. The share issue is underwritten at a guaranteed minimum price. This is designed to minimise the risk of under-pricing the share issue.

 Essential reading

See Chapter 9 section 3 of the Essential reading, available in the digital edition of the Workbook, for more discussion of the motives for, and mechanics of, stock exchange listings.

The Essential reading is available as an Appendix of the digital edition of the Workbook.

4 Islamic finance

Islamic finance is finance that is compliant with Sharia law. Islamic finance has gone through a period of rapid growth in recent years.

4.1 Principles of Islamic finance

Islamic finance transactions are based on the concept of **sharing risk and reward** between the investor and the user of funds.

'Conventional' finance providers make a profit from the difference between interest paid on money deposits and interest received from money lent to customers. However, making profits by lending alone and the charging of interest (**riba**) is forbidden under **Sharia law**. Making money with money is considered to be immoral, and wealth should be generated via trade or investments.

Islamic finance is arranged in such a way that the **bank's profitability is closely tied to that of the client**. The bank stands to take profit or make loss in line with the projects they are financing and as such must be more involved in the investment decision-making.

4.2 Islamic financial instruments

Financial instrument	Explanation
Murabaha (trade credit)	This is a deferred payment sale or an instalment credit sale. It is used mainly for the purchase of goods (eg materials) for immediate delivery on deferred payment. The seller of the asset delivers the goods immediately and the buyer pays for the goods later. To be Sharia compliant a sales contract must satisfy the object in question and its exchange may not be prohibited by Sharia.
Musharaka (joint venture)	This is a **partnership agreement** whereby all partners provide capital and know-how. Profits are **shared** according to a pre-agreed contract. There are no dividends paid. **Losses are shared according to capital contribution**.
Mudaraba (equity)	A contract in which one of the partners (investor) contributes capital and the other (manager) contributes skills and expertise. The partner who contributes capital has no or little involvement in operational decisions and is liable up to the level of capital they provided. Profits are shared in a pre-agreed ratio and **losses are solely attributable to the investor**.
Ijara (leasing)	The lessor is still the owner of the asset and incurs the risk of ownership. This means that the lessor will be responsible for major maintenance and insurance. The lessee must take responsibility for day-to-day maintenance, wear and tear and damage, however.

Financial instrument	Explanation
Sukuk (bonds)	Similar to a bond but in Islamic finance, there is an underlying tangible asset. The Sukuk holder shares in the risk and rewards of ownership, which gives a Sukuk properties of equity as well as debt.

Activity 4: Islamic finance

Dana and Ali have signed a partnership contract that is Sharia compliant. Dana has contributed all the capital and Ali will contribute the expertise and management know-how. Profits will be shared in a ratio of 3:1 between Dana and Ali respectively. In the first year the partnership venture makes a loss of $10,000.

Ali also holds a sukuk which is linked to the future profits of a property which is co-managed with Farid. Under the contract Ali has the right to 20% of the net income from the property. In the first year the property generated a loss of $12,500.

Required

1   What kind of Sharia'a compliant contract do Dana and Ali have between them?

   O   Mudaraba

   O   Musharaka

   O   Ijara

   O   Sukuk

2   How much of the business loss will be attributed to Dana and Ali respectively?

   O $7,500 to Dana, $2,500 to Ali

   O $2,500 to Dana, $7,500 to Ali

   O $10,000 to Dana, none to Ali

   O $5,000 to Dana, $5,000 to Ali

3   How much of the loss on the property will be attributed to Ali?

   O   Nil

   O $2,500

   O $6,250

   O $12,500

Solution

Essential reading

See Chapter 9 section 4 of the Essential reading, available in the digital edition of the Workbook, for more background information on this area.

The Essential reading is available as an Appendix of the digital edition of the Workbook.

Chapter summary

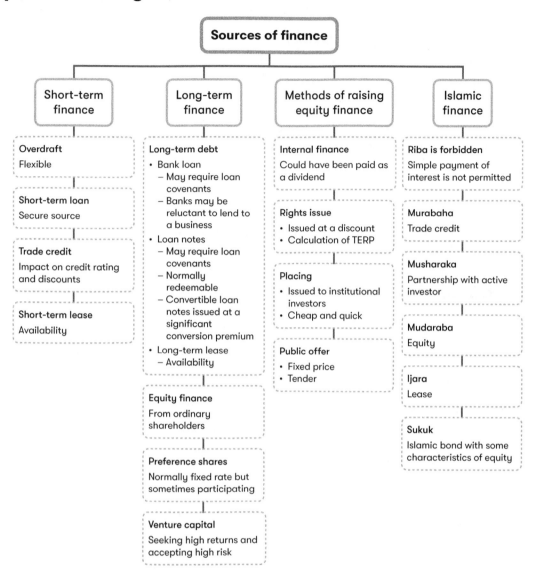

Sources of finance

Short-term finance

Overdraft
Flexible

Short-term loan
Secure source

Trade credit
Impact on credit rating and discounts

Short-term lease
Availability

Long-term finance

Long-term debt
- Bank loan
  - May require loan covenants
  - Banks may be reluctant to lend to a business
- Loan notes
  - May require loan covenants
  - Normally redeemable
  - Convertible loan notes issued at a significant conversion premium
- Long-term lease
  - Availability

Equity finance
From ordinary shareholders

Preference shares
Normally fixed rate but sometimes participating

Venture capital
Seeking high returns and accepting high risk

Methods of raising equity finance

Internal finance
Could have been paid as a dividend

Rights issue
- Issued at a discount
- Calculation of TERP

Placing
- Issued to institutional investors
- Cheap and quick

Public offer
- Fixed price
- Tender

Islamic finance

Riba is forbidden
Simple payment of interest is not permitted

Murabaha
Trade credit

Musharaka
Partnership with active investor

Mudaraba
Equity

Ijara
Lease

Sukuk
Islamic bond with some characteristics of equity

Knowledge diagnostic

1. Short-term finance and working capital

Short-term finance is most appropriate for financing short-term cash flow needs such as working capital fluctuations. A variety of forms of short-term finance exist, each with different advantages and disadvantages.

2. Long-term finance

Long-term finance is most appropriate for financing long-term cash flow commitments such as capital investments. A variety of forms of long-term finance exist, each with different advantages and disadvantages.

3. Loan notes

Loan notes are a key type of long-term debt finance. Convertible loan notes are a type of loan note that allows firms to issue debt that pays a low coupon rate. Convertible loan notes are issued at a conversion premium.

4. Accessing equity finance

This will often require the issue of new shares via a rights issue, a placing or a public offer. A rights issue will normally be at a significant discount to the existing share price, so the theoretical ex-rights price will be below the pre-rights share price. However, this does not in itself damage shareholder wealth because shareholders also benefit from buying the shares at a discount (or by selling the rights).

5. Islamic finance

This requires investors to share risk and return with the company that they are investing in – simply charging interest is not allowed.

Further study guidance

Question practice

Now try the following from the Further question practice bank (available in the digital edition of the Workbook):

Section A questions

Q23–24

Section C questions

Q51 Sagitta

Further reading

There is a useful Technical Article available on ACCA's website, called 'Introduction to Islamic finance'. We recommend that you read this article as part of your preparation for the FM exam.

Activity answers

Activity 1: Debt covenants

The correct answer is: Covenant (1) not breached, Covenant (2) not breached

Interest cover:

Operating profit = $4m × 1.2 = $4.8m

Interest = ($10m × 10%) + ($5m × 12%) = $1.6m

Interest cover = $4.8m/$1.6m = 3

Covenant is an interest cover limit of 2.5, therefore the interest cover needs to exceed 2.5, which it does. **Covenant not breached.**

Debt/Cash flow from operations:

Debt = $10m + $5m = $15m

Cash flow from operations = $5m × 1.15 = $5.75m

Debt/Cash flow from operations = $15m/$5.75m = 2.6

Covenant is a limit of 3, therefore Debt/(Cash flow from operations) needs to be **below** 3 which it is. **Covenant not breached.**

Activity 2: Convertible loan notes

(a)   25 × $3.80 = $95

(b)   Conversion premium = market value of bond – conversion value:

$120 – $95 = $25 or $25/$95 = 26.3%.

The share price would have to rise by 26.3% before the conversion rights became attractive; if this premium is set too high then the convertible bond may not be popular with investors.

(c)   It may be cheaper than a straight loan. It may be preferred to an issue of equity if equity is currently undervalued.

Activity 3: Fantasia

(a) $2.00 × 0.82 = $1.64

So $164m/1.64 = 100m shares

A 1 for 5 rights issue is needed at $1.64

(b)   Using the formula: 1/6 [(5 × $2) + $1.64] = $1.94

Alternatively, not using formula:

Value before rights issue

500m shares × $2 = $1,000m

Rights issue

100m shares × $1.64 = $164m

Value after rights issue

600m shares worth $1,164m

So TERP = $1,164m/600m shares = $1.94

(c)   Value of a right = TERP – issue price = $1.94 – $1.60 = $0.30

Value of a right per existing share = $0.30/5 = $0.06 per existing share

(d) Pre-rights issue, wealth = 10,000 × $2 = $20,000

After the issue

After the rights issue	$
Existing shares = 10,000 × $1.94	19,400
New shares (half of 2,000 entitlement) = 1,000 x $1.94	1,940
Less payment for these shares = 1,000 x $1.64 =	(1,640)
Sale of rights (half of 2,000 entitlement) = 1,000 × $0.30 value of a right = $300	300
Total	20,000

There is no impact on shareholder wealth (ie shareholders are not harmed because they can sell their rights).

Alternatively, the sale of the rights can be calculated as number of shares to which the 'rights' are being sold × value of a right per existing share, ie 5,000 × 0.06 = $300.

Activity 4: Islamic finance

1   The correct answer is: Mudaraba

A partnership where one partner contributes capital and the other contributes management expertise.

2   The correct answer is: $10,000 to Dana, none to Ali

Losses in a mudaraba contract are attributed to the investor partner and none to the manager partner.

3   The correct answer is: $2,500

Losses are attributed to the sukuk holders in the same way as profits.

Dividend policy

10

Learning objectives

On completion of this chapter, you should be able to:

	Syllabus reference
• Identify and discuss internal sources of finance, including:	E1(e)

- retained earnings
- increased working capital efficiency
- the relationship between dividend policy and the financing decision
- the theoretical approaches to, and practical influences on, the dividend decision including legal constraints, liquidity, shareholder expectations and alternatives to cash dividends.

Exam context

In the previous chapter we looked at **external** sources of finance. In this chapter we will consider **internal** finance in the form of surplus cash.

There is a clear link between financing decisions and the wealth of a company's shareholders. **Dividend policy** plays a big part in a company's relations with its equity shareholders, and a company must consider how the stock market will view its results.

The dividend decision is another key part of Financial Management. You may be asked to describe the factors affecting dividend policy in a discussion element of a question in Section C of the exam for a significant number of marks.

Chapter overview

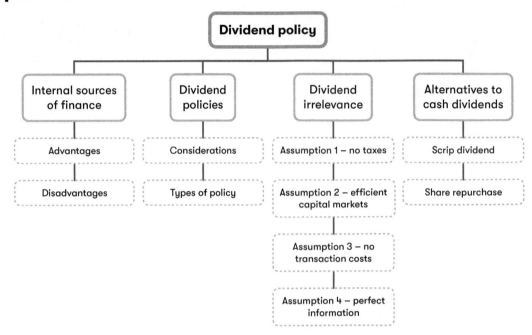

1 Internal sources of finance

If a business is generating surplus **cash** from its operations, then this is an obvious and potentially important source of 'internal' finance (remember that a profitable business may not necessarily be generating surplus cash if its capital expenditure is high).

Linking back to the working capital section of the syllabus, it is important not to forget that internal finance can be generated from more efficient management of trade receivables, inventory, and trade payables.

1.1 Advantages and disadvantages of internal finance

The **main advantages** of internal finance are that it is **immediately available** and is obtained **without the need to pay issue costs**.

However, this **does not mean that internal finance is 'free'**.

The **main disadvantage** of using internal finance is that this cash could have been paid out as a dividend and that in that sense represents the use of shareholders' funds (equity). As we will see in the next chapter, shareholder funds (ie equity) are an **expensive source of finance** in the sense that shareholders expect high returns.

Shareholders may, in fact, prefer surplus cash to be returned to them as a **dividend.**

Essential reading

See Chapter 10 section 1 of the Essential reading, available in the digital edition of the Workbook, for more background information on this area.

The Essential reading is available as an Appendix of the digital edition of the Workbook.

2 Dividend policies

When deciding on the amount of dividend to pay out to shareholders, two of the main considerations of the directors will be the amount of cash needed to meet **investment needs** and the implications of the payment of a dividend for a company's **financing needs**. Other practical considerations will also need to be considered.

2.1 Investment decision

If the company is going through a growth phase, it is unlikely to have sufficient **liquidity** to pay dividends because of the need to invest in non-current assets.

In this case, **shareholder expectations** may well be for the dividend to remain low or zero. This will not be a problem for them if the investments being made are creating value for shareholders and therefore increasing the share price.

2.2 Financing decision

If a company can finance its investments by borrowing, it can finance its investments and still pay dividends as long as it has accumulated net realised profits. However, there may problems associated with higher borrowing levels; these are considered in Chapter 12.

2.3 Shareholder expectations

At its simplest, increases in dividend are seen as a positive sign by shareholders, although sometimes a fall in dividends can be interpreted as a positive signal if it indicates that attractive investment opportunities are being pursued.

Whatever the level of the dividend, if it is not at the level expected by shareholders then this creates an unexpected signal that something is wrong, and this **failure to meet shareholder expectations** will generally cause the share price to fall.

Because **shareholders do not have the same information** as directors about the future prospects of company, the dividend declared can be interpreted as a **signal** from directors to shareholders about the strength of underlying project cash flows.

This means that where possible it is generally better for a company to follow a **consistent dividend policy.**

2.4 Types of policy

Policy	Explanation
Constant payout ratio	Payment of a constant % of profit as a dividend is logical but can create volatile dividend movements if profits are unstable.
Stable growth	Dividends are increased at a level that directors think is sustainable; this signals the growth prospects of the company.
Residual policy	A dividend is paid only if all +NPV projects have been funded. This is often used by companies which have difficulty raising debt finance.

2.5 Life cycle issues

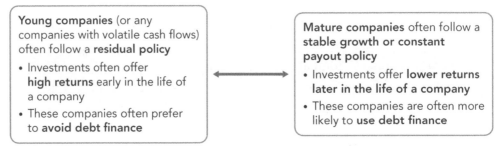

Young companies (or any companies with volatile cash flows) often follow a **residual policy**
- Investments often offer **high returns** early in the life of a company
- These companies often prefer to **avoid debt finance**

Mature companies often follow a **stable growth or constant payout policy**
- Investments offer **lower returns later in the life of a company**
- These companies are often more likely to **use debt finance**

As discussed earlier, whichever policy is formulated, this should be consistent. If a policy is consistent it will attract shareholders who prefer that particular policy; this is sometimes called a clientele effect.

Essential reading

See Chapter 10 section 2 of the Essential reading, available in the digital edition of the Workbook, for more background information on this area.

The Essential reading is available as an Appendix of the digital edition of the Workbook.

3 Dividend irrelevance theory

Modigliani and Miller (M&M) proposed that in a tax-free world, shareholders are **indifferent** between dividends and capital gains, and the value of a company is determined solely by the 'earning power' of its assets and investments. This is sometimes referred to as **dividend irrelevancy theory** (Modigliani and Miller, 1961).

This theory implies that the dividend policy that a company chooses to follow **does not matter.**

Real life example: Dividend irrelevancy 1

A company with attractive investment opportunities **decides to cut the dividend**, to finance these investments.

This does not matter to shareholders because if shareholders do require cash, they can **manufacture dividends** by selling shares which will have risen in value because of the investments.

The **increase in the value of the shares compensates for the loss of dividend.**

Real life example: Dividend irrelevancy 2

A company with attractive investment opportunities **decides to pay a dividend**, so that it requires external finance to fund some/all of its investments.

Although shareholders will have the benefit of receiving the dividend, the shortfall in funds will be made up by **obtaining additional funds** from outside sources. As a result of obtaining outside finance there will be a loss in the value of the firm to the original shareholders.

The loss in value will be equal to the amount of dividend paid, so shareholders have not gained or lost out overall compared to Example 1.

3.1 Assumptions of M&M dividend irrelevancy theory

M&M made a number of simplifying assumptions:

Assumptions
No taxes exist
Capital markets are perfectly efficient: eg funds will always be made available to finance attractive (ie + NPV) investments.
No transactions costs: eg in issuing new shares, or taking out a bank loan, or selling shares.
Information is fully and freely available to shareholders.

Exam focus point

In the real world, dividends do seem to matter which suggests that the case in favour of the relevance of dividend policy is a strong one. Note that this area could be a discussion part of a section C question and was tested in this way in the specimen (pilot) exam.

3.2 Limitations of M&M dividend irrelevancy theory

The arguments **against** M&M's view that dividend policy is irrelevant as a means of affecting shareholders' wealth reflect the **unrealistic nature of the assumptions** made:

Assumptions	Criticism of assumptions (ie limitations)
No taxes exist	**Differing rates** of **taxation** on **dividends** and **capital gains** can create a **preference** for either a **high dividend** or **high earnings retention**. This is one of the key reasons why different clientele are attracted by different dividend policies.
Capital markets are perfectly efficient	Companies may find that funds are **not** always available to finance attractive investments. Where capital rationing is an issue, **dividend retention** may be **preferred** by companies.
No transactions costs	Because of **transaction costs** on the sale of shares, investors who want some cash from their investments will prefer to receive dividends rather than to sell some of their shares to get the cash they want.
Information is fully and freely available	Shareholders are often not fully aware of the **future investment plans** and **expected profits** of their company. Even if management were to provide them

Assumptions	Criticism of assumptions (ie limitations)
	with profit forecasts, these forecasts would not necessarily be accurate or believable unless backed up with a signal of confidence in the form of a rising dividend. So, shareholders may **prefer a current dividend** to future capital gains (or deferred dividends) because the future is more uncertain. This is known as the **bird-in-the-hand** theory.

Activity 1: Dividend irrelevancy

The following information relates to Gerrin Co.

	20X5	20X6	20X7
Earnings after tax ($'000)	25,000	28,000	37,000
Preference dividend	(1,000)	(1,000)	(1,000)
Ordinary shares in issue ('000)	10,000	14,000	14,000
Ordinary dividend per share ($)	0.588	0.42	0.42
Capital expenditure	6,000	72,000	17,000

Gerrin Co has high debt levels and has been unable to take on any new debt over this period.

In 20X6 Gerrin Co's investment plans had to be scaled back because of capital rationing issues.

The following statements have been made in relation to Gerrin Co's dividend policy.

(1) The company is pursuing a dividend policy consistent with Modigliani and Miller's irrelevancy theory.

(2) The company's total dividend payout has fallen between 20X5 and 20X7.

Required

Which of these statements is/are true?

O   (1) only

O   (2) only

O   Both (1) and (2)

O   Neither (1) nor (2)

Solution

4 Alternatives to cash dividends

4.1 Scrip dividends

KEY TERM

> **Scrip dividend:** A dividend paid by the issue of additional company shares, rather than by cash.

A scrip (or share) dividend may be offered to existing shareholders either as a choice (ie a choice between shares or cash) or as an alternative to a cash dividend.

From a company's point of view, this has the following advantages and disadvantages:

Advantages	Disadvantages
If taken up by shareholders, it will conserve cash. This is useful when liquidity is a problem, or when cash is needed for investment.	If the dividend per share is maintained or increased, in future years the total cash payment will increase.
Due to an increase in issued shares, it could lead to a decrease in gearing. This will increase debt capacity.	Due to an increase in supply of shares, the price of an individual share may fall.

4.2 Share repurchases

As an alternative to a cash dividend, a company can choose to return significant amounts of cash to shareholders by means of a **share repurchase** (or share buy-back).

Share repurchase may be appropriate in the following circumstances:

- If there is one-off cash surplus generated from asset sales (higher dividends would increase expectations of further increases).
- The company wants to give an exit route to disaffected shareholders; in this sense it is a defence against a takeover.

Chapter summary

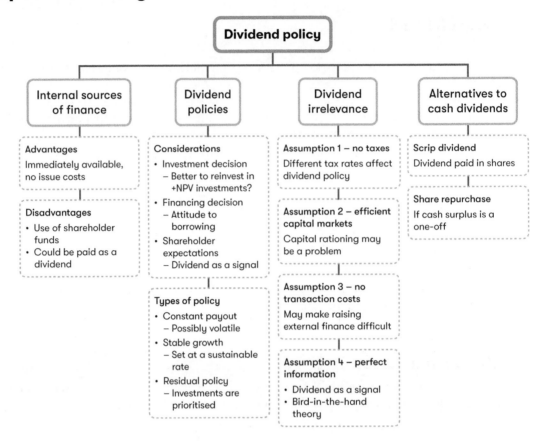

Dividend policy

Internal sources of finance

Advantages
Immediately available, no issue costs

Disadvantages
• Use of shareholder funds
• Could be paid as a dividend

Dividend policies

Considerations
• Investment decision
  – Better to reinvest in +NPV investments?
• Financing decision
  – Attitude to borrowing
• Shareholder expectations
  – Dividend as a signal

Types of policy
• Constant payout
  – Possibly volatile
• Stable growth
  – Set at a sustainable rate
• Residual policy
  – Investments are prioritised

Dividend irrelevance

Assumption 1 – no taxes
Different tax rates affect dividend policy

Assumption 2 – efficient capital markets
Capital rationing may be a problem

Assumption 3 – no transaction costs
May make raising external finance difficult

Assumption 4 – perfect information
• Dividend as a signal
• Bird-in-the-hand theory

Alternatives to cash dividends

Scrip dividend
Dividend paid in shares

Share repurchase
If cash surplus is a one-off

BPP LEARNING MEDIA

Knowledge diagnostic

1. Internal finance is not a free source of finance

Using surplus cash carries an implied cost because it represents the use of shareholders' funds.

2. Different policies

Whichever policy is chosen needs to fit the life cycle of a company and need to be consistent.

3. Life cycle

Normally, dividends are likely to rise over the course of a business's life. In its early years cash flows will be more volatile so external borrowing will be less suitable.

4. Dividend irrelevancy

M&M suggest that dividend policy is irrelevant - however this is based on a number of flawed assumptions and does not seem to be true in reality.

5. Alternatives to cash dividends

If liquidity is poor, then scrip dividends may be appropriate.

If liquidity is unusually high, then a share repurchase may be suitable.

Further study guidance

Question practice

Now try the following from the Further question practice bank (available in the digital edition of the Workbook):

Section A questions

Q25

Section C questions

Q53 ABC

Further reading

There is a useful Technical Article available on ACCA's website, called 'Dividend theory'. We recommend that you read this article as part of your preparation for the FM exam, although it touches on Business Valuation and therefore may be more sensible to read after covering Chapter 13 of this workbook.

Activity answers

Activity 1: Dividend irrelevancy

The correct answer is: Neither (1) nor (2)

If the policy was consistent with Modigliani and Miller's theory, there would be no dividend in 20X6 because there were investment opportunities available then that were not funded.

The total payout is constant. In 20X5 it was 10,000 × $0.588 = $5,880 and in 20X6 and 20X7 the dividend payout was 14,000 × $0.42 = $5,880.

The cost of capital

Learning objectives

On completion of this chapter, you should be able to:

	Syllabus reference

• Estimate the cost of equity including:
   - application of the dividend growth model, its assumptions, advantages and disadvantages
   - explanation and discussion of systematic and unsystematic risk
   - relationship between portfolio theory and the capital asset pricing model
   - application of the CAPM, its assumptions, advantages and disadvantages.
	E2(a)

• Estimating the cost of debt including irredeemable debt, redeemable debt, convertible debt, preference shares and bank debt	E2(b)

• Estimating the overall cost of capital including:
   - distinguishing between average & marginal cost of capital (Chapter 12)
   - calculating WACC using book value and market value weightings.
	E2(c)

• Describe the risk-return relationship and the relative costs of equity and debt.	E3(a)
• Describe the creditor hierarchy and the relative costs of sources of finance.	E3(b)

• Impact of cost of capital on investments including:
   - relationship between company value and cost of capital.
   - circumstances under which WACC can be used in investment appraisal
	E3(e)

Exam context

This chapter covers 'estimating the cost of capital' and 'sources of finance and their relative costs' which are important parts of Section E of the syllabus (Business Finance).

This is an important chapter that is commonly examined in all sections of the exam. In Section C of the exam you may be asked to calculate the **weighted average cost of capital.** Questions won't just involve calculations; you may be asked to discuss the problems with the methods you have used, or their meaning.

The formulae in this chapter are challenging at first, but most are given in the exam and so don't have to be memorised. With practice you will become familiar with them.

Chapter overview

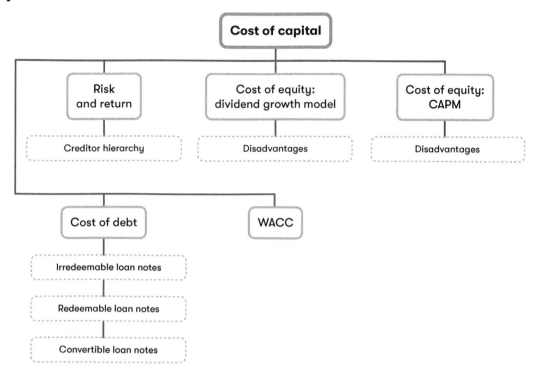

1 Risk and return

To calculate a net present value (NPV), a cost of capital is needed. In this chapter you will see an approach to calculating a cost of capital or, to put it another way, to assessing the return demanded by investors.

The main principle is that the higher the risk faced by the investor, the higher the return they will expect to be paid; this is the risk-return relationship.

1.1 Risk-return relationship

The cost of finance will depend on the level of risk that an investor is taking when they provide funds to a company. **The higher the risk faced, the higher the return that will be expected.**

In reality, **different types of investors will face different levels of risk.**

1.1.1 Debt finance

Providers of debt finance will face relatively low risk, because:

- it is obligatory to make interest payments (unlike dividend payments) each year
- in the event of liquidation debt holders are paid off before providers of share capital.

Debt is especially low risk if:

- it is **secured** on a specific asset (called a fixed charge)
- it is **secured** on the general assets of a business (a floating charge)
- it is due to be repaid in the **short-term**.

Since debt is a relatively low risk source of finance then the return expected by providers of debt will be relatively low, so **debt is a relatively cheap source of finance.**

In addition, debt interest is also corporation **tax deductible** (unlike preference dividends or equity dividends), making it even cheaper to a taxpaying company.

1.1.2 Preference shareholders

Preference shareholders face higher risk because a dividend will only be paid if it can be afforded after the providers of debt have been paid, and because in a liquidation the debt holders will be paid before preference shareholders receive anything.

1.1.3 Ordinary shareholders

Equity (ordinary) shareholders face the highest risk because a dividend will only be paid after the providers of debt and preference shareholders have been paid, and because in a liquidation the debt holders and preference shareholders will be paid before ordinary shareholders receive anything. Therefore, **equity is a relatively expensive source of finance.**

1.1.4 Creditor hierarchy

The differing risk levels faced by investors is sometimes described by the creditor hierarchy. This shows that, in the event of a company being unable to pay its debts and going into liquidation, there is an order in which it must repay its creditors and investors.

1. Creditors with a fixed charge

2. Creditors with a floating charge

3. Unsecured creditors

4. Preference shareholders

5. Ordinary shareholders

(Increasing risk)

1.2 Implications and terminology

The **cheapest finance is debt** (especially if secured and short-term) – the return expected by debtholders is denoted by the term **Kd** or r_d.

The **most expensive finance is equity** (ordinary shares)– the return expected by shareholders (ie the cost of equity) is denoted by the term **Ke** or r_e.

The **cost of preference shares** will be above the cost of debt and below the cost of equity – this is denoted by **Kpref** or **Kp**.

Essential reading

See Chapter 11 section 1 of the Essential Reading, available in the digital edition of the Workbook, for more background information on this area.

The Essential reading is available as an Appendix of the digital edition of the Workbook.

1.3 Reverse yield gap

On rare occasions, shareholders may be prepared to receive **lower** yields than lenders. In the short-term shareholders may be willing to accept low short-term rewards (dividend yield) in the hope of getting greater gains later. It can also arise if firms that are desperate to raise finance offer a yield on their debt in excess of the yield on shares. This called a reverse yield gap and was covered in Chapter 2.

2 The cost of equity (1) – the dividend growth model

Shareholders often expect a dividend to be paid at the end of the year. This is referred to as D_1 (ie the dividend in 1 years' time) or as $D_0(1 + g)$ (where D_0 is the latest dividend paid and g is the annual dividend growth rate).

Shareholders will also expect further dividend growth in future years.

By looking at how much shareholders are prepared to pay for a share today (Po), it is possible to estimate the return that they are expecting using the following formula (which is given in the exam):

$$r_e = \frac{D_0(1+g)}{P_0} + g$$

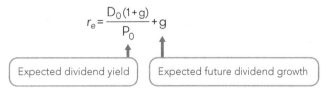

If the expected return is not achieved by a firm then its **share price will fall** which will damage shareholder wealth.

Illustration 1: Dividend growth model

A share has a current market value of 96c, and the last dividend was 12c. The expected annual growth rate of dividends is 4%.

Required

Calculate the cost of equity capital.

Solution

Cost of equity

$$= \frac{12(1.04)}{96} + 0.04$$

= 0.13 + 0.04

= 0.17

= 17%

Activity 1: Dividend growth model

Wright Co has just paid a dividend of 60c and has a market value of $5.50. The dividend growth rate is 8%.

Required

What is Wright Co's cost of equity?

○ 11.8%

○ 21.2%

○ 18.9%

○ 19.8%

Solution

2.1 Assumptions of the dividend growth model

This model makes a number of assumptions, which may not always be valid and therefore can be viewed as weaknesses.

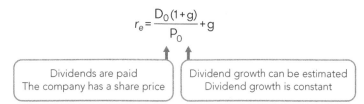

$$r_e = \frac{D_0(1+g)}{P_0} + g$$

Dividends are paid
The company has a share price

Dividend growth can be estimated
Dividend growth is constant

2.1.1 Cum div and ex div share prices

If there is a **dividend about to be paid** the share price is said to be cum div.

In this case, the share price needs to be adjusted by stripping the dividend out of the share price to create an ex div price.

This is needed because the real investment being made by the shareholder is not the cum div price paid for the share if they will immediately receive a dividend.

If the share price is ex div (which is normally the case) then there is no imminent dividend and therefore this adjustment does not need to be made.

2.2 Estimating the dividend growth rate (g)

If the dividend growth rate is not given in the question, you may need to calculate it.

There are two methods of estimating dividend growth that you need to know.

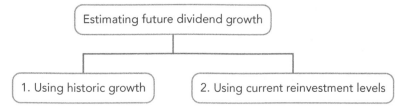

Estimating future dividend growth

1. Using historic growth

2. Using current reinvestment levels

2.2.1 Using historic growth

The future growth rate can be predicted from an **analysis of the growth in dividends** over the past few years.

Real life example: Historic growth

Year	Dividend per share
	$
20X1	1.50
20X2	1.92
20X3	2.06
20X4	2.45
20X5	2.62

Dividends have risen from $1.50 in 20X1 to $2.62 in 20X5. The increase represents four years' growth. (Check that you can see that there are four years' growth, and not five years' growth, in the table.)

The (geometric) average growth rate, g, may be calculated as follows.

Dividend in 20X1 × $(1 + g)^4$ = Dividend in 20X5

∴ $(1 + g)^4$ = Dividend in 20X5/Dividend 20X1 = $2.62/1.50 = 1.747

$$1 + g = \sqrt[4]{1.747} = 1.15$$

Alternatively

$1 + g = 1.747^{1/4} = 1.15$

$\therefore$ g = 0.15, ie 15%

The growth rate over the last four years is assumed to be expected by shareholders into the indefinite future.

Clearly using historic data to predict future growth assumes that past growth achieved is an indication of future growth potential; this may not always be valid.

Formula to learn

$$1 + g = \sqrt[n]{\dfrac{\text{latest dividend}}{\text{earliest dividend}}}$$

or

$$1 + g = \left(\dfrac{\text{latest dividend}}{\text{earliest dividend}}\right)^{\frac{1}{n}}$$

Where n = the number of growth periods

Exam focus point

If you are using a spreadsheet to calculate historic growth, it is easiest to use the second of the above formulae. Note that:

(a)   The ^ symbol is used to 'raise to the power of'

(b)   1/n should either be input in brackets ie as (1/n) or as a decimal.

Activity 2: Historic growth

PB Co

Today is 1 January 20X7.

PB Co has just paid a dividend of 39.25 cents per share. Its current share price is $8.31, ex div. Previous dividends have been paid on 31 December as follows:

20X2	30.00c
20X3	32.40c
20X4	35.40c
20X5	36.50c

Required

What is the growth rate to be used in PB plc's cost of equity calculation?

O   6.76%

O   6.95%

O   14.38%

O   30.83%

Solution

2.2.2 Using current reinvestment levels

The future growth rate can be predicted from an analysis of the amount of profit being re-invested into a business and the expected return on this investment.

 Formula provided

A formula is provided in the exam to enable you to apply this method:

$g = br_e$

where b = balance (%) of profits reinvested and r = return on reinvested funds

Note that br_e means $b \times r_e$

 Real life example: Current reinvestment levels

If a company retains 65% of its earnings for capital investment projects it has identified, and these projects are expected to have an average return of 8%, then dividend growth can be estimated as:

$g = br_e = 65\% \times 8\% = 5.2\%$

 Activity 3: Exam standard

RB Co

RB Co's current cum div share price is $1.45, which will fall to $1.25 after the dividend is paid. RB Co's dividend payout ratio is 60% and the expected return on funds that are reinvested is 30%.

Required

What is the cost of equity of RB Co?

- O 29.92%
- O 36.88%
- O 17.92%
- O 28.00%

Solution

Essential reading

See Chapter 11 section 2 of the Essential reading, available in the digital edition of the Workbook, for more background information on this area.

The Essential reading is available as an Appendix of the digital edition of the Workbook.

3 The cost of equity (2) – using CAPM

The **other method** of calculating the cost of equity (K_e or r_e) is by using the **capital asset pricing model (CAPM)**.

This model is based on portfolio theory which assumes that investors diversify their investments across a wide portfolio to reduce their exposure to risk.

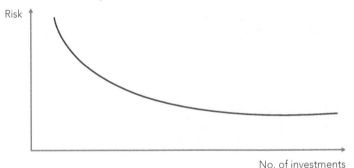

The benefits of diversification can be seen from this graph. Risk (as measured by the standard deviation of the returns from the investment portfolio) decreases rapidly at first as the number of investments rises. The shape of the graph suggests that the benefits of further diversification become marginal after a diverse portfolio has been created (approximately 15-20 investments).

3.1 Unsystematic risk

The reason for the reduction in risk shown in the graph above, is that the impact of **company-specific risks** is spread over the whole investment portfolio (and may actually create benefits to other parts of the portfolio).

> **Unsystematic (or specific) risk:** The component of risk that is associated with investing in a particular company.

KEY
TERM

3.2 Systematic risk

Although diversification helps the investor to eliminate virtually all of the risks that are unique to particular industries or types of business, it does not offer any escape from general market factors that can affect all companies.

For example, a recession will normally have an adverse effect on every company.

> **Systematic (or market) risk:** The component of risk that will still remain even if a diversified portfolio has been created.

The presence of unsystematic and systematic risk is illustrated below:

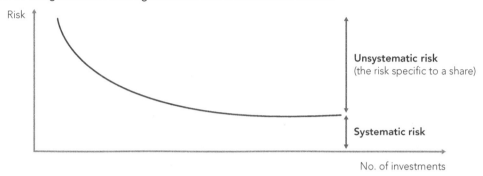

This illustrates that a diversified investor will **only be concerned with systematic risk**. Investors are therefore assumed to be only exposed to the risk that there is a fall in the stock market as a whole.

However, some firms' shares are more sensitive to market downturns than others are. The sensitivity of a firm's share price to a stock market downturn is calculated by measuring the **average change in the return on a share each time there is a change in the stock market as a whole**. This measure is called a beta factor.

Exam focus point

Common errors on this topic in exams include:

- Mixing up systematic and unsystematic risk. Remember that the stock market is a 'system' so systematic risk is linked to movements in the stock market.

3.3 Beta factors

> **Beta factors:** Measures the average change in the return on a share each time there is a change in the stock market as a whole.

3.3.1 Range of beta factor values

Increasing risk →

Beta factor < 1	Beta factor = 1	Beta factor > 1
Below average risk	Average risk	Above average risk
Moves in the same direction as the market, but not by as much	Moves in line with the market	Moves in the same direction as the market, but by more
(eg a stock with a ß of 0.2 would increase by only 0.2% if the market increased by 1%).	(if the market rises by 1% then that security is expected to rise by the same amount).	(eg a stock with a ß of 1.5 would fall by 1.5% if the market suffered a 1% drop).
The return expected by shareholders will be less than the market average as risk is less than the market average.	The return expected by shareholders will be the same as the market average.	The return expected by shareholders will be more than the market average as risk is more than the market average.

3.4 Cost of equity

The CAPM makes use of the principle that **returns on shares** in the **market** as a whole are expected to be higher than the returns on risk-free investments (such as Treasury Bills).

The difference between the market return and the risk-free return is called a **market or equity risk premium**.

For example, if the return on government stocks is 3% and market returns are 8%, the market risk premium is 5%.

> **Market risk premium/equity risk premium:** This is the difference between the expected average market return and the risk-free rate of return over the same period.

The market risk premium shows the **excess return for the market as a whole to compensate for systematic risk**.

To calculate the extra return required to compensate for the risk of an individual share **the market risk premium is multiplied by that share's beta factor**.

The CAPM is shown on your formula sheet as:

Formula provided

$$E(r_i) = R_f + \beta(E(r_m) - R_f)$$

$E(r_i)$ = expected return (eg Ke)

β = the beta of the investment

R_f = risk free rate

r_m = market return

$(E(r_m) - R_f)$ = market risk premium

Illustration 2: CAPM

Shares in Louie Co have a beta of 0.9. The expected market return is 10% and the risk-free rate of return is 4%.

Required

What is the cost of equity capital for Louie Co?

Solution

$E(r_i) = R_f + \beta(E(r_m) - R_f) = 4 + 0.9(10 - 4) = 9.4\%$

Activity 4: CAPM Technique demonstration

The market risk premium is 8%, and the risk-free rate is 3%:

Required

1   What is the required rate of return on a share with an equity beta of 1.6?

2   What is beta factor of a company that has a cost of equity of 10%?

Solution

Exam focus point

Mixing up the terms market return and market risk premium is a common error on this topic in exams.

3.5 Drawbacks of CAPM

Drawbacks	Discussion
Single period model	CAPM does not adjust for different planning horizons. In reality investors will demand a longer return for investment that have a longer planning horizon.
Estimating the beta factor	Beta values are **historic** and will not give an accurate measure of risk if the firm has recently changed its gearing or its strategy. The impact of gearing on beta factors is covered in the **next chapter**.
Other risk factors	It has been argued the CAPM ignores the impact of: • Size of the company (the extra risk of failure for small companies) • The ratio of book value of equity to market value of equity (shares with book values that are close to their market values are more likely to fail)
Assumes diversified portfolios	A beta factor measures systematic risk. However, if shareholders do not hold diversified portfolios then they are exposed to both systematic and unsystematic risk.

3.6 CAPM compared to the dividend growth model

Despite these drawbacks, CAPM is generally perceived as being **a more robust and stable method for calculating the cost of equity,** compared to the dividend growth model.

This is because CAPM gives a **clear link between risk and expected return,** and also because CAPM **does not rely on potentially inaccurate estimates of the future dividend growth rate.**

Essential reading

See Chapter 11 section 3 of the Essential Reading, available in the digital edition of the Workbook, for more background information on this area.

The Essential reading is available as an Appendix of the digital edition of the Workbook.

4 Cost of debt

We have seen that different types of debt have different costs because they will expose investors to different levels of risk. Here we cover how to calculate the cost of debt for different types of debt finance.

4.1 Cost of irredeemable loan notes

Irredeemable (undated) loan notes entitle the holder to receive interest over an indefinite period.

Loan notes are bought on the stock market (like shares) and so an approach that **is similar to the dividend growth model** can be used (however the return is in the form of interest not dividend and there is no growth as the interest is at a fixed rate).

The **formula used here is not given in the exam** but is an **adaption of the dividend growth formula** used earlier (which is given in the exam):

Formula to learn

$$K_d(\text{pre - tax}) = \frac{I}{P_0}$$

I = interest paid

P_0 = market value of the debt

Illustration 3: Irredeemable loan notes ignoring tax

Chappy Co has 8% undated loan notes in issue that are trading at 82% of their nominal value of $100.

Required

What is the cost of debt?

Solution

Cost of irredeemable debt = 8/82 = 9.8% (ignoring tax)

4.1.1 Impact of corporation tax

When a company pays interest, this will reduce its taxable profits which reduces the tax paid on its profits. This has the impact of reducing the net cost of the debt to the company.

The formula then needs to be adapted to include the tax saving:

Formula to learn

$$K_d(\text{post - tax}) = \frac{I(1-t)}{P_0}$$

where t is the tax rate and P_0 is the market value of debt ex-interest.

Activity 5: Technique demonstration

Recalculate the cost of debt for Chappy Co (see previous illustration) given that tax on profits is at 20%.

Solution

4.2 Cost of redeemable debt

Redeemable (dated) loan notes entitle the holder to receive interest over a **defined period**.

Loan notes are bought on the stock market (like shares) and are normally redeemed at their par or nominal value. However, because they are sold to investors at the market price there will normally be a capital gain or loss when they are redeemed. This capital gain/loss on redemption is not captured by the dividend growth model approach, so another approach is needed to assess the cost of redeemable debt.

> ### Exam focus point
>
> (a) Easiest to assess one unit of $100 debt, not the total amount of debt in $000s.
> (b) Tax only affects the cost of the interest payments, not the debt's market value or its redemption value.

4.2.1 Internal rate of return (IRR) approach

In earlier chapters you have used internal rate of return (IRR) to calculate the percentage return given by a project. The same technique can be applied to assess the cost of redeemable debt.

Here, instead of asking what % return is being delivered by a project (the approach taken in Chapter 5), we are asking what % cost is being incurred by using debt.

As with project appraisal, the IRR approach requires the cash flows to be laid out for each year. For redeemable debt the cash flows will be the market value of the debt (this is received by the company), the post-tax interest (paid by the company) and the cash flow (paid by the company) on redemption.

For example, the cashflows from a two-year redeemable loan note are:

Time	0	1	2
	Market value	(Interest × [1 − tax])	(Interest × [1 − tax])
			(Redemption value)

In a computer-based exam the **'=IRR'** spreadsheet function can be used to calculate the IRR. This was covered in Chapter 5.

Alternatively, the IRR formula can be used - this is less important but can be useful if two NPVs are provided in an OT question or if you prefer using this approach.

Formula to learn

IRR formula

$$IRR = a\% + \left(\frac{NPV_a}{NPV_a - NPV_b}\right) \times (b\% - a\%)$$

Activity 6: Redeemable debt

Now is 1 January 20X5.

Willco plc has $100,000 5% 20X8 redeemable loan notes in issue.

Interest is paid annually on 31 December. The ex–interest market value of a loan note on 1 January 20X5 is $90 and the loan notes are redeemable at a 5% premium.

Tax on profits is 20%.

Required

What is the cost of debt?

Solution

4.2.2 CAPM approach

Redeemable loan notes are traded and have a market price. This means a beta factor can be calculated for a loan note.

If an exam question gives you a debt beta, then the cost of debt can be estimated using the CAPM.

Illustration 4: Debt beta and the cost of debt

If the market return is expected to be 10% and the risk-free rate is 5%, on debt which has a debt beta of 0.3.

Required

What is the cost of debt to the company if the tax rate is 20%?

Solution

$r_D = 5 + 0.3 \times (10 - 5) = 6.5\%$

This is the pre-tax return on the debt, so you need to multiply by (1-t) to create a post-tax cost of debt:

$6.5\% \times (1 - 0.2) = \underline{5.2\%}$

4.3 Cost of convertible debt

Convertible debt is debt that can be converted, if the debtholders wish, to equity in the future.

The approach to analysing convertible debt is the same as for redeemable debt except that you will have to use information in the question to analyse whether or not the debt will be converted into shares in the future.

Real life example: Convertible debt

If, in the previous activity on redeemable debt, debtholders had the right to convert each $100 nominal value of debt into 20 shares and you were told to assume that the share price at the redemption date was $4, conversion of debt into shares would not happen (because 20 shares would be worth $80 which is less than the amount available on redemption) and the calculations would therefore not change.

However, if the share price was $6 then conversion would happen (because 20 shares would be worth $120 which is more than the amount due on redemption) so you would need to redo the IRR using the same approach but based on these cash flows (note that the cash on redemption is the market value of the share + interest in time 4):

Time	0	1	2	3	4
Per $100	90	(4)	(4)	(4)	(124)

The =IRR approach shows that the cost of convertible debt is now 11.5% compared to its previous 8.1% when the debt was simply redeemable.

This illustrates the **hidden cost of convertible debt**, because if it is converted into shares (because the share price is high) the company will have to purchase these shares and supply them to convertible debtholders, and this will cost more than simply redeeming the debt.

So, despite the interest cost on convertible debt normally being lower than on redeemable debt, the ultimate cost to the company of using convertible debt may turn out to be high.

4.4 Cost of preference shares

A preference shareholder will receive a fixed income (ie it **does not grow**), based upon the nominal value of the shares held (not the market value).

These dividends, whilst fixed and hence showing debt characteristics, are paid out of post-tax profits and therefore **do not** receive tax relief.

The cost of preference share capital can be calculated adapting the dividend valuation model (which is given in the exam).

$$r_e = \frac{D_0(1 + g)}{P_0} + g$$

Setting the dividend growth rate to zero (because preference dividends are fixed) the dividend growth formula simplifies to:

$$\frac{D_0}{P_0}$$

Activity 7: Cost of preference shares

A company has $100,000 12% preference shares in issue. The nominal value of these shares is $1.

The market value today of the shares is $1.25. A dividend has recently been paid.

Required

Calculate the cost of preference share capital (to one decimal place).

4.5 Cost of bank loan

The cost of a bank loan will be given in the exam. Remember that interest payments will attract tax relief and therefore will need to be multiplied by (1 – t) to obtain the post-tax cost.

 Real life example: Interest rates

If the interest rate on a bank loan is 8% and the rate of tax is 20% then the post-tax cost of the loan is 8% × (1 - 0.2) = 6.4%.

5 Weighted average cost of capital (WACC)

In the exam, you may be required to calculate the weighted average cost **of two or more of the types of capital covered in the previous section**.

This will show the **overall cost of capital** of a business and is called a weighted average cost of capital or **WACC**. This will often be used as the cost of capital in many investment appraisal calculations (where NPV is being used).

As with any cost, management will try to find ways of keeping this cost to a minimum (this is discussed in the next chapter).

5.1 WACC formula

 Formula provided

$$WACC = \left(\frac{V_e}{V_e + V_d}\right)K_e + \left(\frac{V_d}{V_e + V_d}\right)K_d(1-t)$$

Where:

V_e = total market value (ex-div) of shares ie market capitalisation

V_d = total market value (ex-interest) of debt

K_e = cost of equity in a geared company

K_d = cost of debt

Illustration 5: WACC

The current date is the end of 20X5.

Relevant data

	Book values	Market values
	$m	$m
Equity (50m shares)	140	214
Debt: 10% loan notes 20X9	80	90
	Per share	Annual growth rates
Current dividend	24c	6%

Required

If taxation is 30%, calculate the WACC.

Solution

(1) Cost of equity

As there are 50 million shares the share price can be calculated as $214m / 50m = $4.28

The cost of equity can be calculated using either the CAPM model or the dividend valuation model. With the information provided here only the dividend valuation model can be used.

Dividend valuation model: D1/Po + g = [24(1.06) /428] + 0.06 = 0.1194 or 11.94%

(2) Cost of debt

The debt is redeemable so the IRR approach must be used. The total market value of debt is 12.5% higher than the book value (calculated by comparing the total market value of $90m to the total book value of $80m ie 90m / 80m = 1.125). So, the market value of a $100 block of debt (or one loan note) is $112.5

The post-tax cost of debt on a $100 nominal value block of debt is 10% x (1 minus the tax rate of 0.3) = 7%.

The cash flows for a $100 nominal value block of debt are:

Time	0	1	2	3	4
Cash flows (after tax)	112.5	(7)	(7)	(7)	(107)

Using the =IRR function this gives 3.6%.

(3) Market value of equity (Ve)

Given as $214m

(4) Market value of debt (Vd)

Given as $90m

(5) Weighted average cost of capital

$$\text{WACC} = \left(\frac{V_e}{V_e + V_d}\right)K_e + \left(\frac{V_d}{V_e + V_d}\right)K_d(1-t)$$

Now that all the variables have been identified, the WACC can be calculated.

Note that the cost of debt of 3.6% is already post tax and therefore does not need to be multiplied by (1-t) again.

So, the WACC is:

WACC = [(214/304) × 11.94 + (90/304)] × 3.6 = 9.5%

Activity 8: WACC

D Co is financed by 10 million $1 ordinary shares and $8,000,000 8% redeemable loan notes having market values of $1.90 cum-div and $90% ex-interest respectively.

The loan notes are redeemable at par in four years' time

A dividend of 30c is about to be paid and future dividends are expected to grow by 5%.

Required

If taxation is 20%, calculate the WACC.

Solution

5.2 More than two types of finance

The WACC formula provided in the exam assumes that only two sources of finance are being used.

In the exam you may need to **adapt the formula** to accommodate more than two sources of finance.

This is not difficult as the formula is simply calculating a weighted average of two variables and can easily be adapted to include more than two variables.

Real life example: WACC – more than two types of finance

From the previous activity we have the following:

Cost of equity = 24.69%

Cost of debt (post tax) = 9.5%

Value of equity = $16m

Value of debt = $7.2m

If we were now told that the company also had a bank loan of $1.8m costing 10% post-tax, then the total capital becomes $16m + $7.2m + $1.8m= $25m and the WACC formula becomes:

WACC = (16/25) × 24.69 + (7.2/25) × 9.5 + (1.8/25) × 10%

So the WACC is now 19.3%.

5.3 Weightings used in WACC

Two methods of weighting could be used.

Market values should always be used if data is available.

Although book values are often easier to obtain, they are based on historical values and their use will seriously **understate** the impact of the cost of equity finance on the weighted average cost of capital.

This is because the book value of equity is likely to be well below the market value of equity and therefore equity (the more expensive source of finance) will have a lower weighting in the WACC calculation leading to the WACC being underestimated.

If the WACC is underestimated, projects may be accepted that do not in fact deliver a high enough return to satisfy the providers of finance.

5.4 Use of the WACC

The WACC can be used as a discount rate at which to appraise projects; if the project has a positive NPV when discounted using the WACC, it should be accepted.

However, where the risk of an extra project is different from normal, then the return expected by providers of finance will change.

Therefore, the WACC **can only be used for project evaluation** if:

(a) In the long term the company will maintain its existing capital structure ie **same financial risk**

(b) The project has the same risk as the company ie **same business risk**

(c) The project is **marginal in size**; major projects are likely to have a material effect on risk, so the WACC is not normally used for major projects

If there is a change in risk, then there is an argument for a cost of capital to be calculated for that particular project; this is called a **marginal cost of capital** and is **covered in the next chapter**.

Chapter summary

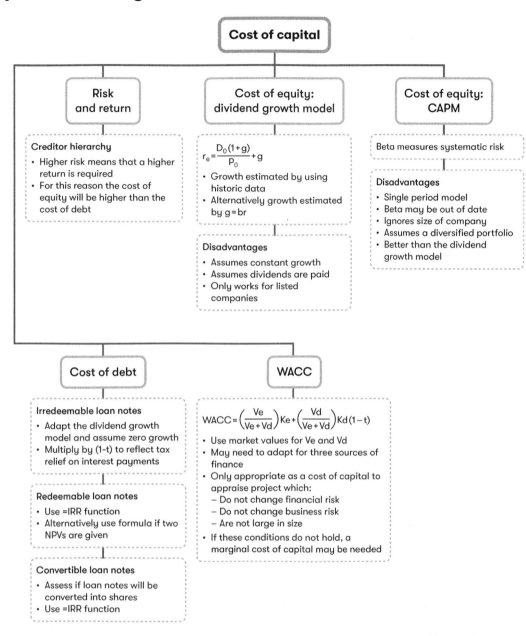

Cost of capital

Risk and return

Creditor hierarchy
- Higher risk means that a higher return is required
- For this reason the cost of equity will be higher than the cost of debt

Cost of equity: dividend growth model

$$r_e = \frac{D_0(1+g)}{P_0} + g$$

- Growth estimated by using historic data
- Alternatively growth estimated by $g = br$

Disadvantages
- Assumes constant growth
- Assumes dividends are paid
- Only works for listed companies

Cost of equity: CAPM

Beta measures systematic risk

Disadvantages
- Single period model
- Beta may be out of date
- Ignores size of company
- Assumes a diversified portfolio
- Better than the dividend growth model

Cost of debt

Irredeemable loan notes
- Adapt the dividend growth model and assume zero growth
- Multiply by (1-t) to reflect tax relief on interest payments

Redeemable loan notes
- Use =IRR function
- Alternatively use formula if two NPVs are given

Convertible loan notes
- Assess if loan notes will be converted into shares
- Use =IRR function

WACC

$$WACC = \left(\frac{Ve}{Ve+Vd}\right)Ke + \left(\frac{Vd}{Ve+Vd}\right)Kd\,(1-t)$$

- Use market values for Ve and Vd
- May need to adapt for three sources of finance
- Only appropriate as a cost of capital to appraise project which:
  – Do not change financial risk
  – Do not change business risk
  – Are not large in size
- If these conditions do not hold, a marginal cost of capital may be needed

Knowledge diagnostic

1. Risk and return

The creditor hierarchy establishes the relationship between risk and return.

2. Dividend growth model

This model for estimating the cost of equity is not as stable as the CAPM but needs to be used to estimate the cost of equity if a beta factor is not given.

3. CAPM

Assuming that shareholders diversify their investments, this model establishes the return that is needed to compensate shareholders for the systematic risk of a company (as measure by its beta factor).

4. Cost of debt

If debt is redeemable or convertible this will require the use of the IRR approach.

5. WACC

This is appropriate for calculating the cost of capital for use in NPV analysis unless a project represents a different level of risk to that normally faced by shareholders.

Further study guidance

Question practice

Now try the following from the Further question practice bank (available in the digital edition of the Workbook):

Section A questions

Q27, Q29

Section C questions

Q55 Cry

Further reading

There is a useful Technical Article written by a member of the FM examining team that is available on ACCA's website; it is called 'CAPM – theory, advantages and disadvantages'. We recommend that you read this article as part of your preparation for the FM exam.

Activity answers

Activity 1: Dividend growth model

The correct answer is: 19.8%

The cost of equity is

$$= \frac{60(1.08)}{550} + 0.08 = 0.198 \text{ or } 19.8\%$$

Activity 2: Historic growth

The correct answer is: 6.95%

$0.30 \times (1+g)^4 = 0.3925$

$\therefore$

$$g = \left(\frac{0.3925}{0.3}\right)^{(1/4)} - 1 = 0.0695$$

$\therefore$ g = 6.95% this is the geometric average growth rate

If the question had asked for the cost of equity, using this growth rate the answer would be: k_e = [0.3925(1.0695)/(8.31)] + (0.0695) = 12%

Activity 3: Exam standard

The correct answer is: 29.92%

Growth = 40% × 30% = 12% p.a.

The difference between the cum div and ex div share price is 20c, so this is the dividend that is about to be paid.

k_e = ((20 × 1.12)/125) + 0.12 = 29.92%

Activity 4: CAPM Technique demonstration

1   15.8%

Use the beta of the company; 1.6

Do not mistake the risk premium for the market return. The risk premium is Rm-Rf.

K_e = 3 + (8 × 1.6) = <u>15.8%</u>

2   0.875

If the cost of equity is 10%, K_e = 3% + (8% × β) = 10%

So 10% - 3%= 8% × β

So 7% ÷ 8% = β = <u>0.875</u>

Activity 5: Technique demonstration

Cost of debt to the company = [8(1 - 0.20)/82] = <u>7.8%</u>

Activity 6: Redeemable debt

CBE exam approach

Post-tax cost of interest = $5 × (1 - 0.2) = $4

Redemption value = $105

There are four years between 1 Jan 20X5 and 31 Dec 20X8.

	A	B	C	D	E	F
1	Time	0	1	2	3	4
2	Per $100	90	-4	-4	-4	-109
3	IRR	=IRR(B2:F2)				

The spreadsheet solution in cell B3 is 8.1%

Using the approach of two NPVs would be slower but the workings are shown below:

Discounting at 7%

Time	0	1 to 4	4
Per $100	90	-4	-105
Df 7%	1.0	3.387	0.763
Present value	90	-13.55	-80.12

NPVa = -3.67

Discounting at 9%

Time	0	1 to 4	4
Per $100	90	-4	-105
Df 10%	1.0	3.240	0.708
Present value	90	-12.96	-74.34

NPVb = +2.70

IRR = 7 + (-3.67/(-3.67 - 2.70) × (9 - 7))

IRR = 7 + (-3.67/(-6.37) × 2) = 8.15%

The CBE method is more accurate

Activity 7: Cost of preference shares

9.6%

Dividend = 12% of nominal value = $0.12

Cost of preference shares = 0.12/1.25 = 9.6%

Activity 8: WACC

The correct answer is: 20.0%

(1) Cost of equity

Because the dividend is about to be paid and the share price is cum div, the ex-div share price needs to be calculated as $1.90 - $0.30 = $1.60

$Ke = [D_0 (1 + g)/P_0] + g = [30(1.05)/160] + 0.05$

= 24.69%

(2) Cost of debt

CBE exam approach

Post tax cost of interest = $8 × (1 - 0.2) = $6.4

Redemption value = $100

	A	B	C	D	E	F
1	Time	0	1	2	3	4
2	Per $100	90	–6.4	–6.4	–6.4	–106.4
3	IRR	=IRR(B2:F2)				

The spreadsheet solution in cell B3 is 9.5%

(3) **Value of equity**

$V_e = 10m × 1.6 = £16m$

(4) **Value of debt**

$V_d = 8,000,000 × 90\% = £7,200,000$

(5) **WACC**

$WACC = [16/(16 + 7.2)] × 24.69\% + [7.2/(16 + 7.2) × 9.5\% = 20.0\%$

12

Capital structure

Learning objectives

On completion of this chapter, you should be able to:

	Syllabus reference
• Estimating the overall cost of capital including distinguishing between average & marginal cost of capital	E2(c)
• Identify and discuss the problem of high levels of gearing	E3(c)
• Assess the impact of sources of finance on financial position, financial risk and shareholder wealth using appropriate measures, including ratio analysis (using statement of financial position gearing, operational and financial gearing, interest coverage ratio and other relevant ratios), cash flow forecasting and leasing or borrowing to buy (Chapter 8)	E3(d)
• Impact of cost of capital on investments including the advantages of the CAPM over WACC in determining a project-specific cost of capital, application of CAPM in calculating a project-specific discount rate	E3(e)
• Describe the traditional view of capital structure and its assumptions	E4(a)
• Describe the views of Miller and Modigliani on capital structure, both without and with corporate taxation, and their assumptions	E4(b)
• Identify a range of capital market imperfections and describe their impact on the views of Miller and Modigliani on capital structure	E4(c)
• Explain the relevance of pecking order theory to selection of sources of finance	E4(d)
• Describe the financing needs of small businesses	E5(a)
• Describe the nature of the financing problem for small businesses in terms of the funding gap, the maturity gap and inadequate security	E5(b)
• Explain measures that may be taken to ease the financing problems of SMEs, including the responses of government departments and financial institutions	E5(c)
• Identify & evaluate the financial impact of sources of finance for SMEs, including sources from syllabus section E1 and business angel financing, government assistance, supply chain financing, crowdfunding/peer-to-peer funding	E5(d)

Exam context

This chapter mainly covers 'capital structure issues' which is part of Section E of the syllabus (Business Finance). Having described a variety of sources of finance in Chapters 9-10, this chapter discusses the appropriate balance of different types of finance, or capital structure. The theories covering capital structure are also useful for calculating a marginal cost of capital which should be used to evaluate investments where risk is changing and so the use of the WACC (Chapter 11) is not appropriate.

Chapter overview

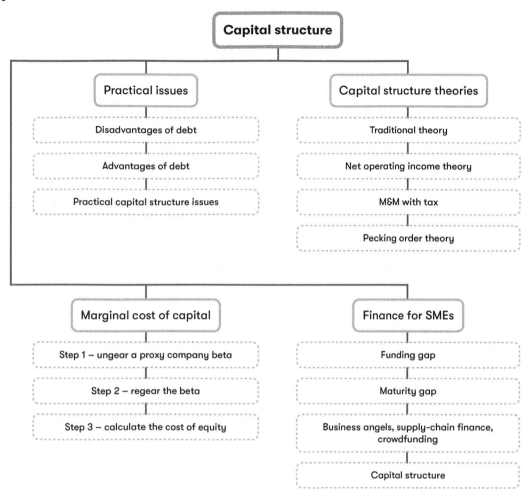

1 Practical capital structure issues

> **PER alert**
>
> Performance objective 11 requires you to 'identify key sources of financial risk to the organisation and how they might arise' and to 'monitor financial risks, reviewing their status and how they should be managed'. You can apply the knowledge you obtain from this chapter of the text to help to demonstrate this competence.

KEY TERM

> **Capital structure:** The capital structure of a company refers to the mixture of equity and debt finance used by a company.

Having looked at a variety of sources of finance in Chapter 9, we now consider the issue of capital structure. We have seen in Chapter 1 that this is measured by the **gearing ratio**.

We start by considering the relative advantages and disadvantages of debt and equity.

1.1 Disadvantages of debt finance compared to equity

Disadvantages of debt	Discussion
Debt creates higher variability in dividends ie higher financial risk.	If there is a downturn in business, there will be a dramatic cut in the funds available to pay a dividend because of the need to pay interest first.
The use of debt worsens interest cover and gearing ratios	Debt creates higher default risk which can lead to **financial distress costs** such as lower sales or higher supplier costs (this is explored later in this chapter).
Debt payments must be made, even if a business is not making profits.	A key advantage of equity is that dividend payments are at the discretion of the Board.

Activity 1: Financial risk

Badtimes Co's latest forecast financial data for the current year is as follows:

	Last year	Forecast
	$m	$m
Profits before interest and tax (PBIT)	12,000	6,000
Interest	3,000	3,000
Tax	2,700	900
Profits after interest and tax	6,300	2,100
Dividends (assuming no change in dividend payout ratio)	2,100	700

Required

Compare the % change in PBIT to the % change in dividends and explain the difference.

Solution

1.2 Advantages of debt finance compared to equity

Advantages of debt	Discussion
Debt is a cheaper source of finance	This has been discussed in Chapter 11 in the section on the creditor hierarchy.
Debt has a better impact on earnings per share (EPS)	Issuing new shares can be expected to have a more dilutive effect on EPS than the issue of debt.
Debt is quicker and cheaper to issue compared to a share issue	Only true if comparing to a share issue, but equity may also be sourced from internal finance.
Interest repayments attract tax relief (ie reduce taxable profit)	This is one of the key reasons why debt is a cheaper source of finance.
The use of debt is a discipline on management	Careful cash flow management is needed eg good management of working capital.
Using debt can be interpreted as a signal of confidence in the company's cash flows	Can be interpreted as a signal that management are confident in the stability of the company's cash flows.

Activity 2: Gearing & EPS

Goodtimes Co plans to spend $5m on expanding its existing business. It is considering raising the finance by issuing 5% loan notes. The expansion of business is expected to increase profit before interest and tax by 10% in the first year.

An ordinary dividend of $425,000 has just been paid and dividends are expected to increase by 4% per year for the foreseeable future.

Summarised financial information on Goodtimes Co for the last financial year is as follows.

	$'000
Profit before interest and tax	3,500
Interest	(250)
Profit before tax	3,250
Tax (30%)	(975)
Profit after tax	2,275

	$'000	$'000
Ordinary shares, par value $1	2,500	
Retained earnings	11,250	
Total equity		13,750
10% loan notes	2,500	
6% preference shares, par value $1	1,250	
Prior charge capital		3,750

Other information

Average sector financial gearing (prior charge capital divided by equity share capital) is 55%.

Required

Evaluate the effect, after one year, of the debt issue and the business expansion on:

(a) Profit after tax

(b) Financial gearing using book values (currently = 3,750/13,750 × 100 = 27.3%)

(c) Earnings per share (currently EPS = [2,275 - (6% × 1,250)]/2,500 = 0.88)

Solution

1.3 Practical capital structure considerations

Each company will need to evaluate the importance of the relative advantages of debt and equity, and to consider practical, company-specific, factors to determine their appropriate capital structure.

Practical issues	Explanation
Life cycle	A new, growing business will find it difficult to forecast cash flows with any certainty so high levels of gearing are unwise.
Operational gearing (ie contribution/PBIT)	If fixed costs are high, then contribution (ie before fixed costs) will be high relative to profits (after fixed costs). High fixed costs mean future cash flows may be volatile, so high gearing is not sensible.
Stability of revenue	If operating in a highly dynamic business environment, then high gearing is not sensible.
Security	If a company is unable to offer security, then debt will be difficult and expensive to obtain.

Essential reading

See Chapter 12 section 1 of the Essential reading, available in the digital edition of the Workbook, for more background information on this area. The Illustration called 'Impact of alternative types of finance' is especially important.

The Essential reading is available as an Appendix of the digital edition of the Workbook.

2 Capital structure theories

Capital structure theories mainly examine the impact of using debt finance on the WACC and **whether debt can be used to lower the WACC - in which case shareholders will benefit** since the market value of a company depends on its cost of capital. The lower a company's WACC, the higher the net present value of its future cash flows and therefore the higher its market value.

2.1 Traditional theory

A traditional approach to gearing suggests that **debt brings benefits, up to a certain level of gearing.** This is illustrated below.

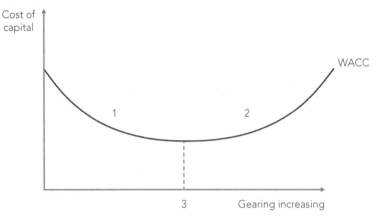

At **point 1** in the diagram, the weighted average cost of capital (WACC) is falling, as gearing rises. This reflects the impact of using more debt, and that debt is a relatively cheap source of finance.

At **point 2** in the diagram, the WACC is rising, as gearing rises. This reflects that the use of high levels of debt makes equity riskier (eg higher bankruptcy risk) which causes the cost of equity to rise exponentially and so the WACC increases.

Point 3 represents the optimal level of gearing, since the WACC is lowest at this point.

2.1.1 Drawbacks of traditional theory

The traditional view does not identify the optimal level of gearing.

Another drawback is that it fails to consider the impact of tax on the cost of debt finance.

2.2 Modigliani and Miller (no tax)

This theory, also known as the net operating income approach, takes a different view of the effect of gearing on WACC. In their 1958 theory, Modigliani and Miller (M&M) proposed that the total market value of a company, in the absence of tax relief on debt interest, will be determined only by two factors:

(a) The **total earnings** of the company

(b) The **level of business risk** attached to those earnings

The total market value would be computed by discounting the total earnings at a rate that is appropriate to the level of business risk. This rate would represent the WACC of the company.

Thus M&M concluded that **the capital structure of a company would have no effect on its overall value or WACC** (quoted in: Watson and Head, 2013, p.299).

This theory can be illustrated as follows:

Like traditional theory, net operating income theory acknowledges that debt is cheaper than equity and that the use of high levels of debt makes equity riskier so the cost of equity will rise as

gearing rises. However, the theory suggests that **these effects exactly offset each other** so the WACC remains constant.

This is illustrated in the following diagram which shows the cost of equity rising in a linear manner, exactly offsetting the impact of using (cheaper) debt finance.

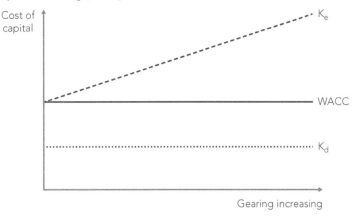

2.2.1 Arbitrage

M&M justified net operating income theory by suggesting that if two companies, that were identical to each other aside from their capital structure, had different values then investors could make a risk free gain by selling shares in company with a higher value and buying shares from the company with a lower value. This would mean that very quickly the market values of the two companies would move into line with each other.

Arbitrage: When a purchase and sale of a security takes place simultaneously in different markets, with the aim of making a risk-free profit through the exploitation of any price difference between the markets.

Exam focus point

The proof of M&M's theory by arbitrage is not examinable.

2.2.2 Drawbacks of net operating income theory

M&M made various assumptions in arriving at this conclusion, including:

(a) A **perfect capital market exists,** in which investors have the same information, on which they act rationally, to arrive at the same expectations about future earnings and risks.

(b) There are no **tax or transaction costs.**

(c) **Debt is risk free** and is freely available at the same cost to investors and companies alike.

2.3 Modigliani and Miller (with tax)

In 1963 Modigliani and Miller modified their theory to recognise that **tax relief** on interest payments does lower the weighted average cost of capital. The savings arising from tax relief on debt interest are the **tax shield.**

Having shown that debt brought no benefit in a zero tax world, M&M were then able to argue that the tax shield is taken into account, then debt brings an extra benefit (not accounted for in net operating income theory).

This means that **a company should use as much debt finance as it can** and its weighted average cost of capital continues to fall as gearing rises (Watson and Head, 2013, p.301).

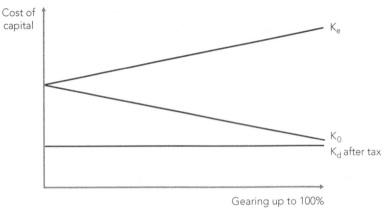

2.3.1 Drawbacks of M&M theory with tax

In reality companies do not maximise their gearing due to the existence of **market imperfections** and **other practical issues** which mitigate the tax advantages of debt finance.

Capital market imperfections	Examples
Direct financial distress costs	M&M's theory assumes perfect capital markets so a company would always be able to raise finance and avoid bankruptcy.
	However, at higher levels of gearing there is an increasing risk of the company being unable to meet its interest payments and being declared bankrupt.
	At these higher levels of gearing, the bankruptcy risk means that shareholders and providers of debt will require a far higher rate of return as compensation.
Indirect financial distress costs	As gearing rises, the risk of bankruptcy may also damage sales (customers may not want to buy from a company that looks financially unstable).
	Suppliers may not want to supply a potentially unstable firm, or may put up prices to compensate for the risk of non-payment.
Agency costs	At higher levels of gearing there are also agency costs as a result of action taken by concerned debt holders.
	Providers of debt finance are likely to impose **restrictive covenants**, such as restriction of future dividends. They may also increase their level of monitoring and require more financial information.

M&M theory with tax also fails to recognise that:

- as companies increase their gearing, they may reach a point where there are not enough profits from which to obtain all available tax benefits (tax exhaustion). They will still be subject to increased bankruptcy and agency costs but will not be able to benefit from the increased tax shield.
- **the impact of personal tax,** which often incentivises share ownership.

Activity 3: M&M

Haridoy Co recently issued some debentures to raise new finance. Before the issue Haridoy Co had a cost of equity of 12% and a weighted average cost of capital of 9%. The company pays tax at 20%. After the issue the cost of equity rose to 12.5% and the weighted average cost of capital (WACC) fell to 8.6%.

Required

With which theory or theories are these movements in cost of capital (Ke and WACC) potentially consistent?

○ Traditional theory only

○ Traditional theory and Modigliani and Miller (with tax)

○ Traditional theory and Modigliani and Miller (both with and without tax)

○ Modigilani and Miller (with tax)

2.4 Pecking order theory

Pecking order theory sees the financing decision in practical terms and suggests that firms will finance projects in the following order:

1. Use internal funds if available

2. Use debt

3. Convertible debt

4. Preference shares

5. Issue new equity

- **Issue costs** (these are zero if retained cash is used, and the issue costs of debt are lower than those of equity).
- Investor preference for **safer securities**; that is, debt with its guaranteed income and priority on liquidation.
- Debt issues have a better **signalling effect** than equity issues ie the market will interpret debt issues as a sign of confidence.
- The market will interpret equity issues as an indication that managers believe that equity is currently **overvalued** and hence are trying to achieve high proceeds while they can.

Essential reading

See Chapter 12 Section 2 of the Essential reading, available in the digital edition of the Workbook, for more background information on this area.

The Essential reading is available as an Appendix of the digital edition of the Workbook.

3 Project specific (marginal) cost of equity

In the previous chapter we saw that **a marginal cost of capital will be needed if a project changes the risk** faced by shareholders. Here we will apply the CAPM and M&M theory (with tax) to estimate a marginal cost of equity.

3.1 Equity betas and asset betas

3.1.1 Equity (geared) beta

The beta of a company's shares reflects both its business risk and its financial risk (the risk of using debt finance in the capital structure).

Since most companies have some level of debt finance, an equity beta can be assumed to be a 'geared' beta ie the beta of a company that employs some debt finance.

3.1.2 Asset (ungeared) beta

M&M theory can be used to adjust an equity beta to show its value if the company was ungeared. This is called an asset beta. An ungeared beta measures **only business risk**, not financial risk.

Equity beta ⟷ Asset beta

An equity beta will be larger than an asset beta because an asset beta only measures business risk, whereas an equity beta measures business risk and financial risk.

KEY TERM

> **Asset beta:** An ungeared beta ie only measures business risk.
>
> **Equity beta:** A measure of the systematic risk of a share, including its business and financial risk.

Formula provided

$$\beta_a = \left[\frac{V_e}{(V_e + V_d(1-T))}\beta_e \right] + \left[\frac{V_d(1-T)}{(V_e + V_d(1-T))}\beta_d \right]$$

Exam focus point

> Often no debt beta is given in the exam and therefore only the first part of the formula is used.

3.2 Calculating a marginal (or project-specific) cost of equity

Where a company is moving into a different business area, it cannot use its current WACC to assess the project because its risk is changing. A marginal cost of capital is therefore needed.

This can be calculated by following 3 steps.

Step 1: Find the asset beta of a company in the same business as the new project

First, find the beta of a company in the same business (a proxy company) as the proposed project; this is an **equity beta**.

This equity beta gives an indication of the business risk of the project but **will be distorted by the gearing of the proxy company** (if a company has a high equity beta this may be because it has high gearing, not because it is a high risk business).

Illustration 1: Beta factors

Train Co is a company experienced in the provision of training courses. Shares in Train have a beta value of 1.2.

Train Co has a **debt: equity ratio of 1:10** which will not change as a result of the project.

The directors of Train plan to expand their business by building hotels which are located near their training centres.

Thirté Co is a listed hotel company with **a debt: equity ratio of 1:1,** its shares have a beta of 1.5.

The **market premium for risk** is 8% and the risk-free rate is 4%.

Required

Which beta factor is a better measure of the risk of the new project?

Solution

The beta of Thirté Co is more relevant as it is in the same business as the proposed project, however it is distorted by the relatively high level of gearing of Thirté Co.

To understand the level of business risk, the **equity beta of the proxy company needs to be adjusted** by stripping out the effect of gearing **to create an ungeared or an asset beta** – this measures the business risk of the project.

Activity 4: Calculating an asset beta

Use the details from the previous illustration and assume the tax rate is 30%.

Required

Calculate the asset beta of Thirté (assume debt has a beta of zero). Work to 3 decimal places.

Solution

Step 2: Re-gear the asset beta to reflect the project's gearing

An asset beta is ungeared and so does not include any allowance for financial risk. However, if a project is financed using some debt finance then it will create financial risk as well as business risk.

Therefore, we now need to adjust the asset beta by including the impact of the gearing of the **project**; this is called re-gearing the beta.

This uses the same formula that we used for ungearing the equity beta.

Formula provided

$$\beta_a = \left[\frac{V_e}{(V_e + V_d(1-T))}\beta_e\right] + \left[\frac{V_d(1-T)}{(V_e + V_d(1-T))}\beta_d\right]$$

Activity 5: Re-gearing the asset beta

Train Co (from the previous activity) has a **debt: equity ratio of 1:10** and Thirté plc is a listed hotel company with an asset beta of 0.882.

The market premium for risk is 8% and the risk-free rate is 4%. Tax is 30%.

Required

Calculate the equity beta of the project to build hotels (assume debt has a beta of zero). Work to 3 decimal places.

Solution

Step 3: Use the re-geared beta to calculate an appropriate cost of equity

The **regeared beta** shows the risk of the project (including both financial and business risk) and is **used to calculate a project-specific cost of equity**.

This uses the CAPM which was covered in the previous chapter:

$E(r_i) = Rf + \beta(E(Rm) - Rf)$

Activity 6: Calculating a project specific cost of equity

Use the equity beta of 0.944 to calculate Train's cost of equity for this project (ie the marginal cost of equity). Work to 2 decimal places.

Solution

In reality, this cost of equity **would be included in a project-specific WACC** if a combination of debt and equity is used to finance the investment. However, **this will not be tested numerically in the exam.**

It is this project-specific cost WACC that represents the marginal cost of capital ie the cost of raising additional finance/the composite rate of return required by shareholders **and** debt-holders for financing new investments of the company.

> ### Exam focus point
>
> Calculation of a marginal/project specific WACC is not examinable, only a project specific cost of equity

A summary of the three-step approach to calculating a project specific cost of equity is:

Step 1   Find the asset beta of a company in the same business as the new project

Step 2   Re-gear the asset beta to reflect the project's gearing

Step 3   Use the re-geared beta to calculate an appropriate cost of equity

Activity 7: Calculating a project specific cost of equity

Company B, a training company, has a debt: equity ratio of 1:2. It wishes to expand into recruitment consultancy. It has identified that the beta of a highly geared recruitment consultancy company (company X) **is 1.8. This is its equity beta and is influenced by its high level of gearing of 1:1 debt to equity.**

Assume that debt has a beta of 0.

Risk-free rate = 4%

Market rate = 12%

Tax = 30%

Required

Calculate the cost of equity that Company B should use to appraise this investment.

Solution

3.3 Problem with approach

A key problem with this approach is **finding a similar company's beta**; this is very difficult in reality.

Essential reading

See Chapter 12 section 3 of the Essential reading, available in the digital edition of the Workbook, for more background information on this area.

The Essential reading is available as an Appendix of the digital edition of the Workbook.

4 Finance for small and medium sized enterprises (SMEs)

4.1 Funding gap

Small and medium-sized enterprises (SMEs) face particular problems in raising external finance which will impact on their capital structure.

The inability of SMEs to raise adequate finance is sometimes referred to as the funding gap.

The funding gap is often the result of the following features of a SME:

- The business is owned by a relatively small pool of investors (very often a family) and is likely to be unquoted
- There is a greater failure rate among small companies
- The companies are less likely to have a discernible track record and generally undergo much less regulatory and public scrutiny
- Knowledge of sources of finance may be limited

4.2 Maturity gap

Even medium-sized companies will sometimes find that they cannot obtain more debt finance, due to **inadequate security** (in the form of assets). This is a particular problem for medium-term projects (eg a new advertising campaign) which often do not have the security offered by long-term investments that land and buildings create.

The difficulty in obtaining medium-term financing is called **the maturity gap**.

Government has recognised these difficulties and has tried to encourage investment in SMEs by underwriting (guaranteeing) a proportion of the value of loans made to SMEs and by direct assistance such as grants.

4.3 Business angel financing

Wealthy individuals or groups of individuals who invest directly in an SME. They are prepared to take large risks in the expectation of large returns on their investment. This finance is also relatively informal which means that the raising of the funds can be speeded up.

4.4 Supply chain finance (SCF)

SMEs are likely to make use of electronic platforms, usually provided by banks or financial institutions, which facilitates the factoring of outstanding trade debts.

Real life example: SCF

(a) Company A buys $50,000 of goods from B on 60-day credit.

(b) Company A approves the invoice for payment and uploads it to a SCF platform.

(c) Company B can see the invoice has been approved for payment and either:

    (i) Waits 60 days to receive cash from A; or

    (ii) Receives the cash within five days from C (the SCF platform provider (the bank)) in return for a discount.

(d) Company A pays the full amount to C.

Company A has the benefit of paying in 60 days as planned but Company B has the cash early and C has earned the discount.

4.5 Crowdfunding

Crowdfunding allows a company to access finance via an online crowdfunding platform (eg, Kickstarter) to pitch for finance from a large number of potential investors.

A successful pitch will require a well thought out business plan setting and a high-quality management team (in terms of their skills and experience).

The use of crowdfunding by companies looking to raise equity finance is becoming increasingly common and is closely tied to growth of internet technology (FinTech), which enables millions of potential investors to be accessed.

Crowdfunding is available to start-up, as well as established, and can be a relatively quick process (sometimes taking as little as a couple of months). It is also a way of building awareness of a business and helping to attract customers.

Some crowdfunding platforms offer both equity and debt finance (debt finance is also called peer to peer lending, and was covered in Chapter 2).

4.6 Capital structure

SMEs are restricted in their sources of new equity finance. They are private companies, with a limited number of shareholders. Unless the shareholders are wealthy, there is a limit to the amount of extra capital they may be able to invest in the company.

SMEs therefore rely heavily on retained profits for new equity finance, but there is a limit to the amount of equity that can be obtained from this source, especially when profits are low.

It is not easy for SMEs to attract venture capital. They must be able to demonstrate strong opportunities for profit growth.

So, if SMEs are restricted in the amount of new equity they can obtain, **they may be forced to rely on borrowing to supplement their finances.**

Essential reading

See Chapter 12 section 4 of the Essential reading, available in the digital edition of the Workbook, for more background information on this area, including examples of government schemes.

The Essential reading is available as an Appendix of the digital edition of the Workbook.

Chapter summary

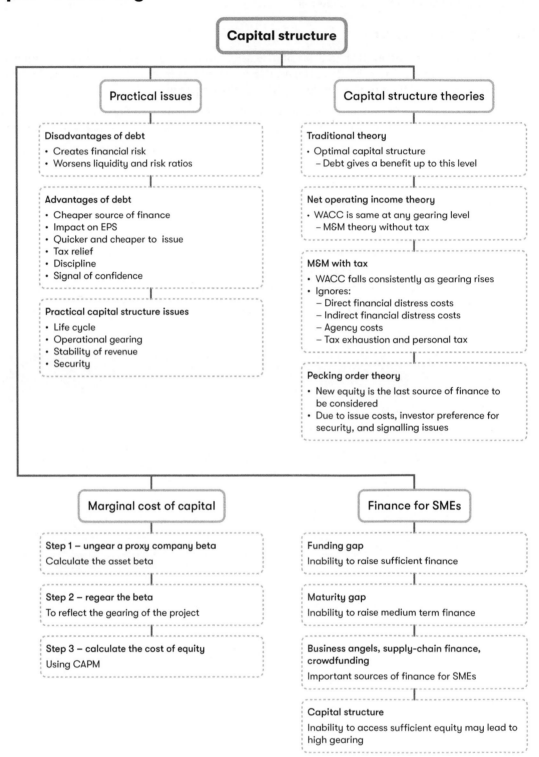

Capital structure

Practical issues

Disadvantages of debt
- Creates financial risk
- Worsens liquidity and risk ratios

Advantages of debt
- Cheaper source of finance
- Impact on EPS
- Quicker and cheaper to issue
- Tax relief
- Discipline
- Signal of confidence

Practical capital structure issues
- Life cycle
- Operational gearing
- Stability of revenue
- Security

Capital structure theories

Traditional theory
- Optimal capital structure
  - Debt gives a benefit up to this level

Net operating income theory
- WACC is same at any gearing level
  - M&M theory without tax

M&M with tax
- WACC falls consistently as gearing rises
- Ignores:
  - Direct financial distress costs
  - Indirect financial distress costs
  - Agency costs
  - Tax exhaustion and personal tax

Pecking order theory
- New equity is the last source of finance to be considered
- Due to issue costs, investor preference for security, and signalling issues

Marginal cost of capital

Step 1 – ungear a proxy company beta
Calculate the asset beta

Step 2 – regear the beta
To reflect the gearing of the project

Step 3 – calculate the cost of equity
Using CAPM

Finance for SMEs

Funding gap
Inability to raise sufficient finance

Maturity gap
Inability to raise medium term finance

Business angels, supply-chain finance, crowdfunding
Important sources of finance for SMEs

Capital structure
Inability to access sufficient equity may lead to high gearing

BPP
LEARNING
MEDIA

Knowledge diagnostic

1. Practical capital structure issues

As well as being aware of the general advantages of debt and equity, you should appreciate that capital structure will be influenced by company-specific factors such as: stage in the life-cycle, operating gearing, stability of cash flows and ability to offer security.

2. Basic ratio analysis

It is vital that you can use basic ratios such as EPS, interest cover and gearing to evaluate a potential capital structure.

3. Capital structure theories

Modigliani and Miller theory with tax suggests that gearing should be maximised, but make sure you understand the limitations of this theory - for example the assumption that financial distress costs (direct and indirect) do not exist.

4. Marginal cost of capital

Where an investment causes a change in risk it will require a project specific cost of capital (as opposed to using the existing WACC). A project specific cost of equity can be calculated by adjusting a proxy company's beta to reflect the gearing of the project.

5. SME finance

SMEs will often experience problems in accessing equity finance and are often exposed to problems in raising finance over the medium and long term.

BPP LEARNING MEDIA

Further study guidance

Question practice

Now try the following from the Further question practice bank (available in the digital edition of the Workbook):

Section A questions

Q28

Section C questions

Q56 Katash

Further reading

There are three useful Technical Articles available on ACCA's website, called:

- 'Business finance for SMEs'
- 'The capital asset pricing model' – parts 1 and 2 (written by a member of the FM examining team).

We recommend that you read these articles as part of your preparation for the FM exam.

Activity answers

Activity 1: Financial risk

PBIT change

$m	Last year	Forecast
Profits before interest and tax	12,000	6,000

% change = 6,000/12,000 × 100 = 50%

Dividends fall by 1,400/2,100 × 100 = 67%

Dividends fall by more than PBIT because interest has to be paid – this is called financial risk.

Activity 2: Gearing & EPS

(a) **Profits after tax**

Interest paid on new debt = 0.05 × $5m = $250,000

	$000s
Revised PBIT (3,500 × 1.1)	3,850
Revised interest (250 + 250)	500
Revised PBT	3,350
Tax (30%)	1,005
Revised PAT	2,345

(b) **Financial gearing**

Financial gearing = Prior charge capital/Equity share capital

	$000s
Revised PAT	2,345
Preference dividend (0.06 × 1,250)	75
Revised earnings	2,270
Ordinary dividend (425 × 1.04)	442
Retained earnings (2,270 – 442)	1,828
Revised equity (13,750 + 1,828)	15,578
Revised prior charge capital (3,750 + 5,000)	8,750

New gearing = 8,750/15,578 = 56.2%

The current financial gearing of Goodtimes Co is around 50% ((55 – 27.3)/55) less than the sector average. After the bond issue, it is predicted to be only 2% ((56.2 - 55)/55) more than the sector average. This increase in, and level of, financial gearing is unlikely to be of concern to investors and the stock market especially as if the company continues to grow at 10% per annum, financial gearing will gradually reduce as the proportion of debt to equity falls.

(c) **Earnings per share (EPS)**

EPS = Profit attributable to ordinary shareholders/Number of ordinary shares

EPS after one year = [2345 - (6% × 1,250)]/2,500 = 0.908 = 90.8 cents per share

EPS has risen which is likely to be welcomed by investors, especially as the increased risk due to extra debt being taken on appears to be manageable.

In conclusion, the plan is likely to have a **positive impact** on the company's financial position.

BPP
LEARNING
MEDIA

Activity 3: M&M

The correct answer is: Traditional theory and Modigliani and Miller (with tax)

With the increase in gearing the traditional theory and all of M&M's theories suggested that the cost of equity would rise. Only the traditional theory and M&M (with tax) suggested that the WACC would potentially fall if gearing was increased.

Activity 4: Calculating an asset beta

0.882

$$\beta_a = \left[\frac{V_e}{(V_e + V_d(1-T))}\beta_e\right] + \left[\frac{V_d(1-T)}{(V_e + V_d(1-T))}\beta_d\right]$$

Asset beta = 1.5 × (1/1.7) = 0.882

This reflects the risk of **Thirté's** business.

Activity 5: Re-gearing the asset beta

0.944

$$\beta_a = \left[\frac{V_e}{(V_e + V_d(1-T))}\beta_e\right] + \left[\frac{V_d(1-T)}{(V_e + V_d(1-T))}\beta_d\right]$$

0.882 = equity beta × (10/10.7)

So the equity beta = 0.882/0.9346 = 0.944

Activity 6: Calculating a project specific cost of equity

11.55%

$E(r_i) = Rf + \beta(E(Rm) - Rf)$

$Ke = 4 + (0.944 \times 8) = 11.55\%$

Activity 7: Calculating a project specific cost of equity

Calculation as follows:

Step 1   Beta of recruitment company = 1.8

             Ungear

             Ba = 1.8 × (1/1.7) = 1.059

Step 2   *Regear*

             Be = 1.059/(2/2.7) = 1.430

Step 3   Ke = 4 + (8)1.43 = 15.44%. This reflects the new scenario – that Company B does have debt finance and that it is investing in a new business area. In other words, it reflects the financial risk and business risk of the investment.

The WACC = (15.44% × 2/3) + (4% × 0.7 × 1/3) = 11.23% (but this is not examinable).

Skills checkpoint 3

Sources of finance and WACC – handling complex calculations

Chapter overview

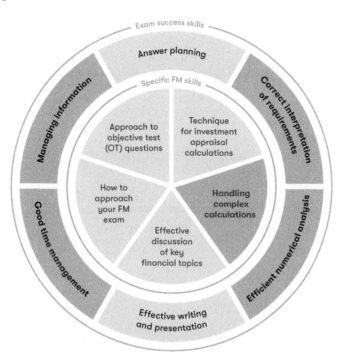

Introduction

The financing decision (section E of the syllabus) is a key part of Financial Management. In section C of the exam you may be asked to advise on the appropriateness and cost of different sources of finance.

Calculating the weighted average cost of capital (WACC) is a popular question in section C of the FM exam. It can be challenging at first, but most of the formulae you'll need will be given in the exam.

You could also be asked to calculate a project specific cost of equity which should be used to evaluate investments where risk is changing and so the use of the WACC is not appropriate. This could involve ungearing and re-gearing beta factors which is a technical area of the syllabus and involves some complex calculations.

Given the complex nature of these calculation it is important that you approach the question in a practical and time-efficient way. Using a standard layout and making good use of the spreadsheet formulae available in the exam is critical to successfully tackling these calculations.

Skills checkpoint 3: Handling complex calculations

FM Skill: Sources of finance and WACC – handling complex calculations

The key steps in applying this skill are outlined below and will be explained in more detail in the following sections as the past exam question 'NN Co' is answered.

> **STEP 1: Understanding the data in the question**
>
> Where a question includes a significant amount of data, read the requirements carefully to make sure that you **understand clearly what the question is asking you to do**. You can use the highlighting function to pull out important data from the question. Use the data provided to think about what formula you will need to use. For example if you are given a beta factor you will use CAPM to calculate the cost of equity; if you are given a dividend growth rate it will be the dividend growth model. If the question states that the debt is redeemable, you will need to use the IRR formula to calculate the cost of debt.

> **STEP 2: Use a standard proforma working.**
>
> For example, if you are asked to calculate the WACC, use your standard proforma or approach for calculating WACC and separately work through the individual parts of the calculation (Ke, Kd, Ve, Vd).

> **STEP 3: Use spreadsheet formulae to perform basic calculations.**
>
> Do not write out your workings; this wastes time and you may make a mistake. Use the spreadsheet formulae instead!

Exam success skills

The following question is an extract from a past exam question; this extract was worth 10 marks.

For this question, we will also focus on the following **exam success skills:**

- **Managing information.** It is easy for the amount of information contained in a section C question to feel over-whelming. **Active reading** is a useful technique to use to avoid this. This involves focusing on the requirement first, on the basis that until you have done this the detail in the question will have little meaning. This is especially important in cost of capital questions where there is likely to be a high level of numerical content.

- **Correct interpretation of requirements.** The requirements clearly ask for two separate calculations. The after-tax cost of debt and the after tax WACC. The cost of debt will be needed to complete the WACC calculation.

- **Efficient numerical analysis.** The key to success here is applying a sensible proforma for typical WACC calculations, backed up by clear, referenced, workings wherever needed. Working through the numerical data in a logical manner will ensure that you stay focused.

- **Good time management.** Complete all tasks in the time available.

Skill activity

STEP 1 Where a question includes a significant amount of data, read the requirements carefully to make sure that you understand clearly what the question is asking you to do.

In this question, the requirement is to calculate a cost of debt and a weighted average cost of capital, so you know that you will need to calculate the cost of, and market value of, various types of finance; this will help you to understand why certain information has been provided.

You can use the highlighting function to pull out important data from the question.

	$m	$m	$m
Assets			
Non-current assets			101
Current assets			
Inventory		11	
Trade receivables		21	
Cash		10	
			42
Total assets			143
Equity and liabilities			
Ordinary share capital		50	
Preference share capital		25	
Retained earnings		19	
Total equity			94
Non-current liabilities			
Long-term borrowings		20	
Current liabilities			
Trade payables	22		
Other payables	7		
Total current liabilities		29	
Total liabilities			49
Total equity and liabilities			143

NN Co has a cost of equity of 12%.[7]

The ordinary shares of the company have a nominal value of $0.50 per share[8] and an ex div market value of $8.30 per share.[9]

The long-term borrowings of NN Co consist of 7%[10] bonds that are redeemable[11] in 6 years' time at their nominal value of $100 per bond. The current ex interest market price of the bonds is $103.50.[12]

The preference[13] shares of NN Co have a nominal value of[14] $0.50 per share and pay an annual dividend of 8%.[15] The ex div market value of the preference shares is $0.67[16] per share.

NN Co pays profit tax at an annual rate of 25% per year.

Required

(a) Calculate the after-tax cost of debt of NN Co.

(4 marks)

Required

(b) Calculate the weighted average after-tax cost of capital of NN Co.

(6 marks)

STEP 2 Use a standard proforma working. For example, if you are asked to calculate the WACC use your standard proforma for calculating WACC and separately work through the individual parts of the calculation (Ke, Kd, Ve, Vd).

There are three sources of finance in this question so the basic WACC formula provided in the exam cannot be used (although it could be adapted).

[7] The cost of equity (Ke) is given.

[8] There are 100 million ordinary shares ($50m/$0.50)

[9] The market value of equity (Ve) = 100m x $8.30 = $830m

[10] Interest on one bond is $7

[11] Use the IRR function to calculate the cost of debt (kd)

[12] The MV of debt (Vd)= $20m/$100 x $103.50 = $20.7m

[13] There is a third source of finance!

[14] There are 50 million preference shares($25m/$0.50)

[15] Dividend = 8% x $0.50 = $0.04

[16] The market value of preference shares (Vp) = 0.67 x 50=33.5

Instead it would make sense to use the following proforma/approach to calculate WACC.

C6	▼	⋮	×	✓	fx	=100*8.3

▲	A	B	C	D	E
1					
2	**WACC Calculation**	Cost	Market value		Weighted cost
3	**Type of finance**	%	$m	%	(B x D)
4	Ordinary shares	12	830	0.94	11.3
5	Preference shares (W1)	6	33.5	0.04	0.2
6	Redeemable bonds (part a)	4.6	20.7	0.02	0.1
7			**884.2**		**11.6**
8					
9					
10					
11	W1 - Preference shares				
12					
13	Do	0.04			
14	Po	0.67			
15	Kpref	6%			
16					

STEP 3 Use spreadsheet formulae to perform basic calculations. Do not write out your workings, this wastes time and you may make a mistake. Use the spreadsheet the spreadsheet formulae instead!

Simple spreadsheet formulae are used to calculate the MV of each source of finance and to weight those values against the cost of each type of finance.

D6	▼	⋮	×	✓	fx	=C4/C7

▲	A	B	C	D	E
1					
2	**WACC Calculation**	Cost	Market value		Weighted cost
3	**Type of finance**	%	$m	%	(B x D)
4	Ordinary shares	12	830	0.94	11.3
5	Preference shares (W1)	6	33.5	0.04	0.2
6	Redeemable bonds (part a)	4.6	20.7	0.02	0.1
7			**884.2**		**11.6**
8					
9					
10					

The IRR spreadsheet function can be used to calculate the cost of debt.

B26 ▼ ⋮ × ✓ *fx* | =IRR(B19:B25)

	A	B	C	D
16				
17	**Cost of debt calculation**			
18				
19	0	-103.5		
20	1	5.25		
21	2	5.25		
22	3	5.25		
23	4	5.25		
24	5	5.25		
25	6	105.25		
26	Cost of debt	4.6%		
27				
28				

Exam success skills diagnostic

Every time you complete a question, use the diagnostic below to assess how effectively you demonstrated the exam success skills in answering the question. The table has been completed below for the 'NN' activity to give you an idea of how to complete the diagnostic.

Exam success skills	Your reflections/observations
Managing information	There is a significant amount of numerical data provided in this question. Did you note that there are 3 sources of finance and therefore the basic WACC formula provided in the exam cannot be used? Did you identify the correct number of shares? Did you note the market value of each instrument?
Correct interpretation of requirements	You need to calculate the post-tax cost of debt and the post-tax WACC. Did you remember to account for tax?
Efficient numerical analysis	Did your answer present a neat WACC calculation in a format that would have been easy for a marker to follow?
Good time management	Did you manage your time to ensure you tackled all workings and completed both requirements in the time available?
Most important action points to apply to your next question	

Summary

Section C of the FM exam could contain a question that focuses on business finance and asks you to perform an WACC calculation.

This is an important area to revise and to ensure that you understand data presented in the question and use it to prepare a WACC calculation.

It is also important to be aware that in the exam you are dealing with detailed calculations under timed exam conditions and time management is absolutely crucial. You therefore need to ensure that you:

- Interpret the data given in the question correctly
- Use a clear, standard WACC layout.
- Use spreadsheet formula to perform basic calculations.
- Show clear workings

Remember that there are no optional questions in the FM exam and that this syllabus section (section E: Business Finance) will definitely be tested!

13

Business valuations

Learning objectives

On completion of this chapter, you should be able to:

	Syllabus reference
• Nature and purpose of the valuation of business and financial assets	
- Identify and discuss reasons for valuing business and financial assets	F1(a)
- Identify information requirements for valuation and discuss the limitations of different types of information	F1(b)
Models for the valuation of shares	
• Discuss and apply asset-based valuation models including:	F2(a)
- Net book value (statement of financial position) basis	
- Net realisable value basis	
- Net replacement cost basis	
• Discuss and apply income-based valuation models including:	F2(b)
- Price/earnings ratio method	
- Earnings yield method	
• Discuss and apply cash flow-based valuation models including:	F2(c)
- Dividend valuation model and the dividend growth model	
- Discounted cash flow basis	
• The valuation of debt and other financial assets. Discuss and apply appropriate valuation methods to: irredeemable debt, redeemable debt, convertible debt, preference shares	F3(a)
• EMH and practical considerations in the valuation of shares	
- Distinguish between weak, semi-strong and strong form efficiency	F4(a)
- Discuss practical considerations, including: marketability & liquidity of shares, availability & sources of information, market imperfections & pricing anomalies and market capitalisation.	F4(b)
- Describe the significance of investor speculation and the explanations of investor decisions offered by behavioural finance.	F4(c)

Exam context

This chapter covers Section F of the syllabus (Business Valuations). This syllabus area is examinable in the OTQ sections of the exam (sections A and B) and commonly forms the central theme of one of the (10 mark) Section B questions.

It is also possible for this syllabus area to be touched on as a part of a Section C question.

Chapter overview

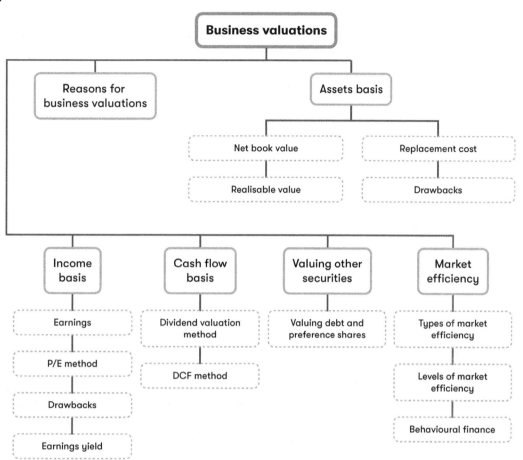

1 Reasons for business valuations

1.1 When share valuations are required

An estimate of the valuation of a share will typically be required if an investor is considering the **purchase or sale of a share**, or in other scenarios such as where a share is being used as **collateral for a loan**.

Shares are valued by stock exchanges, so **an independent share valuation** will not always be required, but may be **necessary if**:

(a) If the company is **unquoted**.

(b) If the stock market **does not value shares accurately** (ie it is not efficient in terms of the efficient markets hypothesis, covered later in this chapter).

(c) If there is a takeover bid and the **value of the company being bought will change** under the management of the new owner.

> **Takeover:** The acquisition by a company of a controlling interest in the voting share capital of another company, usually achieved by the purchase of a majority of the voting shares.
>
> **Market capitalisation:** The total value of all the shares in a company.

1.1.1 Other reasons for valuations

In addition, a **part of a business** may need to be valued because a company is negotiating the sale of a part of its business to a management buyout team or to an external buyer.

1.2 Methods of business valuation

If an independent valuation is needed, it will often be helpful to use a range of techniques in order to create a **range of values** within which a buyer (or seller) will be prepared to negotiate.

There are several different methods of valuing a business. Each of the methods give different values, and are suitable in different situations.

Max → Value the **cash flows** or **earnings** (often under new ownership)

Value the **dividends** (often under the existing management)

Min → Value the **assets** using the net book value or realisable value approaches

Essential reading

See Chapter 13 section 1 of the Essential reading, available in the digital edition of the Workbook, for more background information on this area.

The Essential reading is available as an Appendix of the digital edition of the Workbook.

2 Assets basis (also called net asset value basis)

As an alternative to selling a business as a going concern its owners could sell the assets and use the funds to repay its creditors; any surplus (ie the net asset value) would then belong to the shareholders.

The net asset value approach normally represents the **minimum amount** that shareholders will accept if they are selling the business.

Asset valuation methods are most useful if a business derives most its value from its assets (eg its main business is investing in property), or if it is trying to establish the lowest price that it would find acceptable for its shares.

The net asset valuation (NAV) approach can involve the valuation of assets in three different ways: net book value, realisable value or replacement value.

2.1 Net book value (historic) basis

Using the net book value method of valuation, the value of a share is calculated as the value of **net assets** divided by the **number of shares**.

Net assets are the value in the statement of financial position of:

non-current assets (net of depreciation)

+ **current** assets

− **all liabilities**.

Intangible assets that are not recognised in the statement of financial position are ignored by this method (including workforce skills, customer relationships).

Activity 1: Assets basis

Groady Co wants to buy another company, Bergerbo Co, which operates in the same industry.

Bergerbo Co has non-current assets in its statement of financial position of $50.5m and net current assets of $12.3m. The equity and liabilities of Bergerbo Co are as follows.

	$m
Ordinary shares ($100 par value)	10.4
Reserves	19.3
Medium- and long-term bank loans	33.1
	62.8

Required

What is the net asset value of Bergerbo?

○ $10.4m

○ $62.8m

○ $29.7m

○ $50.5m

Solution

2.2 Realisable asset values

This method works in the same way except that it **adjusts the book value of the assets** to reflect their **market value** and is therefore a more accurate way of assessing the net asset value in the event of a liquidation.

Any adjustments that are required would be **stated in an exam question**.

For example:
- you may be asked to adjust for inventory being **overvalued** by x%
- or the **market value** of non-current assets may be given.

2.3 Replacement cost

This takes a different perspective to the previous two methods.

If a potential buyer of a company can estimate the **replacement cost** of the assets of the target company (ie the cost of acquiring its separate assets on the open market), then it can estimate the **maximum** it should pay for the target company.

In reality, replacement costs are **difficult to estimate** and this basis also ignores the difficulty and cost of creating the intangible assets of a target company (eg its brand name).

Again, any adjustments that are required would be **stated in an exam question**.

2.4 Disadvantages of the asset-based approach

Asset-based methods ignores the value of **intangible assets** and the value of **future profits**.

Asset-based methods are especially limited in their use in valuing **service companies**, which often operate with a low tangible asset base (eg an accountancy practice).

3 Income (or earnings) bases

These approaches use the current earnings or the prospective earnings of a business under new ownership as the basis for valuing a business.

There are two income-based valuation methods: the P/E method, and the earnings yield method.

3.1 P/E method

The P/E ratio (introduced in Chapter 1) indicates the market's assessment of a company's (or a sector's) future cash flows and risk.

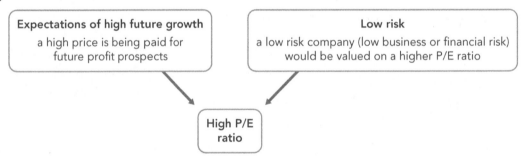

The P/E ratio produces an **earnings-based** valuation of shares by taking the latest earnings of the **target** and multiplying by an **appropriate P/E ratio.**

Income-based value = earnings of target × appropriate P/E ratio

| Shows the **current profitability** of the company | Reflects the **growth prospects/risk** of a company |

Note. If EPS is used in this calculation this gives the value of an **individual share**.

> ### Exam focus point
>
> The ACCA examining team has commented in the past that students often calculate earnings per share incorrectly. Remember that earnings are calculated as profits **after interest and tax and any preference dividends**

Activity 2: P/E method

Groady Co (from activity 1) wants to buy another company, Bergerbo Co, which operates in the same industry.

The statement of profit or loss for Bergerbo for the year just ended is as follows.

	$m
PBIT	5.8
Interest expense	2.3
Taxable profit	3.5
Taxation (25%)	0.9
Profit after tax	2.6
Ordinary dividend	2.0

Groady's P/E is currently 21.2, whilst the industry average is 19.5.

Required

What is the earnings valuation for Bergerbo based on the assumption that it will perform as well as Groady in terms of earnings?

O $55.1m

O $50.7m

O $74.2m

O $66.5m

Solution

3.2   Problems with P/E method

- **Choice of which P/E ratio to use**

The P/E ratio used should reflect the **business and financial risk (ie capital structure) of the company that is being valued**. This is quite difficult to estimate in practice.

Also, the P/E ratio will normally be **reduced** if the company that is being valued is **unlisted**.

Listed companies have a higher value, mainly due to the greater ease in selling shares in a listed company. The P/E ratio of an unlisted company's shares will be 30%–50% lower compared to the P/E ratio of a similar public company.

- **Earnings calculation**

The earnings of the target company may need to be adjusted if it includes one-off items that will tend not to recur.

Historic earnings will not reflect the **potential future** synergies (ie cost savings or revenue increases) that may arise from an acquisition. Earnings may need to be adjusted to reflect such **synergies**.

Finally, the latest earnings figures might have been manipulated upwards by the target company if it has been looking to be bought by another company.

- **Stock market efficiency**

Stock market prices may not be efficient because they are affected by psychological factors (see behavioural finance later in this chapter), so P/E ratios may be distorted by swings in market sentiment.

3.3 Earnings yield method

The earnings yield method produces an **income-based** valuation of shares by taking the latest earnings of the **target** and dividing by earnings yield (defined as earnings / share price).

This is the **same approach as the P/E method** but uses **different terminology**.

Income-based value = earnings of target ÷ earnings yield

In the previous activity, the P/E ratio of 21.2 was used, so the earnings yield would be 1 ÷ 21. 2 = 0.0472 or 4.72%.

The market value of Bergerbo's shares can therefore be calculated as earnings divided by earnings yield ie 2.6 / 0.0472 = $55.1m. This is the **same value obtained by the P/E method.**

4 Cash flow basis

These approaches use a **discounted cash flow approach** to establish the present value of a company either in $m or per share. There are two cash flow-based valuation methods: the dividend valuation method, and the DCF method.

4.1 Dividend valuation method (DVM)

The value of a share is calculated as the present value of the future dividends that are being **generated by the current management team**. This method is suitable for valuing a **minority interest** in the shares of a company, because it ignores forecast synergies arising from a takeover.

Formula provided

Value per share =

$$P_0 = \frac{D_0(1 + g)}{(r_e - g)}$$

d_0 = dividend paid now

r_e = cost of equity of the target

g = annual growth rate in dividends

In Chapter 11 we demonstrated how to estimate 'g', using historic growth or the reinvestment approach, in the context of the dividend growth model for estimating the cost of equity.

Activity 3: Dividend valuation model

Groady Co (from activities 1 and 2) wants to buy another company, Bergerbo Co, which operates in the same industry.

Bergerbo's statement of profit or loss for the year just ended is as follows:

	$m
PBIT	5.8
Interest expense	2.3
Taxable profit	3.5
Taxation (25%)	0.9
Profit after tax	2.6
Ordinary dividend	2.0

There are conflicting views on Bergerbo's future dividend growth potential; some analysts think that the dividend will not grow for the foreseeable future, others estimate that the dividend growth rate will be between 3% and 5% p.a.

Bergerbo's cost of equity is estimated at 7.6%.

Required

1   What is the dividend valuation for Bergerbo assuming zero dividend growth for the foreseeable future?

   ○ $26.3m

   ○ $0.152m

   ○ $34.2m

   ○ $7.9m

2   What is the dividend valuation for Bergerbo assuming 3% dividend growth for the foreseeable future?

   ○ $43.48m

   ○ $44.78m

   ○ $0.092m

   ○ $13.43m

Solution

4.1.1 Disadvantages of the simple dividend valuation model

(a) It is difficult to estimate future dividend growth.

(b) It is inaccurate to assume that growth will be constant (but see section 4.1.2)

(c) It creates zero values for zero dividend companies.

(d) It creates negative values for high growth companies ie if $g > r_e$

4.1.2 Non-constant growth

The DVM formula can be **adapted** to value dividends that are forecast to go through **two phases**:

Phase 1 (eg next 3 years)	Phase 2 (eg year 4 onwards)
• Growth is forecast at an unusually high (or low) rate	• Growth returns to a constant rate
Use a normal NPV approach to calculate the present value of the dividends in this phase.	1. Use the formula to assess the NPV of the constant growth phase, however the **time periods need to be adapted** eg: $$P_0 = \frac{D_0(1 + g)}{(r_e - g)}$$ is adapted to $$P_3 = \frac{D_3(1 + g)}{(r_e - g)}$$ 2. Then adjust the value given above by discounting back to a present value (here using a T_3 discount rate because the first cash flow being assessed is in time 4).

Illustration 1: Dividend valuation model and non-constant growth

Using the information from the previous activity, calculate the dividend valuation to the nearest $m for Bergerbo assuming 5% dividend growth for 3 years and 3% thereafter.

Solution

Time	1	2	3	4 onwards
Expected dividend ($2m)	2.1	2.205	2.315	2.384
Perpetuity factor (1/(0.076 – 0.03))				21.739
DF @ 7.6%	0.929	0.864	0.803	0.803
Present value	1.951	1.905	1.859	41.616

Dividend valuation	47.29 ie $47m to the nearest $m.

4.2 Discounted cash flow (DCF) method

The value of a share is calculated as the present value of the future cash flows that will be **generated by the new management team**. It **includes forecast synergies**.

This method is suitable for valuing a **controlling interest** in the shares of a company, where the owner can act to change the profitability of a company.

The steps in this method of valuation are:

Step 1 Estimate the cash flows that will be obtained each year from the acquired business.

Step 2 Discount these cash flows at an appropriate cost of capital. The cost of capital that is used should be consistent with the cash flow estimates; this means that one of two approaches may be required:

Approach 1	Approach 2
Cash flows are **after interest payments** and after tax (representing returns to ordinary shareholders)	Cash flows are **before interest** and after tax (representing returns to ordinary shareholders **and also** debt holders)
Discount at the **cost of equity** to calculate the present value of the equity (ie ordinary) shares	Discount at the overall **weighted average cost of capital** to calculate the present value of the **company** (ie ordinary shares plus debt) • This value will be used if for a valuation of the whole **company** (eg if the proposal is to buy the entire business, including the debt) • If only the equity needs to be valued then the value of **debt will** then need to **be deducted to calculate the value of equity**

Activity 4: DCF method

Diversification wishes to make a bid for Tadpole. Tadpole makes after-tax profits of $40,000 a year. Diversification believes that if further money is spent on additional investments, the after-tax (and interest) cash flows (ignoring the purchase consideration) could be as follows.

Time	Cash flow (net of tax and interest) in $
0	(100,000)
1	(80,000)
2	60,000
3	100,000
4	150,000
5	150,000

The cost of equity of Diversification is 15%, and the WACC is 10%; the company expects all its investments to pay back, in discounted terms, within five years.

Required

1   What is the maximum price that Diversification should be willing to pay for the shares of Tadpole?

2   What is the maximum price that Diversification should be willing to pay for the shares of Tadpole if it decides to value the business on the basis of its cash flows in perpetuity, and annual cash flows from Year 6 onwards are expected to be $120,000?

Solution

Activity 5: Further practice: Section B example

The following scenario relates to questions a-e

Mathilda Co is a listed company which is seen as a potential target for acquisition by financial analysts. The value of the company has therefore been a matter of public debate in recent weeks and the following financial information is available:

Year	20X4	20X3	20X2	20X1
Profit after tax ($m)	25.3	24.3	22.3	21.3
Total dividends ($m)	15.0	14.0	13.0	12.5

Statement of financial position information for 20X4:

	$m	$m
Non-current assets		227.5
Current assets		
Inventory	9.5	
Trade receivables	11.3	20.8
Total assets		248.3
Equity finance		
Ordinary shares	50.0	
Reserves	118.0	168.0
Non-current liabilities		
8% loan notes		62.5
Current liabilities		17.8
Total financing		248.3

The shares of Mathilda Co have a nominal value of 50c per share and a market value of $10.00 per share. The business sector of Mathilda Co has an average price/earnings ratio of 16 times.

The expected net realisable values of the non-current assets and the inventory are $215.0m and $10.5m, respectively. In the event of liquidation, only 90% of the trade receivables are expected to be collectible.

Required

1   What is the value of Mathilda Co using market capitalisation?

　○ $50m

　○ $250m

　○ $500m

　○ $1,000m

2   What is the value of Mathilda Co using the net asset value on a liquidation basis?

　○ $147.20m

　○ $155.37m

　○ $217.87m

　○ $248.30m

3   What is the value of Mathilda Co using the price/earnings ratio method (business sector average price/earnings ratio)?

　○ $269.87m

　○ $404.8m

　○ $155.37m

　○ $240m

4   What is the geometric average historic dividend growth rate for Mathilda Co?

　○ 4.66%

　○ 5.90%

　○ 6.27%

　○ 35.72%

5   Which of the following statements are problems in using the price/earnings ratio to value a company?

　(1)   It can be difficult to find a quoted company with a similar range of activities.

　(2)   A single year's P/E ratio may not be representative

　(3)   It is the reciprocal of the earnings yield

　(4)   It combines stock market information with corporate information

　○ (1) and (2) only

　○ (3) and (4) only

　○ (1), (3) and (4) only

　○ (1), (2), (3) and (4)

Solution

5 Valuation of other securities

Discounted cash flow techniques can be used to value other securities **including irredeemable debt, redeemable debt, convertible debt and preference shares.**

Because we are valuing these securities from the viewpoint of investors any tax relief due on interest payments is ignored so the **cash flows and the required yield should both be pre-tax**.

For convertible debt and redeemable debt, the DCF should include the interest received during the term of the debt plus the amount received at redemption.

For irredeemable debt and preference shares the cash flows can be treated as being received into perpetuity. In the case the present value is calculated as:

Cash received × (1/required return)

Activity 6: Valuing other securities

Groady has 7% loan notes which are redeemable at their par value of $100 in 3 years' time. Alternatively, each loan note can be converted into 25 shares in 3 years' time. The share price is currently $4.50 and is expected to grow at 5% p.a.

Groady's bond has a yield of 6%.

Required

1   Calculate the market value of this convertible loan note.

2   Calculate the floor value (ie its value if the loan note was not converted into shares).

3   Calculate the value of the 7% loan note if it had been irredeemable.

Solution

Essential reading

See Chapter 13 section 2 of the Essential Reading, available in the digital edition of the Workbook, for more background information on this area.

The Essential reading is available as an Appendix of the digital edition of the Workbook.

---

6 The efficient market hypothesis

KEY TERM

> **The efficient market hypothesis:** A rationale for explaining how share prices react to new information about a company, and when any such change in share price occurs. Stock market reaction to new information depends on the strength of the stock market's efficiency.

6.1 Types of market efficiency

Three different types of efficiency can be distinguished in the context of the operation of financial markets.

6.1.1 Allocative efficiency

This refers to the ability of a financial market to **direct funds** to those organisations (borrowers) which can use them most profitably.

BPP LEARNING MEDIA

6.1.2 Operational efficiency

Operational efficiency describes the ability of a financial market to operate with **minimal transaction costs**.

6.1.3 Information processing (or pricing) efficiency

The market price for securities **reflects all the relevant and available information** relating to the securities and the company which issued them.

6.2 Levels of market efficiency

Capital markets can potentially display three varying levels of information processing efficiency.

Levels of efficiency	Definition / explanation	Implication(s)
Zero efficiency	Share prices **fail to reflect** a wide range of factors that should impact on the share price.	Share prices will regularly be mis-priced and investors can make excess profits over the long-term by studying the market to spot over- or under-priced shares eg by **analysing past share price movements** (this is called Chartism, or technical analysis).
Weak form	Share prices reflect **historical information** including information about past share price movements.	If true, investors **can't** make excess profits over the long-term by studying past share price movements. Share prices move due to the unpredictable arrival of favourable and unfavourable information, because this information cannot be predicted share prices are said to follow a 'random walk'. This is called random walk theory. However, investors **can** make excess profits by analysing any new information and reacting to it quicker than the stock market does. This is because a weak-form efficient market is not quick at responding to new information coming into the public domain that should affect share prices.
Semi-strong form	In addition to **historical information,** share price movements **also reflect all publicly available information quickly and accurately**.	Here, professional investors can't beat the market in the **long term** either by analysing past price patterns (as for weak form efficiency) or by analysing the implications of new publicly available information. Over the long-term investors will not be able to make above average profits by consistently identifying shares that have a **fundamental value** that is materially different from their market value.
Strong form	Share prices reflect **all** information, whether publicly available or not:	In this case, share prices will respond to new developments and events before they even become public knowledge. This happens using **information held privately by the directors; in theory directors are not allowed to trade shares using this information** (this would be insider trading and is **not legal**).

Most studies support the view that the sophisticated markets like the London Stock Exchange are **semi-strong form efficient**. If this is the case, then the implications are that:

(a) The **share price of a company is the best basis for a takeover bid**; a company should only pay more than the market price if there are synergies (eg extra cash flows) arising from a takeover.

(b) The directors should take the correct investment/financing/risk management decisions and **make this information public** (press release, annual accounts).

The central paradox of efficient markets is that an efficient market requires people to believe that the market is **inefficient**, so that they trade securities in an attempt to outperform the market. This is sometimes called the **market paradox**.

Activity 7: EMH

1   Given a strong form efficient market which of the following actions by the directors of a company listed on the market would impact the share price?

O   Window dressing the accounts to make financial performance appear more impressive

O   Releasing information relevant to the riskiness of the organisation

O   Making a decision to launch a new product with innovative technology

O   Increasing the dividend in the current year to make shareholders more satisfied with their investment

2   Sergey has devised an investment strategy whereby shares will be bought and sold based on patterns discerned from a graph of past share price movements.

Which level of efficiency does Sergey think the market has?

O   Not efficient on any level

O   Weak form efficient

O   Semi-strong form efficient

O   Strong form efficient

6.3   Practical considerations in the valuation of shares

Marketability and liquidity of shares	How easy it is to find a buyer for a share (**marketability**) and how **liquid** a share is (how easy it is to convert into cash at a fair value) will influence the value of a share.
	In general, shares in large companies are relatively easy to sell, which has a positive impact on their share value compared to small companies. It may be difficult to sell shares in a private company, particularly a minority shareholding, which will have the effect of lowering the share value.
Availability and sources of information	If investors are **unable to obtain accurate information** (eg if there are doubts over the accuracy of a company's financial statements) this is likely to lead to a drop in the value of a share as they react adversely to uncertainty.
Market imperfections and pricing anomalies	Various types of anomaly appear to support the views that irrationality often drives the stock market, including **calendar effects** such as share prices often falling at particular times of the week (eg Monday mornings) and high returns often occurring in particular months.

Market capitalisation	Shares in small companies may be neglected. The return from investing in **smaller** companies has been shown to be **greater** than the average return from all companies in the long run. This increased return may compensate for the greater risk associated with smaller companies, or it may be due to a start from a lower base reflecting that they are often undervalued.

6.4 Behavioural finance

Behavioural finance is an alternative view to the efficient market hypothesis. It attempts to explain the market implications of the **psychological** factors behind investor decisions and suggests that **irrational investor behaviour** may significantly affect share price movements.

6.4.1 Herding

An example of irrational behaviour is the tendency for investors to follow trends, this can lead to stock market bubbles in particular sectors, or in the stock market as a whole.

6.4.2 Loss-aversion

Some investors will place undue emphasis on avoiding short-term losses even if long-term performance looks strong.

Essential reading

See Chapter 13 section 3 of the Essential reading, available in the digital edition of the Workbook, for more background information on this area.

The Essential reading is available as an Appendix of the digital edition of the Workbook.

Chapter summary

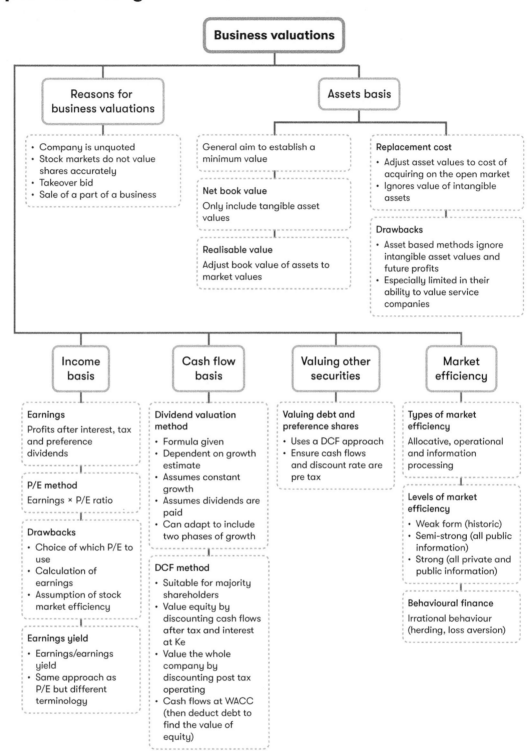

Business valuations

Reasons for business valuations
- Company is unquoted
- Stock markets do not value shares accurately
- Takeover bid
- Sale of a part of a business

Assets basis

General aim to establish a minimum value

Net book value
Only include tangible asset values

Realisable value
Adjust book value of assets to market values

Replacement cost
- Adjust asset values to cost of acquiring on the open market
- Ignores value of intangible assets

Drawbacks
- Asset based methods ignore intangible asset values and future profits
- Especially limited in their ability to value service companies

Income basis

Earnings
Profits after interest, tax and preference dividends

P/E method
Earnings × P/E ratio

Drawbacks
- Choice of which P/E to use
- Calculation of earnings
- Assumption of stock market efficiency

Earnings yield
- Earnings/earnings yield
- Same approach as P/E but different terminology

Cash flow basis

Dividend valuation method
- Formula given
- Dependent on growth estimate
- Assumes constant growth
- Assumes dividends are paid
- Can adapt to include two phases of growth

DCF method
- Suitable for majority shareholders
- Value equity by discounting cash flows after tax and interest at Ke
- Value the whole company by discounting post tax operating
- Cash flows at WACC (then deduct debt to find the value of equity)

Valuing other securities

Valuing debt and preference shares
- Uses a DCF approach
- Ensure cash flows and discount rate are pre tax

Market efficiency

Types of market efficiency
Allocative, operational and information processing

Levels of market efficiency
- Weak form (historic)
- Semi-strong (all public information)
- Strong (all private and public information)

Behavioural finance
Irrational behaviour (herding, loss aversion)

Knowledge diagnostic

1. Asset based models

The main methods (net book value and realisable value) establish a minimum price for a share.

2. Income based models

Main model is the P/E model, the P/E ratio reflects the risk and growth potential of a business.

3. Dividend growth model

This is based on a company's existing growth rate and dividend policy and is therefore mainly used to value minority stakes.

4. DCF model

Be careful to use the WACC if cash flows are pre-interest and the cost of equity if the cash flows are post interest.

5. Stock market efficiency

Most studies suggest the London Stock market is a semi-strong form efficient.

Further study guidance

Question practice

Now try the following from the Further question practice bank (available in the digital edition of the Workbook):

Section A questions

Q26, Q30

Section B questions

Q34, Q35, Q36 *(also recaps on earlier chapters)*

Section C questions

Q57 Bases of valuation (this longer question is to allow further study of this area, but this chapter is not directly examinable in Section C of the real exam).

Further reading

There is a useful Technical Article written by a member of the FM examining team that is available on ACCA's website; it is called 'Behavioural finance'. We recommend that you read this short article to improve your understanding of this area.

Activity answers

Activity 1: Assets basis

The correct answer is: $29.7m

$62.8m − debt of $33.1m = **$29.7m**

But we have no information about the industry, the nature of the assets or any intangible values.

Activity 2: P/E method

The correct answer is: $55.1m

P/E valuation: 21.2 × 2.6 = **$55.1m**

This uses the P/E of 21.2 on the assumption that Bergerbo shares Groady's growth prospects.

Activity 3: Dividend valuation model

1   The correct answer is: $26.3m

   P = 2/0.076 = 26.3m

2   The correct answer is: $44.78m

   P = 2.06/(0.076 - 0.03) = 44.78m

Activity 4: DCF method

1   $101,910

   The maximum price is one which would make the return from the total investment exactly 15% over five years, so that the NPV at 15% would be 0. It is suitable to use the cost of equity because the cash flows are after interest.

Time	Cash flows	DF (15%)	PV
	$		$
0	(100,000)	1.000	(100,000)
1	(80,000)	0.870	(69,600)
2	60,000	0.756	45,360
3	100,000	0.658	65,800
4	150,000	0.572	85,800
5	150,000	0.497	74,550

   Maximum purchase price: 101,910

2   $499,510

   If the shares are valued on the basis of cash flows in perpetuity, we need to add the PV of annual cash flows from Year 6 onwards.

   The value of the cash flows from Time 6 onwards, in perpetuity, at a Time 5 present value = $120,000/0.15 = $800,000.

   Discounting this to a Time 0 PV: $800,000 × 0.497 = $397,600.

   This increases the valuation from $101,910 to $499,510 ($101,910 + $397,600).

   The difference between this valuation and the valuation in (a) is huge. It may illustrate that business valuations depend crucially on the assumptions that are used to reach the valuation.

Activity 5: Further practice: Section B example

1   The correct answer is: $1,000m

Market capitalisation = number of shares × market value.

= ($50m / $0.5) × $10.00 = $1,000m

2   The correct answer is: $155.37m

The net realisable value of assets at liquidation = non-current assets + inventory + trade receivables − current liabilities − loan notes

= $215m + $10.5m + ($11.3m × 90%) − $17.8m − $62.5m

= $155.37m

3   The correct answer is: $404.8m

Historic earnings based on 20X4 profit are after tax = $25.3m

Average P/E ratio in industry = 16 times

Assuming no adjustment required to P/E ratio (Mathilda is a listed company so no need to adjust for transferability) and using historic earnings:

P/E ratio value = 16 × $25.3m = $404.8m

4   The correct answer is: 6.27%

A geometric average is the compound average growth rate.

Historic growth dividend rate = $[(15m/12.5m)^{1/3}-1]$ = 0.0627 = 6.27%

5   The correct answer is: (1) and (2) only

It can be difficult to find a quoted company with a similar range of activities.

Quoted companies are often diversified.

A single year's P/E ratio may not be a good basis if earnings are volatile or the quoted company's share price is at an abnormal level.

Notes on incorrect answers:

The P/E ratio is the reciprocal of earnings yield (which is E/P), but this is not a problem in using the P/E ratio.

The P/E ratio does combine stock market information (e.g. the general state of the market) and company specific factors (eg forecast growth), but both are relevant for valuing a business so these are not problems.

Activity 6: Valuing other securities

1   $128.1

Share price in 3 years' time = 4.50 × 1.05 × 1.05 × 1.05 = **$5.21**

25 shares × $5.21 = $130.25 so conversion will be preferred

Assume in Year 3 $7 interest is received as well.

Time	1	2	3
Cash flow	7	7	137.25
DF @ 6%	0.943	0.890	0.840
PV	6.6	6.2	115.3

Total **$128.1**

2 $102.7

Time	1	2	3
Cash flow	7	7	107
DF @ 6%	0.943	0.890	0.840
PV	6.6	6.2	89.9

Total **$102.7**

3 $116.7

$7 × 1/r = $7 × 1/0.06 = **$116.7**

Activity 7: EMH

1 The correct answer is: Making a decision to launch a new product with innovative technology

In a strong form efficient market, the release of insider information or information designed to manipulate shareholder sentiment will have no effect on the share price as the share price will already reflect the directors' view of the company's true value.

However, making a decision on a new product will change the present value of future cash flows and will therefore change the fundamental value of the company.

2 The correct answer is: Not efficient on any level

If the market was efficient (even weak form efficient) share prices would be based on the available information relevant to the individual companies listed. If share prices are expected to continue to follow past trends then the market is not reacting to available information. On a weak form efficient market, those past share price movements would already be reflected in the share price.

Skills checkpoint 4

Effective discussion of key financial topics

Chapter overview

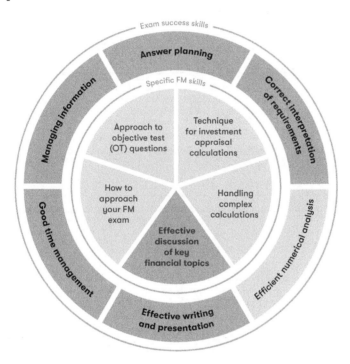

Introduction

Section C of the FM exam will contain two questions which will be scenario-based and will contain both discursive and computational elements.

A key skill in Section C, and one that candidates are **often weak on**, is that of **discussing and explaining Financial Management concepts** as applied to a given scenario.

This may be a weakness because candidates preparing for this exam focus on practising numerical questions, as they are easy to mark because the answer is right or wrong, whereas written questions are more subjective. Even when attempting written questions, it is tempting to write a brief answer plan and then look at the answer rather than writing a full answer to plan. However, **unless you practise written questions in full to time, you will not acquire the necessary skills to tackle discussion questions.**

The FM examining team provide the following useful feedback on answering discursive question responses:

Question requirements must be read carefully and answered directly. Candidates writing 'all that they know about the topic' without addressing the question requirement will invariably score few marks. Instead, **the focus must be on the question requirement and relating this to the scenario provided.**

Question requirements will often refer to the company in the scenario, eg 'Discuss THREE ways in which K Co can ...'. This means that candidates **must refer to the company's circumstances** in order to score the marks on offer.

As in previous diets, some candidates failed to score marks where a recommendation and/or a comment was required on calculated figures. For instance, if asked whether a company should undertake an investment project, it **is not enough for a candidate to simply say 'Good project so invest', without justifying the decision**. Saying 'the project is financially acceptable as it has a positive NPV' offers a suitable justification.

Finally, in terms of general comments about Section C, it must be emphasised that if asked to discuss factors/benefits/reasons/merits, it is not enough to simply list a few words. ACCA's guidance is that **'Discuss' means 'Consider and debate/argue about the pros and cons of an issue. Examine in detail by using arguments in favour or against'.**

Effective discussion of key financial topics.

FM Skill: Effective discussion of key financial topics.

The key steps in applying this skill are outlined below and will be explained in more detail in the following sections as an extract of the past exam question 'Corfe Co' is answered.

STEP 1: Read and analyse the requirement.

The active verb used often dictates the approach that written answers should take. For example, 'discuss' means to examine in detail by using arguments in favour or against.
Work out how many minutes you have to answer each sub requirement.

STEP 2: Read and analyse the scenario.

Identify the type of company you are dealing with and how the financial topics in the requirement relate to that type of company. As you go through the scenario you should be highlighting important information which you think will play a key role in answering the specific requirements.

STEP 3: Plan your answer

Ensure your answer is balanced in terms of identifying the potential benefits **and** limitations of topics that are being discussed or recommended.

Step 4: Write your answer

As you write your answer, **try wherever possible to apply your analysis to the scenario**, instead of simply writing about the financial topic in generic, technical terms.
As you write your answer, explain what you mean – in one (or two) sentence(s) – and then explain **why this matters in the given scenario**. This should result in a series of short paragraphs that address the specific context of the scenario.

Exam success skills

The following question is an extract from a past exam question; this extract was worth 9 marks.

For this question, we will also focus on the following **exam success skills:**

- **Managing information.** There is a lot of information to absorb in this question and the best approach is active reading. This involves focusing on the requirement first, on the basis that until you have done this the detail in the question will have little meaning.

- **Correct interpretation of requirements.** The requirements clearly ask you to discuss the views of three directors, it may therefore be helpful to think of this as three sub-requirements worth three marks each. Remember that the verb 'discuss' means that you should debate/argue about the pros and cons of each director's view.

- **Answer planning.** Everyone will have a preferred style for an answer plan. For example, it may be a mind map, bullet-pointed lists or simply annotating the question paper. Choose the approach that you feel most comfortable with or, if you are not sure, try out different approaches for different questions until you have found your preferred style. You will typically be awarded 1 mark per relevant, well explained point so you should aim to generate sufficient points to score a comfortable pass.

- **Effective writing and presentation.** This is particularly important in discussion questions. Use headings and sub-headings in your answer, and write in full sentences, ensuring your style is professional. To achieve the necessary depth of discussion and to explain your points, it is recommended that you include illustrative examples in your answer.

- **Good time management.** The exam will be time-pressured, and you will need to manage it carefully to ensure that you can make a good attempt at every part of every question. It is tempting to spend more time on numerical requirements and then rush through the discursive elements. Please try to avoid this. You will have 1.8 minutes per mark in the exam. The following question is worth 9 marks so you should allow 16 minutes in the exam.

Skill activity

STEP 1   Read and analyse the requirement.

The active verb used often dictates the approach that written answers should take. For example, discuss means examine in detail by using arguments in favour or against. Work out how many minutes you have to answer each sub requirement. Here the requirement was:

Discuss[17] the views expressed by the three[18] directors on

how the investment should be financed.

9 marks

[17] You must provide a reasoned approach to your answer discussing the pros and con of each directors' view

[18] 3 marks will be allocated to the view of each director, you will score one mark for each relevant, well explained point

STEP 2   Read and analyse the scenario.

Identify the type of company you are dealing with and how the financial topics in the requirement relate to that type of company. As you go through the scenario you should be highlighting key information which you think will play a key role in answering the specific requirements.

Corfe Co is a listed[19] company, the board is looking to

finance investments in facilities over the next three

years[20], forecast to cost up to[21] $25m. The board does

not wish to obtain further long-term debt finance and is

also unwilling to make an equity issue. This means that

investments have to be financed from cash which can

be made available internally.[22]

[19] Corfe Co is a listed co; therefore any advice on how to finance the new investment must focus on the key objective of maximising shareholder wealth

[20] The suggested source of finance will need to be available over the next three years

[21] Amount to be raised

[22] Make sure you do not discuss raising new external debt or equity as this is not relevant to the scenario

Board members have made a number of suggestions about how this can be done:

Director A has suggested that the company does not have a problem with funding new investments, as it has cash available in the reserves[23] of $29m. If extra cash is required soon, Corfe Co could reduce its investment in working capital.[24]

Director B has suggested selling the building[25] which contains the company's headquarters in the capital city for $20m.[26] This will raise a large one-off sum and also save on ongoing property management costs. Head office support functions[27] would be moved to a number of different locations rented outside the capital city.

Director C has commented that although a high dividend has just been paid, dividends could be reduced[28] over the next three years, allowing spare cash for investment.

[23] Reserves do not represent cash

[24] What would be the pros and cons of reducing working capital to release extra cash?

[25] Is the property used as security for a loan?

[26] Insufficient amount.

[27] What are the pros and cons of moving the head office function?

[28] What are the expectations of shareholders? What are the pros and cons of cutting the dividend payment?

STEP 3 **Plan your answer**

Ensure your answer is balanced in terms of identifying the potential benefits **and** limitations of topics that are being discussed or recommended.

Type up your answer plan using the word-processing function available in the constructive response workspace. A brief answer plan could look like this:

	Pros	Cons
Director A	Better management of WC	Must maintain liquidity
		Risks associated with reducing WC
Director B	Savings in costs	Used as security?
		Additional costs – Restructuring costs?
		Lose future increase in value
Director C	Capital growth in share price	Negative signal to market
		Shareholders expectations

STEP 4 **Write your answer**

As you write your answer, try wherever possible to apply your analysis to the scenario, instead of simply writing about the financial topic in generic, technical terms. As you write your answer, explain what you mean – in one (or two) sentence(s) – and then explain why this matter in the given scenario. This should result in a series of short paragraphs that address the specific context of the scenario.

A well-structured answer would address each director's comments (3 marks were available for each) and would look like this:

Director A[29]

Reserves are not cash

Director A is incorrect in saying that $29m of cash reserves are available. **Reserves are $29m**, but this figure represents backing for all Corfe Co's assets and not just cash.

Must maintain liquidity

Some of this could be used for investment, although the company will need a minimum balance of cash to maintain liquidity for its day-to-day operations. **Corfe Co's current ratio is (20/7) = 2:86**. This may be a high figure (depending on the industry Corfe Co is in), so Corfe Co may have scope to generate some extra cash by reducing working capital.

Risks associated with reducing WC

Inventory levels could be **reduced by just-in-time policies[30], trade receivables reduced by tighter credit control and payments delayed to suppliers.** All of these have possible drawbacks. Just-in-time policies may result in running out of inventory, and tighter policies for trade receivables and payables may worsen relations with customers and suppliers. Again also, Corfe Co would have to maintain minimum levels of each element of working capital, so it seems **unlikely that it could raise the maximum $25m solely by doing what Director A suggests.[31]**

Director B

Lose future increase in value

Selling the headquarters would raise most of the sum required for investment, assuming that Director B's assessment of sales price is accurate. However, Corfe Co would lose the benefit of the value of the site increasing in future, which may happen if the headquarters is in a prime location in the capital city.

[29] Use headings and sub headings to provide good structure.

[30] Illustrate your point with an example

[31] Provide a conclusion

Security

Being able to sell the headquarters would be subject to the agreement of lenders if the property had been used as security for a loan. Even if it has not been used as security, the sale could reduce the borrowing capacity of the company by reducing the availability of assets to offer as security.

Additional costs

An ongoing commitment to property management costs of an owned site would be replaced by a commitment to pay rent, which might also include some responsibility for property costs for the locations rented. It is possible that good deals for renting are available outside the capital city. However, in the longer term, the rent may become more expensive if there are frequent rent reviews. There may also be visible and invisible costs attached to moving and splitting up the functions. There will be one-off costs of moving and disruption to work around the time of the move. **Staff replacement costs may increase** if staff are moved to a location which is not convenient for them[32] and then leave. Senior managers may find it more difficult to manage functions which are in different locations rather than the same place. There may be a loss of synergies through staff in different functions not being able to communicate easily face-to-face anymore.

[32] Illustrate your point with an example

Director C

Capital growth in share price

If the funds are invested in a project with a positive NPV this will lead to a **capital growth in the share price.** Shareholders[33] may be happy to forego their dividend knowing that they achieve a growth in the share price.

[33] Provide a balanced discussion illustrating the pros and cons of the director's view

Shareholder expectations

Shareholders may well expect a consistent or steadily growing dividend. A cut in dividend may represent a significant loss of income for them. If this is so, shareholders may be unhappy about seeing dividends cut or not paid, particularly if they have doubts about the director's future investment plans.

Negative signal to market

They may see this as a signal that the company has poor prospects, particularly if they are unsure about why the directors are not seeking finance from external sources. The director's dividend policy may also be questioned if the dividend just paid was a one-off, high payment. Such a payment is normally made if a company has surplus cash and does not have plans to use it. However, the directors are planning investments, and shareholders may wonder why a high dividend was paid when the directors need money for investments.

Exam success skills diagnostic

Every time you complete a question, use the diagnostic below to assess how effectively you demonstrated the exam success skills in answering the question. The table has been completed below for the 'Corfe Co' activity to give you an idea of how to complete the diagnostic.

Exam success skills	Your reflections/observations
Managing information	Did you identify that Corfe Co is a listed Co? Did you identify that internal financing was to be used for this investment?
Correct interpretation of requirements	Did you present a reasoned argument of the pros and cons of each of the three director's views?
Answer planning	Did you take time to prepare an answer plan and note three relevant points for each director?
Effective writing and presentation.	Did you use headings and sub headings? Did you write in clear, concise paragraphs? Did you explain your points in enough detail using illustrative examples?
Good time management	Did you manage your time to ensure you discussed all three director's views in the time available?
Most important action points to apply to your next question	

Summary

Section C of the FM exam will contain two questions which will be scenario-based and will contain **both discursive and computational elements.** This Skills Checkpoint should help with your approach to all narrative requirements. Make sure you practice discussion questions in full, to time. The most important aspects to take away are:

- Prepare a brief answer plan to gather your thoughts and make sure you address all parts of the requirement.
- Structure your answer with headings, sub-headings and concise and clear paragraphs.
- Provide a balanced discussion.
- Do not overlook the scenario in the question – it is likely to provide you with some ideas for your answer.

14

Foreign currency risk

Learning objectives

On completion of this chapter, you should be able to:

	Syllabus reference
The nature and types of risk and approaches to risk management	
• Describe and discuss different types of foreign currency risk:	G1(a)
- Translation risk	
- Transaction risk	
- Economic risk	
Causes of exchange rate differences	
• Describe the causes of exchange rate fluctuations, including:	G2(a)
- Balance of payments	
- Purchasing power parity theory	
- Interest rate parity theory	
- Four-way equivalence	
• Forecast exchange rates using:	G2(b)
- Purchasing power parity theory	
- Interest rate parity theory	
Hedging techniques for foreign currency risk	
• Discuss and apply traditional and basic methods of foreign currency risk management, including: currency of invoice, netting and matching, leading and lagging, forward exchange contracts, money market hedging, asset and liability management	G3(a)
• Compare and evaluate traditional methods of foreign currency risk management	G3(b)
• Identify the main types of foreign currency derivatives used to hedge foreign currency risk and explain how they are used in hedging (no numerical questions will be set on this topic)	G3(c)

Exam context

This chapter, and the next, cover Section G of the syllabus (Risk Management). This syllabus section is examinable in the OT sections of the exam (Sections A and B) and commonly forms the central theme of one of the (10 mark) Section B questions.

It is possible for an aspect of risk management to be tested as a part of a Section C question, mainly because exchange rate risk can arise due to foreign currency receivables and payables, and these working capital issues are examinable in Section C of the exam. However, it is rare for this chapter to be tested in Section C of the exam.

Chapter overview

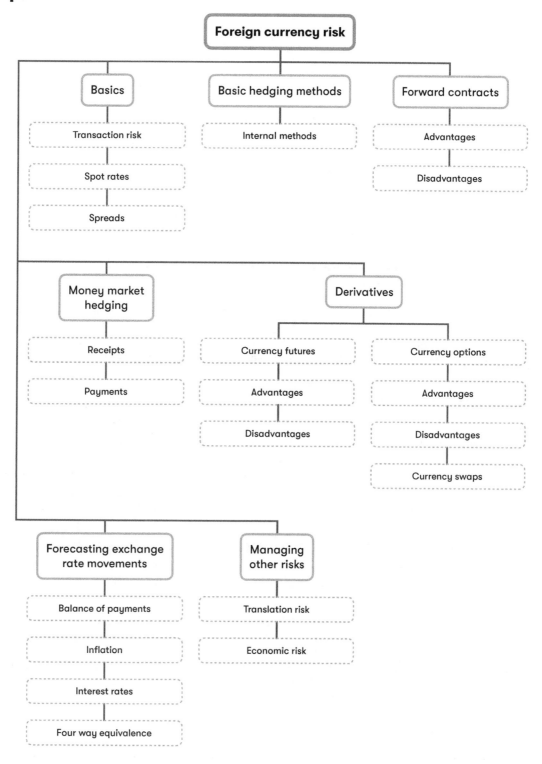

1 Exchange rate risk management basics

PER alert

Performance objective 11 requires you to 'advise on using instruments or techniques to manage financial risk'. This chapter covers the management of foreign currency risk.

Exchange rate: The rate at which one country's currency can be traded in exchange for another country's currency.

This chapter focuses on exchange rate risk management, which is sometimes referred to as **hedging**.

There are three categories of exchange rate risk: transaction risk, translation risk and economic risk. The main focus of this chapter, and of the exam, is the management of **transaction risk;** the other types of risk are briefly covered in the final section of the chapter.

Exam focus point

In the exam, the **domestic currency is normally dollars.** The use of dollars as the domestic currency does not mean that we are dealing with the US dollar – it is simply being consistent with the fact that cash flows in the ACCA exams are usually expressed in dollars. In this chapter **the domestic currency is normally in dollars and the foreign currency is in pesos.**

1.1 Transaction risk

Transaction risk: The risk that a transaction in a foreign currency is recorded at one rate and then settled at a different rate because of a change in the exchange rate.

Transaction risk arises due to the **timing** between **entering into the transaction** (agreeing the price) and the time that the **actual cash flows** will materialise. It can arise for a number of reasons, for example:

* a company **exports** to foreign countries and has foreign currency receivables
* a company **imports** from foreign countries and has foreign currency payables
* a company is making **interest payments** on a foreign currency loan (or is receiving interest from a foreign investment)

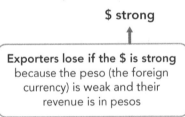

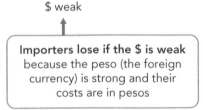

Illustration 1: Transaction risk

Company A is based in Country Z where the currency is the dollar.

Company A exports to Country C where the currency is the peso and has receivables of 154,000 pesos due in 1 month.

During the month the value of the dollar increased by 10% against the peso; from 2 pesos to the dollar to 2.2 pesos to the dollar.

Required

Calculate the impact of this exchange rate movement on Company A.

Solution

154,000 peso / 2 = $77,000 revenue expected

1 month later:

154,000 peso / 2.2 = $70,000 revenue received

Foreign currency loss = $7,000

Exporters in Country Z lose when the $ gets stronger

Activity 1: Transaction risk

Company B is based in Country Z where the currency is the dollar.

Company B imports from Country C where the currency is the peso and has payables of 180,000 pesos due in 1 month.

During the month the value of the dollar decreased by 10% against the peso; from 2 pesos to the dollar to 1.8 pesos to the dollar.

Required

Calculate the impact of this exchange rate movement on Company B.

Solution

You should note that **foreign currency risk is a two-way risk**. This means that exchange rate movements may be **favourable as well as adverse**, so the term 'risk' can be misleading.

1.2 Spot rate

Spot rate: The exchange rate currently offered on a currency for **immediate delivery**.

1.2.1 Exports

Export sales create revenue in a foreign currency (eg pesos), this will normally be converted by a company into dollars (the domestic currency) at the spot rate available when the money is received.

1.2.2 Imports

Costs that are payable in a foreign currency will require a company to sell dollars (the domestic currency) to buy the foreign currency required for the transaction, at the spot rate that is available. This will mean that an importer will sell dollars and buy the foreign currency.

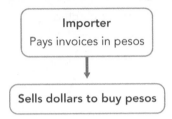

Importer
Pays invoices in pesos

Sells dollars to buy pesos

1.3 Spreads

Sometimes an exam question will simply provide you with a single spot rate to use eg 1.7800 peso per dollar.

However, exam questions may also provide the spot rate as a spread eg 1.7600 – 1.8000 pesos per dollar.

This is more realistic since a bank would not offer a rate of 1.7800 pesos per dollar to both exporters (selling pesos) and importers (buying pesos); instead, it will charge them different rates and make a profit on the **spread**.

A spread shows the different rates at which a bank will transact with an exporter and an importer.

In order to make a profit, a bank sells dollars (the domestic currency) to an exporter at a high price (1.8000 pesos) and buys dollars from an importer at a low price (1.7600 pesos) and make a **profit on the spread** (ie the difference between 1.8000 and 1.7600).

Lower rate 1.7600 – a bank buys dollars at this rate	Higher rate 1.8000 – a bank sells dollars at this rate
An importer sells dollars to a bank in exchange for foreign currency, and so receives the lower rate when selling dollars to a bank.	An exporter buys dollars from a bank in exchange for foreign currency and so pays the higher rate when buying dollars from a bank.

Spreads can be shown in different ways; you **do not have to remember** these different methods, just make sure you can interpret them.

Spot rate 1.7600 – 1.8000 pesos per dollar

Spot rate 1.7800 +/- 0.0200 pesos per dollar

> ### Exam focus point
>
> If in doubt as to which part of the spread to use, remember that a company will always be offered the **worse rate in order that the bank generates a profit on the transaction.**

Activity 2: Spreads

The spot rate at the time that a company wishes to convert its export revenue of 360,000 peso into dollars is quoted as 1.4000-1.5000 pesos per dollar.

Required

Calculate the receipts in dollars.

Solution

Essential reading

See Chapter 14 section 1 of the Essential reading, available in the digital edition of the Workbook, for more background information on this area.

The Essential reading is available as an Appendix of the digital edition of the Workbook.

2 Managing transaction risk – basic methods

Basic techniques can be used by a company to eliminate transaction risk or to reduce it to an acceptable level. These are illustrated below for a company with dollars as its domestic currency and with revenue in pesos (a foreign currency).

Real life example: Illustration of basic methods

The risk is that the value of the peso will fall so that the peso revenue is worth fewer dollars.

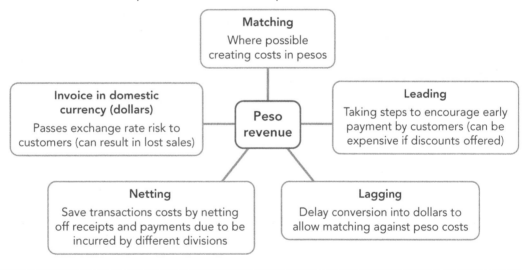

Essential reading

See Chapter 14 section 2 of the Essential reading, available in the digital edition of the Workbook, for more background information on this area.

The Essential reading is available as an Appendix of the digital edition of the Workbook.

BPP LEARNING MEDIA

3 Managing transaction risk – forward contracts

KEY TERM

> **Forward contract:** A **contract** with a bank (sometimes called an over the counter or OTC contract) **fixing** the exchange rate on a **specific** amount of foreign currency (FX) receivable or payable at a **future date at an exchange rate agreed now**.

The purpose of a forward contract is to **fix an exchange rate** now for the settlement of a transaction at a future date. This removes uncertainty about what the exchange rate will be at that future date.

Currency risk is a **two-way risk**. By arranging a forward contract, a company can hedge against the risk of an adverse movement in the spot exchange rate up to the date of settlement, but at the same time it loses the opportunity to gain from a favourable movement in the spot rate.

Forward contracts can be arranged for settlement up to several months ahead, or possibly as much as one year ahead (or even slightly longer) but **cannot be used as a hedge against currency risk in the long term**.

Forward contracts are arranged directly with a bank and are sometimes referred to as **over-the-counter** or OTC transactions.

3.1 Quotation of forward rates

As with spot rates, a forward rate may be given as a single figure or as a spread, the same rules apply for interpreting the spread.

Activity 3: Forward rates

The spot exchange rate is 1.2500- 1.3500 pesos to the dollar and the three-month forward rate is 1.3000-1.5000 pesos to the dollar.

Required

1   Calculate the receipts from a 1,400,000 peso sale, due to be received in 3 months' time if forward rates are used.

2   Calculate the cost of paying an invoice of 1,500,000 pesos in 3 months' time, if forward rates are used.

Solution

3.2 Advantages of forward rates

Forward contracts are the most popular method of hedging currency risk.

Advantages	Discussion
• Simple	Easy to organise for the exact amount of money required and the exact timing of the transaction

Advantages	Discussion
• Low or zero up-front costs	Unlike currency options (see later)
• Available for many currencies	Likely to be available in the required currency.

3.3 Disadvantages of forward rates

Disadvantages	Discussion
• Fixed date	The forward contract must be exercised on a specific date, and the bank that has provided the forward contract can enforce this.
• Unattractive rate	The fixed rate that is offered may not be attractive.
• Counter-party risk	The agreement is between two parties, there is therefore a risk of default on either side.

Essential reading

See Chapter 14 section 3 of the Essential reading, available in the digital edition of the Workbook, for more background information on this area.

The Essential reading is available as an Appendix of the digital edition of the Workbook.

4 Managing transaction risk – money market hedging

4.1 Foreign currency receipt (eg an export)

Because of the close relationship between forward exchange rates and the interest rates in currencies, it is possible to 'manufacture' a forward rate by using the spot exchange rate and money market lending or borrowing.

Where foreign currency revenue is expected, exchange rate risk can be eliminated by:

(a) borrowing in the foreign currency **today**, converting these funds into dollars (the domestic currency) at **today's spot rate** (so there is no exchange rate risk)

(b) using the future revenue (in foreign currency) to repay the foreign currency loan.

Because this involves a short-term loan in a foreign currency it is called money-market hedging.

To create a money market hedge for a receipt, follow the steps below.

Step 1 Identify the **loan repayment** required in the future (this should match the expected revenue)

Step 2 Using the interest rate provided, calculate the amount that needs to be **borrowed** today in the foreign currency (adjusting the interest rate, if given in annual terms, to reflect the period of the loan).

Step 3 Convert this immediately to domestic (home) currency at the **spot rate**. Place this on **deposit** in the home currency.

Step 4 Include the interest earned on the **deposit** in the home currency, using the interest rate provided (adjusting the interest rate, if given in annual terms, to reflect the period of the deposit).

These same steps can be easier to remember as a table, the following table assumes that the transaction is in 3 months' time:

	Receipts	
	Domestic currency $	Foreign currency (peso)
Now	(3) Pay peso loan into your bank account today at the spot rate	(2) Take out loan in pesos: this will be the amount in step 1 divided by (1 + borrowing rate)
	(1 + deposit rate) *	(1 + borrowing rate) *
Three months	(4) Adjust step 3 by multiplying by (1 + deposit rate), to allow comparison to a forward contract	(1) Receive pesos from export. This is the amount of loan repayment required

*You will need to take the interest rate quoted and multiply by 3/12 if a three-month loan, if interest rates are given in annual terms.

Illustration 2: Money market hedge

A company whose domestic currency is the dollar is owed 2,500,000 pesos, receivable in three months' time. The spot exchange rate is 1.4498 – 1.4513 pesos per $1. The company can deposit in dollars for three months at 2.00% per annum and can borrow pesos for three months at 1.5% per annum.

Required

What is the receipt in dollars with a money market hedge?

Solution

The interest rates for **three months** are calculated by adjusting the annual rates given by multiplying them by 3/12. This gives a 0.5% rate to deposit in dollars and 0.375% to borrow in pesos.

(1) The company should aim to repay 2,500,000 pesos in 3 months' time.

(2) The company should aim to borrow 2,500,000/1.00375 = 2,490,660 pesos today (after three months, 2,500,000 pesos will be repayable, including interest).

(3) These pesos will be converted to $ at 2,490,660/1.4513 = $1,716,158. This is placed on deposit in the US.

(4) The company will deposit this amount for three months, when it will have increased in value with interest (2% for the three months) to: $1,716,158 × 1.005 = $1,724,739

In three months, the loan will be repaid out of the pesos proceeds from the trade receivable.

The company has 'manufactured' a forward rate of 1.4495 (2,500,000/$1,724,739)

Activity 4: Money market hedging: receipts

Three-month interest rates are currently as follows:

	US	Country P
Borrowing rates	5.59% per year	5.38% per year
Deposit rates	5.50% per year	5.31% per year

The spot rate is 1.9612-1.9618 pesos to the dollar.

Required

Calculate the receipts from a 1m peso sale, due to be received in 3 months' time if money market hedging is used by a US company.

Solution

4.2 Foreign currency payable (eg an import)

Where foreign currency expenses are due, money market hedging can eliminate exchange rate risk by:

(a) Withdrawing funds from your local bank account in the domestic currency (eg dollars) and putting them on deposit in a **foreign currency** bank account **today** (so there is no exchange rate risk)

(b) Using these funds (plus interest) to pay the foreign currency expense **in future**.

Because this involves a short-term investment in a foreign currency it is a money-market hedge. To create a money market hedge for an expense, follow the steps below.

Step 1 Identify the cash required to **pay the foreign currency expense**

Step 2 Using the interest rate provided, calculate the amount that needs to be **invested** today in the foreign currency.

Step 3 Convert this immediately to home currency at the **spot rate**. This is the amount of $s that needs to be borrowed today from your domestic bank account.

Step 4 Include the cost of **borrowing** in the domestic country to compare to a forward contract.

Again, these same steps can be pictured as a table, here assuming a transaction is in 3 months' time:

	Expenses	
	Domestic currency $	**Foreign currency (peso)**
Now	(3) Withdraw funds from $ bank account today	(2) Put money into a foreign currency bank account (in pesos)
	(1 + borrowing rate) *	(1 + deposit) *
Three months	(4) Include the cost of borrowing (to compare to a forward)	(1) Pay peso invoice from supplier Pay off invoice with pesos in foreign currency bank account

*Remember to take the interest rate quoted and multiply by 3/12, if interest rates are given in annual terms.

Illustration 3: Money market hedge

A company whose local currency is the dollar owes a Danish supplier Kr3,500,000 which is payable in three months' time. The spot exchange rate is Kr7.5509 – Kr7.5548 per $1. The company can borrow in dollars for three months at 8.60% per annum and can deposit kroner for three months at 4.92% per annum.

Required

What is the cost in dollars using a money market hedge?

Solution

The interest rates for three months are calculated by adjusting the annual rates given by multiplying them by 3/12. This gives 2.15% to borrow in dollars and 1.23% to deposit in kroner.

(1) The company needs to deposit enough kroner now so that the total including interest will be Kr3,500,000 in three months' time.

(2) This means depositing: Kr3,500,000/ 1.0123 = Kr3,457,473 today.

(3) These kroner will be converted to $ at the spot rate of Kr7.5509 giving a cost $457,889 today.

(4) The company must borrow this amount now and will have to repay: $457,889 × (1 + 0.0215) = $467,734 in 3 months' time.

So, in three months, the Danish supplier will be paid out of the Danish bank account and the company will effectively be paying $467,734 to satisfy this debt. The company has 'manufactured' a forward rate of 7.4829 (3,500,000/$467,734).

Activity 5: Money market hedging: expenses

Current three-month interest rates are as follows:

	US	Country P
Borrowing rates	5.59% per year	5.38% per year
Deposit rates	5.50% per year	5.31% per year

The spot rate is 1.9612-1.9618 peso to the $.

Required

Calculate the dollar cost of an invoice for 1m pesos payable in three months' time if money market hedging is used.

Solution

4.3 Money market hedging compared to forward contracts

As we will see later in this chapter, **interest rate parity theory** explains that **forward contracts are determined by interest rate differences** between two countries. This means that money market hedging is unlikely to deliver a significantly different outcome from that delivered by a forward contract.

Money market hedging may deliver a slightly better outcome if **used by an exporter with a cash flow deficit,** (so that step 4 in the method brings a greater benefit in the form of saved overdraft interest).

Alternatively, if used by an **importer with a cash flow surplus** (so that step 4 in the method brings a lower cost as interest lost on a cash flow surplus will be lower than the cost of borrowing).

Money market hedging is likely to be more time consuming than a forward contract and could involve issue costs as borrowing is involved.

Activity 6: Mini-case practice 1

Fidden is a medium-sized company in a country whose currency is the dollar, with export and import trade with country P, whose currency is the peso. The following transactions are due within the next nine months:

(1) Sale of finished goods, cash receipt due in three months: 197,000 pesos

(2) Purchase of finished goods for resale, cash payment due in six months: 293,000 pesos

(3) Sale of finished goods, cash receipt due in nine months: 154,000 pesos

Exchange rates		Peso per $
Spot		1.9612-1.9618
Three months' forward		1.9598- 1.9612
Six months' forward		1.9585-1.9607
Nine months' forward		1.9477-1.9621
Annual interest rates (3, 6 or 9 months)	Borrowing	Lending
Dollars	5.59%	5.5%
Country P	5.38%	5.31%

Required

1   What is the value in dollars of the receipt in three months if a forward contract is used?
   O   389,356 dollars
   O   386,475 dollars
   O   100,417 dollars
   O   100,449 dollars

2   What is the value in dollars of the payment in six months if a money market hedge is used?
   O   149,556 dollars
   O   149,502 dollars
   O   149,602 dollars
   O   145,534 dollars

3   What is the value in dollars of the payment in six months if a forward contract is used?

4   If the receipt in nine months was hedged using a money market hedge how would the hedge be initiated?

    ○ Deposit in pesos now

    ○ Deposit in dollars now

    ○ Borrowing in pesos now

    ○ Borrowing in dollars now

Solution

5   Managing transaction risk – derivatives

> **Exam focus point**
>
> This section **will not be tested numerically in the exam.**

5.1 Currency futures

> **Currency futures:** A **contract** to purchase or sell a **standard quantity** of a currency by an **agreed future date** at a **specified exchange rate**.

Currency futures have a similar impact to forward contracts in that they **fix the exchange rate** to use in the future.

Currency futures are traded on a market and are mainly available from the US markets. Each contract fixes the exchange rate on a large, standard amount of currency and contracts expire at the end of each quarter (March, June, September and December) but **can be used on any date up to the expiry date.**

However, unlike a forward, a futures contract is **separate from the actual transaction** and is designed in such a way that:

- If a company makes an exchange loss on a transaction, then it will make a profit in the futures market to compensate for this.

- If a company makes an exchange profit on a transaction, then it will make a loss in the futures market.

So, the outcome is **fixed** whatever happens to the exchange rate.

5.1.1 Setting up a futures transaction

There are three steps to a futures transaction.

For a foreign currency (peso) **receipt**, the steps are as follows:

Step 1   Today: Enter into a futures contract to **sell pesos** at a fixed rate

Contracts should be due to be fulfilled on a standardised date **after** the transaction date.

Step 2   Complete the **actual** transaction on the **spot market**.

Step 3   **Close out the futures contract** by doing the opposite of what you did in Step 1 ie by entering into **contracts to buy pesos**.

Any profits or losses that arise as futures are settled will offset the impact of exchange rate movements on the actual transaction that is being hedged. So, the outcome is **fixed** whatever happens to the exchange rate.

- **If the peso devalues**
  - There will be a **gain on the future** as it will be bought back at a lower price than it was sold in step 1.
  - However, on the **actual transaction** there will be **an exchange loss** because the peso receipts from the actual transaction would be worth less in dollars.

- **If the peso increases in value**
  - There will be a **loss on the future** as it will be bought back at a higher price than it was sold in step 1.
  - However, on the **actual transaction** there will be **an exchange gain** because the peso receipts from the actual transaction would be worth more in dollars.

5.1.2 Advantages of currency futures

Futures are valid for a **period of time.** Eg a September future can be used on any day between the day it was entered into up to the end of September. This is more flexible than a forward, which is only valid on a specific day.

Counterparty risk is lower since the futures exchange guarantees the transaction.

5.1.3 Disadvantages of currency futures

Currency futures are **only available in large, standard, contract sizes, and for a narrow range of currencies** (compared to forward contracts). This makes currency futures less suitable for small transactions.

To cover potential losses a company using futures will be required to place **a deposit** (called a margin) with the futures exchange, which may need to be topped up on a daily basis if the contract is incurring losses.

There is a risk that futures exchange rates do not move exactly in line with spot exchange rates so that the hedge is not effective (this is an example of **basis risk**).

5.2 Currency options

KEY TERM

> **Currency options:** A right of an option holder to buy (call) or sell (put) a quantity of one currency in exchange for another, at a specific exchange rate on or before a future expiry date.

Companies can choose whether to buy:

(a)   A tailor-made currency option from a bank, suited to the company's specific needs. These are **over the counter** (OTC) or **negotiated** options; or

(b)   A standard **exchange- traded option,** in certain currencies only, from an options exchange.

With either type of option, the holder can choose whether or not to exercise the option – this **allows the holder to enjoy the upside without a risk of suffering the downside of exchange rate movements.**

Obtaining a currency option involves **paying a premium upfront to the option seller.**

The option acts as an **insurance policy** and can be used by the purchaser to compensate for adverse exchange rate movements.

If the exchange rate moves favourably then the option will **not be exercised.**

5.2.1 Advantages of currency options

Exchange-traded options (but not OTC options) are valid for a **period of time.** This is more flexible than a forward, which is only valid on a specific day.

Exchange traded options **can be sold on** if not needed.

Any type of option allows a company to **benefit from favourable exchange rate movements.**

5.2.2 Disadvantages of currency options

Exchange-traded options are only available in **large, standard, contract sizes**, and for a narrow range of currencies (compared to forward contracts).

Any type of option will need to be purchased, and the **premium** can be expensive.

5.3 Currency swaps

> **Swap:** A formal agreement whereby two organisations contractually agree to exchange payments on different terms, eg in different currencies.

In a **currency swap**, the parties agree to swap equivalent amounts of currency for a period. This effectively involves the exchange of debt from one currency to another. Liability on the main debt (the principal) **is transferred** and the parties are liable to **counterparty risk**: if the other party defaults on the agreement to pay interest, the original borrower remains liable to the lender.

Currency swaps may be used to **restructure the currency base** of the company's liabilities. This may be important where the company is trading overseas and receiving revenues in foreign currencies, but its borrowings are denominated in the currency of its home country.

Currency swaps therefore provide a means of reducing exchange rate exposure over the **long-term.**

Essential reading

See Chapter 14 section 4 of the Essential reading, available in the digital edition of the Workbook, for more background information on this area.

The Essential reading is available as an Appendix of the digital edition of the Workbook.

6 Forecasting exchange rate movements

There are several factors that influence exchange rates over the long term, these include the balance of payments, inflation and interest rates.

6.1 Balance of payments

If an economy is importing more than it is exporting, then this means that over time more of the domestic currency is being sold (to pay for imports) than is being bought (as export revenue is converted into the domestic currency). A balance of payments deficit can therefore **weaken** the domestic currency over the long-term.

6.2 Inflation

High rates of inflation in a foreign country erode the **purchasing power** of that currency ie what a unit of the currency can buy in terms of goods and services.

Over time this fall in purchasing power will affect what a unit of the currency can buy on the currency markets and **leads to a fall in the value of its currency.**

Purchasing power parity theory predicts that the exchange value of foreign currency depends on the relative purchasing power of each currency in its own country and that **spot exchange rates will vary over time according to relative price changes.**

So, **if inflation is relatively high** in one country, then that country will, over the long-term, experience a **fall in the value of its currency.**

$$S_1 = S_0 \times \frac{(1 + h_c)}{(1 + h_b)}$$

Where

S_1 = expected spot rate

S_0 = current spot rate

hb = base country inflation

hc = inflation in foreign country

Real life example: Purchasing power parity theory

The spot exchange rate between Country A (where the currency is the dollar) and Country B (where the currency is the kroner) is $1 = 8.00 kroner.

Assuming that there is now purchasing parity, an amount of a commodity costing $110 in Country A will cost 880 kroner in Country B.

Over the next year, price inflation in Country B is expected to be 5% while inflation in Country A is expected to be 8%. What is the 'expected spot exchange rate' at the end of the year?

Forecast rate, S_1

$$= 8 \times \frac{1.05}{1.08}$$

= 7.7778

This is the same figure as we get if we compare the inflated prices for the commodity. At the end of the year:

Country A price = $110 × 1.08 = $118.80

Country B price = Kr880 × 1.05 = Kr924

Forecast rate, S_1 = 924 ÷ 118.80 = 7.7778

In the real world, exchange rates move towards purchasing power parity only over the **long term.**

Essential reading

See Chapter 14 section 5 of the Essential reading, available in the digital edition of the Workbook, for more background information on this area.

The Essential reading is available as an Appendix of the digital edition of the Workbook.

Activity 7: Mini-case practice 2

The currency of Country A is the dollar ($).

The currency of Country B is the euro (€).

The value of one dollar is currently €1.5000.

Inflation in Country A is 2.7%, and in Country B is 2.1%.

Inflation in Country C, where the currency is the peso. is expected to remain constant at 2.5% for the foreseeable future.

Required

1   What is the value of a dollar expected to be in one year?

  O   €0.6628

  O   €0.6706

  O   €1.5088

  O   €1.4912

2   What is the value of a dollar expected to be in six years?

  O   €0.6436

  O   €1.4482

  O   €0.6905

  O   €1.5537

3   What is the value of a dollar expected to be in six months?

  O   €0.6647

  O   €1.4956

  O   €1.5044

  O   €0.6686

4   According to the purchasing power parity theory what is the most likely effect on the value of Country C's currency, the peso, over the coming years?

  O   The peso will weaken against the $ and the €

  O   The peso will strengthen against the $ and the €

  O   The peso will weaken against the $ but strengthen against the €

  O   The peso will strengthen against the $ but weaken against the €

Solution

6.3 Interest rates

6.3.1 Long-term

In the **long term** two countries of similar risk should offer similar rates of return to international investors so **any differences in interest rates should reflect differences in inflation.**

High rates of inflation in a foreign country weaken its exchange rate **so high interest rates are associated with weakening currencies, in the long-term.**

This is sometimes called the international Fisher effect.

6.3.2 Short-run

In the **short-run** banks use **interest rates** to **calculate forward exchange rates**; this is **interest rate parity theory.**

$$F_0 = S_0 \times \frac{(1 + i_c)}{(1 + i_b)}$$

Where: F_0 = forward rate

S_0 = current spot rate

b = base country and c = foreign country

Activity 8: IRP theory

A company based in country A, where the currency is the $, is expecting to receive Kuwaiti dinars in six months' time. The spot rate is 5.4670 dinars per $. Annual interest rates are 8% in country A and 6% in Kuwait.

Required

Calculate the forward exchange rate in 6 months' time.

Solution

6.4 Four-way equivalence

The **four-way equivalence model** states the theories that we have been examining are linked.

If interest rates are only different between two countries due to inflation (ie real interest rates are the same in both countries) then:

(a) **Inflation** rates can be used to predict the future spot rate (purchasing power parity theory), and

(b) **Long-term interest rates** can also be used to predict the future spot rate (international fisher effect).

It is also logical to assume that if short-term interest rate differences explain the differences between the forward rate and the spot rate then over the long-term this can also be seen as an **unbiased indicator** of expected changes in the spot rate.

In other words, the theories that we have been examining are linked.

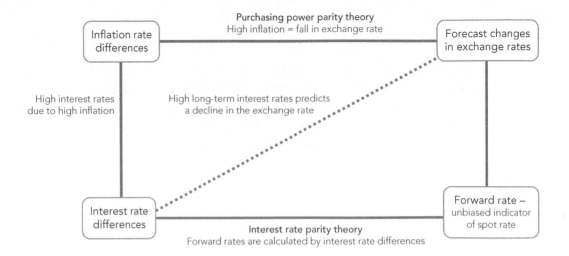

7 Managing other risks

This chapter has focussed on transaction risk, but you also need to be aware of other exchange rate risks.

7.1 Translation risk

KEY TERM

> **Translation risk:** The risk that the domestic currency value of foreign currency assets falls, or the value of foreign currency liabilities rises.

If a change in the exchange rate causes an adverse change in the domestic currency value of foreign currency assets and liabilities then the difference may be written off as a loss.

Unlike transaction risk, this is **not a cash flow,** but it is still a worry for some companies because of its potential profit impact.

To manage translation risk, a company that has assets in a foreign currency can **match** these assets with liabilities (eg debt finance) in the same foreign currency.

One way of obtaining foreign currency debt finance is to use a **currency swap** (not examinable with numbers).

7.2 Economic risk

KEY TERM

> **Economic risk:** Due to long-term movements in the exchange rate that damage the value of a company because the net present value of the business's cash flows is diminished by expected exchange rate trends.

Companies should carefully analyse potential exchange rate fluctuations so that they minimise the risk of export revenue being damaged over the **longer-term** due to **sustained exchange rate movements** (or the cost of imported goods rising).

However, even companies that do not export or import can be exposed to economic risk if a sustained movement in the exchange rate **benefits an overseas rival**.

Economic risk is difficult to manage effectively, but a recognised strategy is to **diversify its international operations** so that it is not overly exposed to a change in a single exchange rate.

Chapter summary

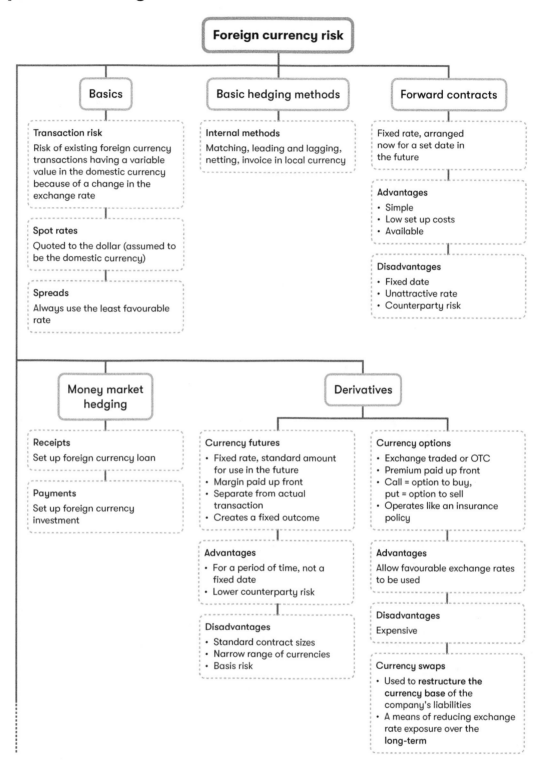

Foreign currency risk

Basics

Transaction risk

Risk of existing foreign currency transactions having a variable value in the domestic currency because of a change in the exchange rate

Spot rates

Quoted to the dollar (assumed to be the domestic currency)

Spreads

Always use the least favourable rate

Basic hedging methods

Internal methods

Matching, leading and lagging, netting, invoice in local currency

Forward contracts

Fixed rate, arranged now for a set date in the future

Advantages
- Simple
- Low set up costs
- Available

Disadvantages
- Fixed date
- Unattractive rate
- Counterparty risk

Money market hedging

Receipts

Set up foreign currency loan

Payments

Set up foreign currency investment

Derivatives

Currency futures
- Fixed rate, standard amount for use in the future
- Margin paid up front
- Separate from actual transaction
- Creates a fixed outcome

Advantages
- For a period of time, not a fixed date
- Lower counterparty risk

Disadvantages
- Standard contract sizes
- Narrow range of currencies
- Basis risk

Currency options
- Exchange traded or OTC
- Premium paid up front
- Call = option to buy, put = option to sell
- Operates like an insurance policy

Advantages

Allow favourable exchange rates to be used

Disadvantages

Expensive

Currency swaps
- Used to **restructure the currency base** of the company's liabilities
- A means of reducing exchange rate exposure over the long-term

Forecasting exchange rate movements

Balance of payments

Deficit causes a weaker exchange rate in the long-term

Inflation
- PPP theory suggests relatively high inflation causes a weakening of the exchange rate
- Only true over the longer term

Interest rates
- Long-term: international fisher effect
- Short-term: interest rate parity (IRP) theory
- IRP used to calculate forward rates

Four-way equivalence

Links together interest rate and inflation rate theories

Managing other risks

Translation risk
- Risk of changes in the domestic value of foreign assets and liabilities
- Use foreign currency liabilities to match to foreign currency assets
- Foreign currency liabilities may be obtained via a currency swap

Economic risk
- Change in company value due to long-term exchange rate movements
- Manage by diversifying operations

Knowledge diagnostic

1. Basic hedging methods

Internal methods such as leading & lagging, netting, matching and invoicing in own currency are simple techniques that can be considered independently by a company.

2. Forward contracts

The most popular form of hedging because of the ability to use a range of currencies and to tailor the amount and the timing to a company's specific circumstances.

3. Money market hedging

Matches to the transaction: an export will require a foreign currency loan; an import will require a foreign currency investment.

4. Derivatives

Derivatives include futures, options and swaps.

5. Causes of fluctuations in exchanges rates

Primary explanations centre on inflation (PPP theory) and interest rates. Four-way equivalence links these theories.

BPP LEARNING MEDIA

Further study guidance

Question practice

Now try the following from the Further question practice bank (available in the digital edition of the Workbook):

Section A questions

Q31, Q32

Section B questions

Q37 (a), (b), and (c)

Section C questions

Q58 Expo (this longer question is to allow further study of this area, but this chapter is not directly examinable in Section C of the real exam).

Further reading

There is a useful Technical Article that is available on ACCA's website; it is called 'Foreign currency risk and its management'. We recommend that you read this article as part of your preparation for the FM exam.

Activity answers

Activity 1: Transaction risk

$10,000 loss

180,000 peso/2 = $90,000 cost expected

180,000 peso/1.8 = $100,000 cost incurred

Losses = $10,000

Importers in Country Z lose when the $ gets weaker

Activity 2: Spreads

$240,000

An exporter buys dollars from a bank in exchange for foreign currency and so **pays the higher rate when buying dollars from a bank.**

360,000 peso/1.5 = $240,000 revenue received

Activity 3: Forward rates

1   $933,333

   An exporter buys dollars from a bank in exchange for foreign currency and so **pays the higher rate when buying dollars from a bank**. Using the forward spread the rate is therefore 1.5 pesos to the dollar.
   1,400,000 peso /1.5 = $933,333 revenue received

2   $1,153,846

   An importer sells dollars to a bank in exchange for foreign currency and so **receives the lower rate**. Using the forward spread the rate is therefore 1.3 pesos to the dollar.1,500,000 peso /1.3 = $1,153,846 cost incurred

Activity 4: Money market hedging: receipts

$509,887

The interest rates for **three months** are calculated by adjusting the annual rates given by multiplying them by 3/12. This gives a 1.375% rate (5.5% × 3/12) to deposit in dollars and 1.345% to borrow in pesos (5.38% × 3/12).

(1)   The company should aim to repay 1,000,000 pesos in 3 months' time.

(2)   The company should aim to borrow 1,000,000/1.01345 = 986,729 pesos today (after three months, 1,000,000 pesos will be repayable, including interest).

(3)   These pesos will be converted to $ at 986,729/1.9618 = $502,971. This is placed on **deposit** in the US.

(4)   The company will deposit this amount for three months, when it will have increased in value with interest (5.5% for the three months) to: $502,971 × 1.01375 = **$509,887**

In three months, the loan will be repaid out of the pesos proceeds from the trade receivable.

The company has 'manufactured' a forward rate of 1.9612 (1,000,000/$509,887).

Solution presented as a table:

	$	Peso
Now	(3) 986,729/1.9618= $502,971	(2) 1000000/1.013245 = 986,729 pesos
	(1 + interest rate) = 1.01375	1.01345
Three months	(4) $502,971 × 1.01375 = **$509,887**	(1) −1,000,000 pesos to pay +1,000,000 pesos required 0

Activity 5: Money market hedging: expenses

$510,224

The interest rates for three months are calculated by adjusting the annual rates given by multiplying them by 3/12. This gives 1.3975% to borrow in dollars and 1.3275% to deposit in pesos

(1) The company needs to deposit enough pesos now so that the total including interest will be 1,000,000 pesos in three months' time.

(2) This means depositing: 1,000,000/ 1.013275 = 986,899 pesos today.

(3) These pesos will be converted to $ at the spot rate of 1.9612 giving a cost $503,212 today.

(4) The company must borrow this amount now and will have to repay: $503,212 × (1 + 0.013975) = $510,244 in three months' time.

So, in three months, the supplier will be paid out of the peso bank account and the company will effectively be paying $510,244 to satisfy this debt. The company has 'manufactured' a forward rate of 1.9598 (1,000,000/$510,244)

Again, these same steps can be pictured as a table

IMPORTER – three months		
Now	(3) 986,899/1.9612 = $503,212	(2) 1,000,000/1.013275 = 986,899 pesos
	5.59% × 3/12 = 1.3975% ie 1.013975	5.31% × 3/12 = 1.3275% ie 1.013275
6 months	(4) 503,212 × 1.013975 = **$510,244**	(1) −1,000,000 pesos +1,000,000 pesos

Activity 6: Mini-case practice 1

1 The correct answer is: 100,449 dollars

Value

	Three months
Net transactions	+197,000 pesos
Forward rate	1.9612
Forward outcome	**+$100,449**

2 The correct answer is: 149,602 dollars

The interest rates for six months are calculated by adjusting the annual rates given by multiplying them by 6/12. This gives 2.795% to borrow in dollars and 2.655% to deposit in pesos.

(1) The company needs to deposit enough pesos now so that the total including interest will be 293,000 pesos in six months' time.

(2) This means depositing: 293,000/ 1.02655 = 285,422 pesos today.

(3) These pesos will be converted to $ at the spot rate of 1.9612 giving a cost $145,534 today.

(4) The company must borrow this amount now and will have to repay: $145,534 × (1 + 0.02795) = $149,602 in 6 months' time.

So, in six months, the supplier will be paid out of the peso bank account and the company will effectively be paying $149,602 to satisfy this debt. The company has 'manufactured' a forward rate of 1.9585 (293,000/$149,602).

Again, these same steps can be pictured as a table

IMPORTER – Six months		
Now	(3) 285,422/1.9612 = $145,534	(2) 293,000/1.02655 = 285,422 pesos
	5.59% × 6/12 = 2.795% ie 1.02795	5.31% × 6/12 = 2.655% ie 1.02655
6 months	(4) 145,534 × 1.02795 = **$149,602**	(1) −293,000 pesos +293,000 pesos ———————— 0

3 $149,604

	Six months
Net transactions	-293,000 pesos
Forward rate	1.9585
Forward outcome	**-$149,604**

This is $2 worse than the money market hedge (an immaterial difference as would normally be expected because forward rates are determined by interest rate differences)

4 The correct answer is: Borrowing in pesos now

The underlying transaction is an asset in pesos therefore the hedge must begin with the creation of an equivalent peso liability (some borrowings) which are turned immediately into dollars.

Activity 7: Mini-case practice 2

1 The correct answer is: €1.4912

€1.5000 × 1.021/1.027 = €1.4912 in 1 year

2 The correct answer is: €1.4482

€1.5000 × (1.021/1.027)^6 = €1.4482 in 6 years

3 The correct answer is: €1.4956

Inflation rate over 6 months = 2.1% x 6/12 = 1.05% and 2.7% x 6/12 = 1.35% so the exchange rate in ½ year is estimated as 1.5000 × 1.0105/1.0135 = 1.4956 or €1.5000 × (1.021/1.027)$^{1/2}$

4 The correct answer is: The peso will strengthen against the $ but weaken against the €

The currency whose inflation rate is higher will weaken. Here the Country C (peso) has a lower inflation rate than Country A ($) and so will strengthen against the $, the reverse is true for Country B.

Activity 8: IRP theory

5.4144

Using interest rate parity, the dinar is the numerator and the $ is the denominator.

Interest rates need to be multiplied by 6/12 to create a rate for a 6 month period.

So, the forward rate is given by:

5.4670 × 1.03/1.04 = 5.4144

Interest rate risk

Learning objectives

On completion of this chapter, you should be able to:

	Syllabus reference
The nature and types of risk and approaches to risk management	
• Describe & discuss types of interest rate risk: gap exposure, basis risk	G1(b)
Causes of interest rate fluctuations	
• Describe the causes of interest rate fluctuations, including:	G2(c)
– Structure of interest rates and yield curves	
– Expectations theory	
– Liquidity preference theory	
– Market segmentation	
Hedging techniques for interest rate risk	
• Discuss and apply traditional and basic methods of interest rate risk management, including: matching and smoothing, asset and liability management, forward rate agreements	G4(a)
• Identify the main types of interest rate derivatives used to hedge interest rate risk and explain how they are used in hedging (no numerical questions will be set on this topic)	G4(b)

Exam context

This chapter, and the previous chapter, cover Section G of the syllabus (Risk Management). Syllabus section G, risk management, is examinable in the OT sections of the exam (sections A and B) and commonly forms a theme of one of the (10 mark) Section B questions.

It is also possible for an aspect of this chapter to be tested as a part of a Section C question, mainly because interest rate risk can impact on investment appraisal and the financing decision; but this is rare.

Chapter overview

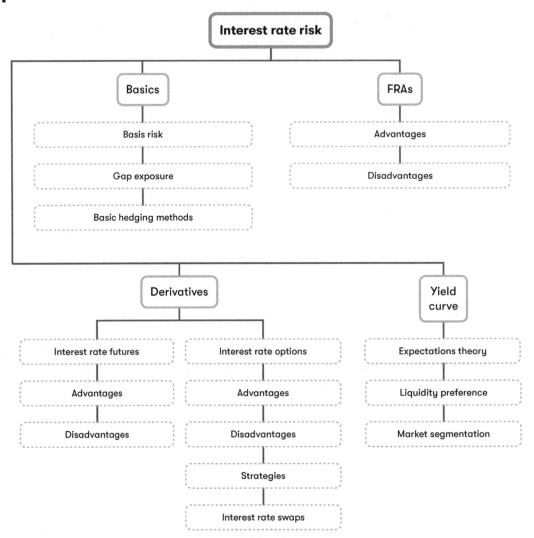

1 Introduction to interest rate risk

> **PER alert**
>
> Performance objective 11 requires you to 'advise on using instruments or techniques to manage financial risk'. This chapter covers the management of interest rate risk.

1.1 Types of interest rate risk

A company may face interest rate risk on:

> **Borrowings:** higher interest rates will increase financing costs

> **Investments:** lower interest rates will reduce the return on cash investments

Even if a company has **both borrowings and investments** of similar sizes, there may still be a risk if:

(a) Interest is **earned at a fixed rate** on investments but interest is **paid at a variable rate** on borrowings (so there is a risk if interest rates rise).

(b) Interest is **earned at a variable rate** on investments but interest is **paid at a fixed rate** on borrowings (so there is a risk if interest rates fall).

1.1.1 Base rate

The base rate may be referred to by using the precise name given to the benchmark rate at which banks lend to each other in different countries, such as:

- SONIA (the Sterling overnight index average) in the UK (this used to be known as LIBOR)
- ESTR (the Euro short-term rate) in Europe
- TONAR (Tokyo overnight average rate) in Japan
- SARON (Swiss overnight rate) in Switzerland
- SOFR (the secured overnight financing rate) in the US

1.1.2 Basis risk and gap exposure

Even if a company has both cash assets and liabilities of similar sizes, and both investments and borrowings are at a variable rate of interest, there may still be a risk if:

(a) The variable interest rates are **not determined by the same basis** eg one might be linked to the central bank base rate, and the other to SONIA.

This is an example of **basis risk**.

(b) There is a **time gap** that gives rise to risk.

This is called **gap exposure.**

Gap exposure may arise because:

- the interest rates on investments and borrowings are revised **at different points in time** eg assets might be at a variable rate based on the base rate that is revised every three months and liabilities might be variable rate based on the base rate but revised every six months

- at a given point in time there is **a difference between the value of the** (interest-sensitive) **assetsmaturing at that time and the value of the** (interest sensitive) **liabilities maturing at that time**. If liabilities are greater than assets, there is a risk of interest rates rising (a negative gap). If assets are greater than liabilities, there is a risk of interest rates falling (a positive gap).

1.2 Basic methods of managing risk

From the perspective of a company **borrowing** money, interest rate risk can be managed by:

- Smoothing

This involves using a prudent mix of fixed and floating rate finance to mitigate the impact of interest rate changes.

- Matching

This involves creating assets that are based on the same interest rates (eg base rate) as their liabilities (mainly used by banks).

1.3 Protecting against future interest rate exposure

If the company is risk averse or expects interest rates to rise, then the emphasis will be on using fixed rate finance.

If, however, a loan (or investment) is being **planned in the future**, then the risk is **harder to manage.**

| A company is planning to take out a loan **in one months' time** | In one months' time, when the loan is taken out, interest **rates may have risen.** |

This risk can be managed by the **techniques covered in the following sec**tions, which either aim to **fix** the interest rate (FRAs, futures, swaps) or **cap** the interest rate (options).

2 Forward rate agreements (FRAs)

KEY TERM

> **FRA:** A contract with a bank covering a **specific amount** of money to be borrowed over a specific time period in the future **at an interest rate agreed now**.

A forward rate agreement (FRA) for interest rates is similar in many respects to a forward exchange contract for currencies.

- FRAs are arranged with a bank as an **over the counter transaction**.
- An FRA is a binding contract that **fixes an interest rate** for short-term lending/investing or short-term borrowing, for an interest rate period that begins at a future date.

However, an FRA is **not identical** to a currency forward because it is **not** an agreement that is directly linked to a transaction (eg to lend or borrow). Instead, it is a **derivative agreement** that fixes an interest rate on a **notional amount** of money (the principal).

A company can enter into an FRA with a bank that **fixes the rate of interest** for short-term borrowing from a certain time in the future.

- If the actual interest rate at that date proves to be higher than the rate in the FRA, **the bank** supplying the FRA **pays the company the difference.**
- If the actual interest rate is lower than the FRA rate, **the company pays the bank** supplying the FRA the difference.

The FRA does not need to be with the same bank as the loan, as the FRA is a hedging method independent of any loan agreement.

This allows a company to take out the loan in future at the best rate available.

2.1 Quotation of FRAs

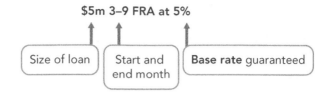

$5m 3–9 FRA at 5%

Size of loan | Start and end month | **Base rate** guaranteed

Activity 1: FRA

Frantic plc is planning to take out a 6-month loan of £5m in 3 months' time. It is concerned about the base rate rising above its current level of 4.75%.

Frantic has been offered a three to nine FRA at 5%.

Frantic can borrow at approximately 1% above the base rate.

Required

1   Advise Frantic of the likely outcome if in 3 months' time the base rate is 5.5%.

2   Advise Frantic of the likely outcome if in 3 months' time the base rate is 4.5%.

Solution

2.2 Advantages of FRAs

FRAs have similar advantages to currency forwards.

Advantages	Discussion
• Simple	Easy to organise for the exact amount of money required and the exact timing of the transaction
• Low or zero up-front costs	Unlike interest rate options (see later)
• Fix the interest rate	This protects the borrower from higher interest rates in future

2.3 Disadvantages of FRAs

Disadvantages	Discussion
• Fixed date	The outcome of the FRA will be determined on a specified date, even if the actual borrowing is on a different date.
• Unattractive rate	The fixed rate that is offered may not be attractive
• Counter-party risk	The agreement is between two parties, there is therefore a risk of default on either side

FRAs are usually only available on large loans and are likely to be **difficult to obtain for periods of over one year**.

Activity 2: FRA discussion

Today is 1 January 20X6. Deverosity Ltd will borrow $6 million on 31 March 20X6 and will repay this debt on 31 December 20X6.

The base rate is currently at 1.0% and Deverosity Ltd can borrow short-term debt at 8% above the base rate.

A forward rate agreement is available for Deverosity Ltd at 1.25%.

On 31 March 20X6, the base rate is 0.75%.

Required

State whether the following statements are true or false.

(1)   The appropriate type of forward rate agreement in this case would be a 3–9 FRA

(2)   The FRA rate would be 9.25%

(3)   If the base rate was actually 0.75% on 31 March 20X6 this would result in an obligation on Deverosity Ltd to make an FRA payment

(4)   If the base rate was actually 0.75% on 31 March 20X6 this would result in an FRA payment or receipt of $22,500

Solution

Essential reading

See Chapter 15 section 1 of the Essential reading, available in the digital edition of the Workbook, for more background information on this area.

The Essential reading is available as an Appendix of the digital edition of the Workbook.

---

3 Interest rate derivatives

> ### Exam focus point
>
> This section **will not be tested numerically in the exam**.

3.1 Interest rate futures

> **Interest rate futures:** An interest rate **futures contract** is a **contract** to receive or pay interest on a notional **standard quantity** of money at an **agreed future date** at a **specified interest rate**.

Like an FRA, a futures contract is intended to **fix the outcome of a hedge**. However, a futures contract is for a **standard amount of money** and is traded on an exchange.

Like an FRA, an interest rate futures hedge is designed so that:

- If a company makes a loss on a transaction (borrowing or investing) due to interest rate movements, then it will make a profit in the futures market to compensate for this.
- If a company makes a profit on a transaction (borrowing or investing) due to interest rate movements, then it will make a loss in the futures market.

So, the outcome is **fixed** whatever happens to the exchange rate.

Types of interest rate futures contract	
Contract to buy	**Contract to sell**
With interest rate futures what is being **bought** is the entitlement to **interest receipts**.	With interest rate futures what is being **sold** is the promise to make **interest payments**.
A contract to receive interest at a fixed rate would be appropriate for an investor; this is called a **contract to buy**.	A contract to pay interest at a fixed rate would be appropriate for a borrower; this is called a **contract to sell**.

3.1.1 Setting up a futures transaction

There are three steps to a futures transaction. For a **borrower**, these are as follows:

Step 1 Today: Enter into a futures contract to sell (pay interest) at a fixed rate

Contracts should be due to be fulfilled on a standardised date **after** the transaction date.

Step 2 Complete the **actual** transaction on the **spot market**.

Step 3 **Close out the futures contract** by doing the opposite of what you did in Step 1 ie by entering into contracts to buy (receive interest).

A profit or loss will arise as futures are settled.

- If interest rates rise then there will be a gain on the future as the interest received in step 3 will be higher than the interest paid in step 1.

However, there will also be an interest rate loss because the interest rate (ie repayments) on the actual loan will be higher.

- If interest rates fall then there will be a loss on the future as the interest received in step 3 will be lower than the interest paid in step 1.

However, there will also be an interest rate gain because the interest rate (ie repayments) on the actual loan will be lower.

3.1.2 Advantages of interest rate futures

As for currency futures.

- Futures are valid for a period of time eg a September future can be used on any day between the day it was entered into up to the end of September. This is more flexible than a forward, which is only valid on a specific day.
- **Counterparty risk is lower** since the futures exchange guarantees the transaction.

3.1.3 Disadvantages of interest rate futures

As for currency futures.

- Interest rate futures are **only available in large, standard, contract sizes** (compared to forward contracts). This makes interest rate futures less suitable for small transactions.
- To cover potential losses a company using futures will be required to place a **deposit** (called a margin) with the futures exchange, which may need to be topped up on a daily basis if the contract is incurring losses.
- There is a risk that futures interest rates do not move exactly in line with spot interest rates so that the hedge is not effective (this is an example of **basis risk**).

Essential reading

See Chapter 15 section 2 of the Essential reading, available in the digital edition of the Workbook, for more background information on this area.

The Essential reading is available as an Appendix of the digital edition of the Workbook.

3.2 Interest rate options

> **Interest rate options:** Gives an option holder the right to pay or receive interest on an agreed quantity of money, at a specific interest rate on or before a future expiry date.

As for currency options, companies can choose whether to buy:

(a) A tailor-made interest rate option from a bank, suited to the company's specific needs. These are **over the counter** (OTC) or **negotiated** options; or

(b) A standard interest rate option, from an options exchange. Such options are **traded** or **exchange-traded** options.

Options offer the flexibility to the holder of **enjoying the upside without a risk of suffering the downside of adverse interest rate movements.**

However, buying an option involves **paying a premium to the option seller**. The option premium is a cost of using an option.

The option acts as an **insurance policy** and will be used by the purchaser to compensate for adverse interest rate movements. If the interest rate moves favourably then the option will not be exercised.

3.2.1 Advantages of options

- Exchange -traded options (not OTC options) are, like futures, valid for a period of time. This is more flexible than a forward, which is only valid on a specific day.
- Exchange traded options can be sold on if not needed.
- Any type of option allows the company to benefit from favourable interest rate movements.

3.2.2 Disadvantages of options

- Exchange-traded options are only available in large, standard, contract sizes
- Any type of option will need to purchased and the **premium** can be expensive.

> **Put option:** An option to **pay interest** at a pre-determined rate on a standard notional amount over a fixed period in the future.
>
> **Call option:** An option to **receive interest** at a pre-determined rate on a standard notional amount over a fixed period in the future.

3.2.3 Option strategies

An interest rate cap protects against interest rate rises for a borrower.

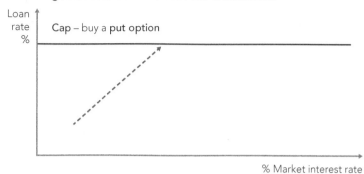

An interest rate floor protects against interest rate falls for an investor.

An interest rate collar is **cheaper** than a cap or a floor. For a borrower, a collar would be as follows:

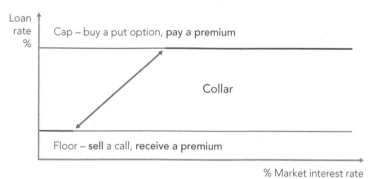

The cost of a collar is lower than for buying an option alone. However, the borrowing company forgoes the benefit of movements in interest rates **below the floor limit** in exchange for this cost reduction.

For an **investor** a collar involves buying a call option (a floor) and selling a put option (at a higher interest rate than the floor). The investor therefore forgoes the benefit of movements in interest rates above the put option rate.

Activity 3: Interest rate collar

A company wishes to arrange a collar to fix a future interest rate on a variable rate five-year loan it has obtained from its bank.

Required

Which of the following transactions will enable the company to arrange an appropriate collar?

- O   Buying a cap and buying a floor
- O   Buying a cap and selling a floor
- O   Selling a cap and selling a floor
- O   Selling a cap and buying a floor

Solution

3.3   Interest rate swaps

> **Interest rate swap:** An agreement whereby the parties to the agreement exchange interest rate commitments.

Finally, a company may be able to swap variable rate debt for fixed rate debt if it is worried about interest rate rises. This type of swap is sometimes known as a '**plain vanilla**' swap.

A swap allows a company to organise a new loan without incurring redemption penalties for early repayment of an existing loan.

3.3.1   Why bother to swap?

Obvious questions to ask are:

- Why do the companies bother swapping interest payments with each other?
- Why don't they just terminate their original loan and take out a new one?

The answer is that **transaction costs** may be too high. Terminating an original loan early may involve a significant termination fee and taking out a new loan will involve issue costs. Arranging a swap can be significantly cheaper, even if a banker is used as an intermediary. Because the banker is simply acting as an agent on the swap arrangement and does not have to bear any default risk, the arrangement fee can be kept low.

4 Yield curve

The term structure of interest rates refers to how the yield on bonds of a certain type eg government bonds varies according to the term of the borrowing.

Normally, the longer the term of an asset to maturity, the higher the rate of interest paid on the asset. This can be shown as a **yield curve**.

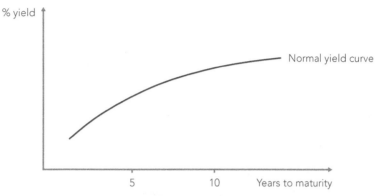

4.1 Explanations of the yield curve

There are a number of explanations of the yield curve; these are not competing explanations, and at any one time all may be influencing the shape of the yield curve.

(a) Expectations theory – the curve may reflect expectations that interest rates will rise in the future, so the Government has to offer higher returns on long-term debt.

(b) Liquidity preference theory – the curve reflects the compensation that investors require higher returns for sacrificing liquidity on long-dated bonds.

(c) Market segmentation theory – short-dated bonds tend to be more popular with banks, and long-dated bonds are more popular with pension funds, ie there are different markets. This theory suggests that the slope of the yield curve will reflect conditions in different segments of the market.

4.1.1 The significance of yield curves to financial managers

Financial managers can inspect the shape of the yield curve when deciding the term of borrowing or deposits. The curve is influenced by the market's expectations of future interest rate movements.

For instance, a yield curve that is sloping steeply upwards suggests a rise in interest rates in the future; in this case a company will be more concerned about **managing interest rate risk**.

Essential reading

See Chapter 15 section 3 of the Essential reading, available in the digital edition of the Workbook, for more background information on this area.

The Essential reading is available as an Appendix of the digital edition of the Workbook.

4.2 Comprehensive example on risk management

Section B of the exam will often have a 10-mark question focusing on risk management. This type of question can combine elements of both currency risk and interest rate risk as illustrated in the following comprehensive activity.

Activity 4: Risk management: Section B style OTQ

Robin Co expects to receive €800,000 from a credit customer in the European Union in six months' time. The spot exchange rate is €2.413 per $1 and the six month forward rate is €2.476 per $1. The following commercial interest rates are available to Robin Co:

	Deposit rate	Borrow rate
Euros	3.0% per year	7.0% per year
Dollars	1.0% per year	2.5% per year

Robin Co does not have any surplus cash to use in hedging the future euro receipt.

Required

1 What could Robin Co do to reduce the risk of the euro value dropping relative to the dollar before the €800,000 is received?

(1) Deposit €800,000 immediately as part of a money market hedge

(2) Enter into a forward contract to sell €800,000 in six months

(3) Enter into an interest rate swap for six months

○ (1) or (2) only

○ (2) only

○ (3) only

○ (1), (2) or (3)

2 What is the dollar value of a forward market hedge?

○ $323,102

○ $331,538

○ $1,930,400

○ $1,980,800

3 If Robin Co used a money market hedge, what would be the percentage borrowing rate for the period?

○ 1.25%

○ 2.5%

○ 3.5%

○ 7%

4 Which of the following statements about forward rate agreements (FRAs) are true?

(1) They fix the borrowing rate on a sum of money for an agreed period

(2) They are arranged with a bank as an over-the-counter transaction

(3) The allow companies to benefit from favourable interest rate movements

(4) They can be used to hedge against foreign exchange risk

○ (1), (2), (3) and (4)

○ (1) and (2) only

○ (3) and (4) only

○ (2), (3) and (4) only

5 Which of the following statements about interest rate theories are true?

(1) Expectations theory provides a reason why the interest yield curve is normally upward sloping

(2) Market segmentation theory states that interest rates reflect expectations of future changes in interest rates

○ Statement (1) is true and statement (2) is false

○ Statement (2) is true and statement (1) is false

○ Both statements are true

○ Both statements are false

Solution

Chapter summary

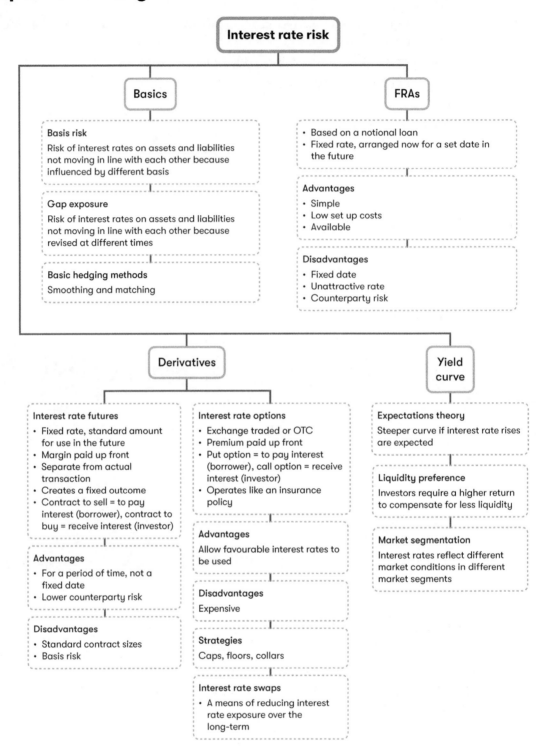

Interest rate risk

Basics

Basis risk
Risk of interest rates on assets and liabilities not moving in line with each other because influenced by different basis

Gap exposure
Risk of interest rates on assets and liabilities not moving in line with each other because revised at different times

Basic hedging methods
Smoothing and matching

FRAs
- Based on a notional loan
- Fixed rate, arranged now for a set date in the future

Advantages
- Simple
- Low set up costs
- Available

Disadvantages
- Fixed date
- Unattractive rate
- Counterparty risk

Derivatives

Interest rate futures
- Fixed rate, standard amount for use in the future
- Margin paid up front
- Separate from actual transaction
- Creates a fixed outcome
- Contract to sell = to pay interest (borrower), contract to buy = receive interest (investor)

Advantages
- For a period of time, not a fixed date
- Lower counterparty risk

Disadvantages
- Standard contract sizes
- Basis risk

Interest rate options
- Exchange traded or OTC
- Premium paid up front
- Put option = to pay interest (borrower), call option = receive interest (investor)
- Operates like an insurance policy

Advantages
Allow favourable interest rates to be used

Disadvantages
Expensive

Strategies
Caps, floors, collars

Interest rate swaps
- A means of reducing interest rate exposure over the long-term

Yield curve

Expectations theory
Steeper curve if interest rate rises are expected

Liquidity preference
Investors require a higher return to compensate for less liquidity

Market segmentation
Interest rates reflect different market conditions in different market segments

Knowledge diagnostic

1. Basic hedging methods

Internal methods such as smoothing and matching are simple techniques that can be considered independently by a company.

2. FRAs

FRAs fix the interest rate on borrowing that is planned for the future but unlike currency forwards are based on a notional loan (separate from the actual loan).

3. Interest rate futures

Like FRAs but based on a standard amount of money. A contract to sell is required by a borrower, and a contract to buy is required by an investor.

4. Interest rate options

A put option is required by a borrower, and a call option is required by an investor.

5. Yield curve

The shape of the yield curve gives an indication of the likely trend in interest rates (expectations theory) but is also influenced by liquidity preference and market segmentation.

Further study guidance

Question practice

Now try the following from the Further question practice bank (available in the digital edition of the Workbook):

Section B questions

Q37 (d) and (e)

Further reading

There is a useful Technical Article that is available on ACCA's website; it is called 'Hedging techniques for interest rate risk'. We recommend that you read this article as part of your preparation for the FM exam.

Activity answers

Activity 1: FRA

1   Net cost = 6%

    Bank pays compensation of 0.5% to Frantic

    Frantic borrows at the best rate available eg 5.5 + 1 = 6.5%

    Net costs = 6% in £s this is 0.06 × £5m × 6/12 = £0.15m

2   Net cost = 6%

    Frantic pays bank compensation of 0.5%

    Frantic borrows at the best rate available eg 4.5 + 1 = 5.5%

    Net costs = 6%

Activity 2: FRA discussion

Answer as follows:

(1)   False – the contract starts in 3 months and lasts for 9 months and therefore is a 3-12 FRA

(2)   False – the FRA rate is 1.25%

(3)   True – the base rate has fallen so the company must pay extra as they have entered an FRA at a higher rate.

(4)   True – as the base rate is 0.5% below the FRA rate, Deverosity will pay 0.5/100 × $6m × 9 months /12 months = $22,500.

Activity 3: Interest rate collar

The correct answer is: Buying a cap and selling a floor

Buying a cap (ie a put option) sets the maximum rate for borrowing. Selling a floor (ie a call option) reduces the cost of the hedge, but also sets a minimum effective rate.

Activity 4: Risk management: Section B style OTQ

1   The correct answer is: (2) only

    Statement 1 is incorrect. Robin Co could use a money market hedge but €800,000 would have to be borrowed, then converted into dollars and then placed on deposit. Statement 3 is also incorrect. An interest rate swap swaps one type of interest payment (such as fixed interest) for another (such as floating rate interest). Therefore, it would not be suitable.

2   The correct answer is: $323,102

    Future value = €800,000/2.476 = $323,102.

3   The correct answer is: 3.5%

    Robin Co is expecting a euro receipt in six months' time and it can hedge this receipt in the money markets by borrowing euros to create a euro liability.

    Euro borrowing rate for six months = 7.0%/2 = 3.5%.

4   The correct answer is: (1) and (2) only

    Statement 3 is false. A company is locked into the FRA borrowing rate and so it cannot benefit from favourable rate movements. Statement 4 is false. FRAs hedge against interest rate risk (although they are similar to a forward exchange contract for currencies).

5   The correct answer is: Both statements are false

Statement 1 is false. It is liquidity theory which provides a reason why the interest yield curve is normally upward sloping. Expectations theory states that interest rates reflect expectations of future changes in interest rates. Therefore statement 2 is also false.

Skills checkpoint 5

How to approach your FM exam

Chapter overview

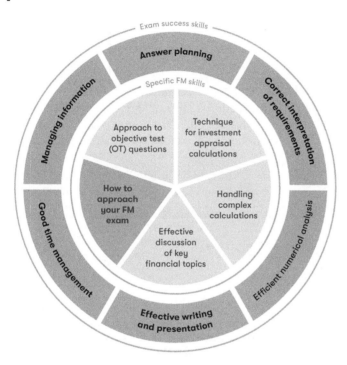

Introduction

You can answer your FM exam in whatever order you prefer. It is important that you adopt a strategy that works best for you. We would suggest that you decide on your preferred approach and practice it by doing a timed mock exam before your real exam.

Remember you FM exam will be structured as follows:

Section A – 15 **individual OT questions** worth 2 marks each. Questions in Section A can come from any syllabus area. There will be an equal mix of numerical and discursive style questions.

Section B – Three **OT case questions** worth 10 marks each. Each case question will consist of five individual OT questions worth two marks each. There will normally be two numerical questions followed by three discussion style questions. Again, questions in Section B can come from any syllabus area. Each individual case does however tend to focus on a particular syllabus area for example, working capital management, investment appraisal, risk management or business finance.

Section C – Section C will contain two, 20 mark questions which will be **scenario based** and will contain both discursive and computational elements. Section C questions will mainly focus on the following syllabus areas, but a minority of marks can be drawn from any other area of the syllabus.

*   Working capital management (syllabus area C)
*   Investment appraisal (syllabus area D)
*   Business finance (syllabus area E)

This Skills Checkpoint will provide you with one suggested approach for tackling your FM exam.

Good luck!

How to approach your FM exam

FM Skill: How to approach your FM exam

We would suggest the following approach for tackling your FM exam. It is important that you adopt an approach that works best for you and practice it by completing a mock exam to time prior to your real exam.

Complete Section A first – allocated time 54 minutes

*   Tackle any easier OT questions first. Often discursive style questions can be answered quickly, saving more time for calculations. Do not leave any questions unanswered. Even if you are unsure make a reasoned guess. Skills Checkpoint 1 covers how to approach OT questions in more detail.
*   If you do not feel that you need the full 54 minutes to complete Section A you can carry this time forward to your Section C questions which tend to be more time pressured. With practice, it may be possible for you to complete section A up to 10 minutes quicker than the allocated time of 54 minutes.

Complete Section B next – allocated time 54 minutes

*   You will have 18 mins of exam time to allocate to each of the three OT case questions in Section B. Use the same approach to OT questions as discussed for Section A.
*   Each individual case tends to focus on a specific syllabus area. Start with the OT case question you feel most confident with.
*   There will normally be three discussion type and two numerical questions within each case. Again, it is better to tackle the discussion type questions first as they tend to be less time consuming.
*   If you do not feel that you need the full 54 minutes to complete section B you can carry this time forward to your Section C questions which tend to be more time pressured. With practice, it may be possible for you to complete Section A approximately 5 minutes quicker than the allocated time of 54 minutes.

Finally, complete Section C – allocated time 72 minutes

*   Section C will contain two, 20-mark questions which will be scenario based and will contain both discursive and computational elements. Allocate at least 36 minutes to each question (remembering to split your time between each of the sub requirements) but you may have up to 15 minutes of extra time if you have completed Sections A and B of the exam in less than the allotted time.
*   Start with the question you feel most confident with. The first sub requirement will normally involve some detailed calculations, these tend to be very time pressured. Ensure that you don't spend too much time on the calculations and then lose out on the easier discursive marks. Make it clear to your marker which sub requirement you are answering.
*   Skills Checkpoints 2 and 3 look specifically at the techniques you should use for investment appraisal and complex cost of capital calculations. NPV and WACC are popular areas examined in Section C so make sure you are confident using the techniques covered in these skills checkpoints

Set some time aside to practice this approach through the completion of a mock exam to time.

Appendix 1:
Formulae, ratios and mathematical tables

Appendices

Appendix A: Formulae and ratios that you need to learn

Profitability ratios:

$$\text{ROCE} = \frac{\text{Profit from operations (before interest and tax)}}{\text{Capital employed}}$$

Debt ratios include:

$$\text{Gearing} = \frac{\text{Value of debt}}{\text{Value of equity (or debt + equity)}}$$

$$\text{Interest cover} = \frac{\text{Profit from operations}}{\text{Interest}}$$

Liquidity ratios:

$$\text{Current ratio} = \frac{\text{Current assets}}{\text{Current liabilities}}$$

Shareholder investor ratios include:

$$\text{Dividend yield} = \frac{\text{Dividend per share}}{\text{Share price}} \times 100$$

$$\text{Earnings per share (EPS)} = \frac{\text{Profits after tax - preference dividend}}{\text{Number of ordinary shares}}$$

$$\text{Price to earnings ratio (P/E)} = \frac{\text{Share price}}{\text{EPS}}$$

Working capital ratios

Operating cycle = inventory days + receivable days − payables days

Inventory days = inventory/cost of sales × 365

Receivables days = trade receivables/(credit) sales × 365

Payables days = trade payables/(credit) purchases × 365

Sales to net working capital ratio = sales/net working capital (excl cash)

Cost of capital formulae:

$$K_d = \frac{I(1-t)}{P_0}$$

$$K_p = \frac{d}{p}$$

Other useful formulae to learn:

$$IRR = a\% + \left[\frac{NPV_a}{NPV_a - NPV_b} \times (b\% - a\%) \right]$$

$$\text{Total shareholder return} = \frac{\text{dividend gain} + \text{capital}}{\text{share price at start year}}$$

$$EAC = \frac{NPV \text{ of costs}}{\text{Annuity factor for life of the project}}$$

$$\text{Profitability index} = \frac{\text{Present value of cash inflows (or NPV of the project)}}{\text{Present value of cash outflows}}$$

Appendix B: Mathematical tables

Present Value Table

Present value of $1, that is $(1+r)^{-n}$ where r = interest rate; n = number of periods until payment or receipt.

Periods (n)	\multicolumn{10}{c}{Interest rates (r)}									
	1%	2%	3%	4%	5%	6%	7%	8%	9%	10%
1	0.990	0.980	0.971	0.962	0.952	0.943	0.935	0.926	0.917	0.909
2	0.980	0.961	0.943	0.925	0.907	0.890	0.873	0.857	0.842	0.826
3	0.971	0.942	0.915	0.889	0.864	0.840	0.816	0.794	0.772	0.751
4	0.961	0.924	0.888	0.855	0.823	0.792	0.763	0.735	0.708	0.683
5	0.951	0.906	0.863	0.822	0.784	0.747	0.713	0.681	0.650	0.621
6	0.942	0.888	0.837	0.790	0.746	0705	0.666	0.630	0.596	0.564
7	0.933	0.871	0.813	0.760	0.711	0.665	0.623	0.583	0.547	0.513
8	0.923	0.853	0.789	0.731	0.677	0.627	0.582	0.540	0.502	0.467
9	0.914	0.837	0.766	0.703	0.645	0.592	0.544	0.500	0.460	0.424
10	0.905	0.820	0.744	0.676	0.614	0.558	0.508	0.463	0.422	0.386
11	0.896	0.804	0.722	0.650	0.585	0.527	0.475	0.429	0.388	0.350
12	0.887	0.788	0.701	0.625	0.557	0.497	0.444	0.397	0.356	0.319
13	0.879	0.773	0.681	0.601	0.530	0.469	0.415	0.368	0.326	0.290
14	0.870	0.758	0.661	0.577	0.505	0.442	0.388	0.340	0.299	0.263
15	0.861	0.743	0.642	0.555	0.481	0.417	0.362	0.315	0.275	0.239

Periods (n)	\multicolumn{10}{c}{Interest rates (r)}									
	11%	12%	13%	14%	15%	16%	17%	18%	19%	20%
1	0.901	0.893	0.885	0.877	0.870	0.862	0.855	0.847	0.840	0.833
2	0.812	0.797	0.783	0.769	0.756	0.743	0.731	0.718	0.706	0.694
3	0.731	0.712	0.693	0.675	0.658	0.641	0.624	0.609	0.593	0.579
4	0.659	0.636	0.613	0.592	0.572	0.552	0.534	0.516	0.499	0.482
5	0.593	0.567	0.543	0.519	0.497	0.476	0.456	0.437	0.419	0.402
6	0.535	0.507	0.480	0.456	0.432	0.410	0.390	0.370	0.352	0.335
7	0.482	0.452	0.425	0.400	0.376	0.354	0.333	0.314	0.296	0.279
8	0.434	0.404	0.376	0.351	0.327	0.305	0.285	0.266	0.249	0.233
9	0.391	0.361	0.333	0.308	0.284	0.263	0.243	0.225	0.209	0.194
10	0.352	0.322	0.295	0.270	0.247	0.227	0.208	0.191	0.176	0.162
11	0.317	0.287	0.261	0.237	0.215	0.195	0.178	0.162	0.148	0.135
12	0.286	0.257	0.231	0.208	0.187	0.168	0.152	0.137	0.124	0.112
13	0.258	0.229	0.204	0.182	0.163	0.145	0.130	0.116	0.104	0.093
14	0.232	0.205	0.181	0.160	0.141	0.125	0.111	0.099	0.088	0.078
15	0.209	0.183	0.160	0.140	0.123	0.108	0.095	0.084	0.079	0.065

Annuity Table

Present value of an annuity of 1 ie $\frac{1-(1+r)^{-n}}{r}$

Where r = discount rate; n = number of periods

Periods (n)	\multicolumn{10}{c}{Discount rate (r)}									
	1%	2%	3%	4%	5%	6%	7%	8%	9%	10%
1	0.990	0.980	0.971	0.962	0.952	0.943	0.935	0.926	0.917	0.909
2	1.970	1.942	1.913	1.886	1.859	1.833	1.808	1.783	1.759	1.736
3	2.941	2.884	2.829	2.775	2.723	2.673	2.624	2.577	2.531	2.487
4	3.902	3.808	3.717	3.630	3.546	3.465	3.387	3.312	3.240	3.170
5	4.853	4.713	4.580	4.452	4.329	4.212	4.100	3.993	3.890	3.791
6	5.795	5.601	5.417	5.242	5.076	4.917	4.767	4.623	4.486	4.355
7	6.728	6.472	6.230	6.002	5.786	5.582	5.389	5.206	5.033	4.868
8	7.652	7.325	7.020	6.733	6.463	6.210	5.971	5.747	5.535	5.335
9	8.566	8.162	7.786	7.435	7.108	6.802	6.515	6.247	5.995	5.759
10	9.471	8.983	8.530	8.111	7.722	7.360	7.024	6.710	6.418	6.145
11	10.368	9.787	9.253	8.760	8.306	7.887	7.499	7.139	6.805	6.495
12	11.255	10.575	9.954	9.385	8.863	8.384	7.943	7.536	7.161	6.814
13	12.134	11.348	10.635	9.986	9.394	8.853	8.358	7.904	7.487	7.103
14	13.004	12.106	11.296	10.563	9.899	9.295	8.745	8.244	7.786	7.367
15	13.865	12.849	11.938	11.118	10.380	9.712	9.108	8.559	8.061	7.606

(n)	11%	12%	13%	14%	15%	16%	17%	18%	19%	20%
1	0.901	0.893	0.885	0.877	0.870	0.862	0.855	0.847	0.840	0.833
2	1.713	1.690	1.668	1.647	1.626	1.605	1.585	1.566	1.547	1.528
3	2.444	2.402	2.361	2.322	2.283	2.246	2.210	2.174	2.140	2.106
4	3.102	3.037	2.974	2.914	2.855	2.798	2.743	2.690	2.639	2.589
5	3.696	3.605	3.517	3.433	3.352	3.274	3.199	3.127	3.058	2.991
6	4.231	4.111	3.998	3.889	3.784	3.685	3.589	3.498	3.410	3.326
7	4.712	4.564	4.423	4.288	4.160	4.039	3.922	3.812	3.706	3.605
8	5.146	4.968	4.799	4.639	4.487	4.344	4.207	4.078	3.954	3.837
9	5.537	5.328	5.132	4.946	4.772	4.607	4.451	4.303	4.163	4.031
10	5.889	5.650	5.426	5.216	5.019	4.833	4.659	4.494	4.339	4.192
11	6.207	5.938	5.687	5.453	5.234	5.029	4.836	4.656	4.486	4.327
12	6.492	6.194	5.918	5.660	5.421	5.197	4.988	4.793	4.611	4.439
13	6.750	6.424	6.122	5.842	5.583	5.342	5.118	4.910	4.715	4.533
14	6.982	6.628	6.302	6.002	5.724	5.468	5.229	5.008	4.802	4.611
15	7.191	6.811	6.462	6.142	5.847	5.575	5.324	5.092	4.876	4.675

Formula Sheet

Economic Order Quantity

$$= \sqrt{\frac{2C_0D}{C_H}}$$

Miller-Orr Model

$$\text{Return point} = \text{Lower limit} + \left(\frac{1}{3} \times \text{spread}\right)$$

$$\text{Spread} = 3\left[\frac{\frac{3}{4} \times \text{transaction cost} \times \text{variance of cash flows}}{\text{Interest rate}}\right]^{\frac{1}{3}}$$

The Capital Asset Pricing Model

$$E(n) = R_f + \beta_i(E(r_m) - R_f)$$

The asset beta formula

$$\beta_a = \left[\frac{V_e}{(V_e + V_d(1-T))}\beta_e\right] + \left[\frac{V_d(1-T)}{(V_e + V_d(1-T))}\beta_d\right]$$

The Growth Model

$$P_O = \frac{D_O(1 + g)}{(r_e - g)} \qquad r_e = \frac{D_O(1 + g)}{P_O} + g$$

Gordon's Growth Approximation

$g = br$

The weighted average cost of capital

$$WACC = \left[\frac{V_e}{V_e + V_d}\right]k_e + \left[\frac{V_d}{V_e + V_d}\right]k_d(1 - T)$$

The Fisher formula

$$(1 + i) = (1 + r)(1 + h)$$

Purchasing Power Parity and Interest Rate Parity

$$S_1 = S_0 \times \frac{(1 + h_c)}{(1 + h_b)} \qquad F_0 = S_0 \times \frac{(1 + i_c)}{(1 + i_b)}$$

Index

A

Acceptance credits, 31

Accounting rate of return, 107

Adjusted payback, 106

Agency problem, 9

Agency theory, 9

Aggregation, 29

Annuities, 110

Arbitrage, 257

Asset beta, 259

Asset replacement decisions, 165

Audit committee, 9

B

Bank bills, 31

Basis risk, 341

Baumol model, 80

Behavioural finance, 296

Beta factor, 231

Bill of exchange, 31

C

Capital asset pricing model (CAPM), 230

Capital rationing, 171

Capital structure, 252

Cash flow forecast, 75

Cash operating cycle, 47

Cash shortages, 78

Cash surpluses, 79

Certainty-equivalent method, 154

Certificates of deposit, 31

Clientele effect, 212

Commercial paper, 31

Competition policy, 27

Conservative forecasting, 154

Contractionary macroeconomic policies, 24

Conventions used in DCF, 110

Conversionpremium, 194

Conversion ratio, 194

Conversion value, 194

Convertible loan note, 194

Corporate governance, 9

Cost of bank loan, 238

Cost of convertible debt, 237

Cost of debt, 234

Cost of irredeemable loan notes, 234

Cost of preference shares, 237

Cost of redeemable debt, 235

Credit period, 56

Creditor hierarchy, 225

Cum div, 227

Currency futures, 324

Currency options, 325

Currency swaps, 326

D

Debt beta, 236

Debt ratios, 12

Delayed annuities, 112

Discount factors, 109

Discounted payback period, 106

Discounting, 108

Disintermediation, 29

Dividend growth model, 225

Dividend irrelevance theory, 212

Dividend policies, 211

Dividend valuation method, 286

Divisible projects, 172

E

Early settlement discount, 57

Earnings per share, 4

Earnings yield method, 286

Economic risk, 330

Efficient market hypothesis, 293

EOQ model, 51

Equity beta, 259

Equity finance, 195

Equivalent annual benefit, 167

Equivalent annual cost, 165

Eurobond, 33

Eurocurrency, 33

Ex div, 227

Exchange rate policy, 25

Expansionary macroeconomic policies, 24

Expectations theory, 349

Expected values, 151

Bibliography

Arnold, G. (2015) *Corporate Financial Management*. 5th edn. Harlow, Pearson Education Limited.

Chisolm, A. (2007) *Derivatives demystified*. Chichester, Wiley Finance.

Pike, R., Neale, B. and Linsley, P. (2016) *Corporate Finance & Investment*. 8th edn. Harlow, Pearson Education Limited.

Watson, D. and Head, A. (2013) *Corporate Finance principles and practice*. 6th edn. London, Pearson Education Limited.

Tell us what you think

Got comments or feedback on this book? Let us know.
Use your QR code reader:

Or, visit:
https://bppgroup.fra1.qualtrics.com/jfe/form/SV_9TrxTtw8jSvO7Pv